A Question of Loyalty

A volume in the Series

CORNELL STUDIES IN SECURITY AFFAIRS

edited by Robert Jervis
Robert J. Art
Stephen M. Walt

A full list of titles in the series appears at the end of the book.

A Question of Loyalty

Military Manpower Policy in Multiethnic States

ALON PELED

Cornell University Press

ITHACA AND LONDON

First published 1998 by Cornell University Press

Printed in the United States of America

Library of Congress Cataloging-in-Publication Data

Peled, Alon, 1962–
    A question of loyalty : military manpower policy in multiethnic
states / Alon Peled.
        p.   cm.—(Cornell studies in security affairs)
    Includes index.
    ISBN 0-8014-3239-1 (cloth : alk. paper)
    1. Armed Forces—Minorities—Case studies.   2. Military policy—
Case studies.   I. Title.   II. Series.
    UB416.P45   1998
    355'.0089—dc21   97-51489

Cornell University Press strives to use environmentally responsible suppliers
and materials to the fullest extent possible in the publishing of its books.
Such materials include vegetable-based, low-VOC inks and acid-
free papers that are also either recycled, totally chlorine-free,
or partly composed of nonwood fibers.

Cloth printing   10 9 8 7 6 5 4 3 2 1

To my parents,
Sylvia and Arye Peled,
with great love

Contents

Figures and Tables

Preface

At the beginning of 1990, the People's Army of Yugoslavia (the Jugoslovenska Narodna Armija or JNA) was the only truly national institution in an ethnically divided society that was on the verge of civil war. Since 1945, the JNA had remained a genuinely Yugoslav institution, both in its ethnic composition and in its ideology. For most Yugoslavs, the multinational JNA embodied the concept of "brotherhood and unity" and acted as a meeting ground for all ethnic groups in the country. Article 242 of the 1974 Yugoslav constitution guaranteed that all promotions in the Yugoslav military from the rank of colonel upward would be according to a "national key" formula so that each nation within the Yugoslav confederation obtained its quota in the uppermost ranks.[1]

Yet only two years later, in 1992, western and Yugoslav media portrayed the JNA as a bloodthirsty Serbian militia. Under the direct orders of Slobodan Milosevic, the ultranationalistic Serbian leader, JNA units extended the Serbian war into Croatia and, later, into Bosnia. How could a conservative military organization that for over forty years had been structured and indoctrinated to embody the concept of multinationalism become a xenophobic ethnic militia overnight?

Almost at the same time in 1991, astounded Western military experts watched tens of thousands of frontline Iraqi soldiers capitulate to the allies virtually without firing a shot. Today, we forget the tense hours

---

1. John Zametica, *The Yugoslav Conflict*, Adelphi Paper 270 (London: International Institute for Strategic Studies, 1992), pp. 11, 40.

preceding the commencement of Desert Storm but, back then, horrified Western viewers watched distinguished military analysts predict that the Iraqis would inflict a blood bath on American and allied forces in Kuwait. According to these experts, American and allied forces would encounter miles of massive mine fields, trenches, strongpoints and hellish fire on their way to Kuwait City. Yet, shortly after the beginning of Desert Storm—and well before the Iraqis encountered the brilliant pincer maneuver of General Schwarzkopf in the western desert—thousands of Iraqi frontline soldiers abandoned their posts, left behind their heavy weapons, and surrendered en masse to the allies. How could the fourth largest military organization in the world, with all the experience it had gained from the Iran–Iraq War (1980–1987), collapse so rapidly and unconditionally?

The unconditional surrender of the Iraqi frontline units and the internal ethnic degradation of the Yugoslav military have one important common denominator: the failure of government officials, military officers, and ethnic leaders to manage the complex problems resulting from the military's multiethnic composition. In Yugoslavia, the principal blame falls on Croat, Slovene, Muslim, and Macedonian ethnic leaders. They did everything within their powers to antagonize the JNA and to push it into the hands of the Serbs. For example, they called on the members of their ethnic groups to desert the Yugoslav military, stopped sending new conscripts, confiscated military equipment, built their own militias, and unjustifiably denigrated the military, calling it a "Serb-dominated army."[2] In Iraq, the principal fault lay with the government. Saddam Hussein filled the ranks of the frontline units with disgruntled Kurdish and Shiite soldiers who were starved and brutalized for years to secure their obedience to the state. During the bloody Iran–Iraq War, these soldiers served as human shields against the onslaught of Iranian suicide units (Pasadrans). To the poor ethnic soldiers in Saddam's military, the allied forces appeared as saviors rather than enemies, and the mass desertion was inevitable.[3]

The ethnic predicament of the Yugoslav and Iraqi militaries is not unique. Today, across the globe, politicians, officers and ethnic leaders

2. Zametica, *Yugoslav Conflict*, pp. 14, 40–45.

3. U.S. News & World Report, *Triumph without Victory: The Unreported History of the Persian Gulf War* (New York: Random House, 1992), p. 320; Samir al-Khalil, *Republic of Fear: The Politics of Modern Iraq* (Berkeley: University of California Press), p. 165.

grapple with the same dilemmas as did the Yugoslav and Iraqi militaries. How can the state recruit, train, integrate, and promote members of ethnic groups whose loyalty is questioned by the government or by the general public? Why and how do military organizations become ethnically integrated? What features characterize a military organization that successfully integrates? What are the more successful paths to military integration of youth from subordinated ethnic groups?

These questions are not new. Throughout history, most military organizations have been multiethnic in nature, and this phenomenon is even more common in the post-Soviet era. Most important, the fate of multiethnic armies is not sealed in advance for better or worse. In some cases, diverse ethnic groups have come together, fought bravely and defeated much more ethnically cohesive enemies. In other cases, armies have fallen apart from within (the Yugoslav military) or collapsed on the battlefield (the Iraqi military). In every case, political, military, and ethnic leaders have made policy choices that determined how the multiethnic military performed on the battlefield. This book reviews three examples of such choices and their consequences. It suggests how the military can bring together ethnic groups that are frequently hostile toward each other to serve as an effective defense shield for the state. These ethnic manpower decisions and policies determine the quality of the state's armed forces, the overall credibility of its conventional deterrence, and the effectiveness of its military on the battlefield.

Ethnic military manpower policy is important for another reason. Many developing countries face strong threats from their neighbors. Lacking the funds to build a powerful professional military, these developing nations rely on conscripting of all male citizens for their defense. Military service becomes a precondition for full and equal citizenship. When an ethnic group is excluded from the military, its members are condemned to second-class citizenship. Members of such groups are not able to obtain good jobs, work on classified projects, or get full social benefits from the state. In countries that honor the tradition of the citizen-soldier, those not permitted into the military are neither citizens nor soldiers. The study of ethnic military manpower policy is therefore also a study of citizenship and how to extend first-class citizenship to more people.

The scarcity of studies on this issue stems partly from its sensitive nature. Politicians avoid it for fear that public discussions will upset the delicate ethnic balance in their countries. Military officers impose secrecy on all decisions of ethnic manpower policy in order to avoid compromising the military's professional and ethnically neutral image; outsiders may question the rationale behind the establishment of ethnic units or ethnic officers' unusual promotion tracks. Ethnic leaders themselves refrain from discussing this issue with outsiders, fearing that the status and promotion of their youth in the military will suffer a setback if the public becomes aware that the state is putting arms into the hands of allegedly disloyal ethnic groups. A personal anecdote illustrates this secrecy. Before traveling to Singapore, I called a journalist who had worked there many years to ask for his advice on how to facilitate my research. The journalist, who knew nothing about the topic of my work, attempted to allay my fears. "The reports in the West on the so-called Singaporean secrecy are grossly exaggerated," he told me. "You can research anything you wish to research in Singapore with the exception of two topics: the military and ethnic relations."

There are, however, many sources on the topic of ethnic military manpower policy in developing states. In most such countries, the recruitment and arming of ethnic groups whose allegiance the dominant ethnic group doubts is a long-standing issue. Thus, numerous articles, archive sources, and publications on the subject are available locally. A researcher can also interview former politicians and officers who may discuss this issue more freely than their successors do. I relied on more than a hundred interviews with former chiefs of staff, defence ministers, generals, ethnic leaders, and journalists in Singapore, Israel, and South Africa. Finally, radical ethnic groups that oppose the service of ethnic youth in the armed forces compose and publish much on this topic. Thus, information on the history of various ethnic groups in the armed forces *is* available, though incomplete and scattered, and the researcher must carefully collect and scrutinize it.

My ethnic histories of the armed forces of Israel, Singapore, and South Africa have had to rely heavily on the military archives of these states and on interviews with officials, military leaders, and ethnic officers who played key roles in ethnic soldiers' recruitment, training, deployment and promotion. I selected these particular militaries from among a group of 150 because these countries differed greatly in the degree to which ethnic groups were included in the state and military. This book includes new details on the systematic exclusion of Malay Muslims from military service in the Singapore Armed Forces (SAF) after 1967, on the integration of non-Jewish soldiers into the Israeli Defence Forces (IDF) during the 1950s, and on internal decision making in the South African Defence Force (SADF) during the 1970s to open up the military to nonwhites.

By comparing these three historical narratives, the book highlights the important role that professional military officers can play in recruiting and integrating members of subjugated ethnic groups. I suggest that ethnic integration in a professional military organization is often the result of the professional needs of the organization rather than the allegedly "liberal" or "enlightened" character of its officers. The book also narrates a common path through which ethnic youth find a home in the armed forces of many multiethnic countries. At first, professional officers oppose the recruitment of a new ethnic group because they fear that external political demands for military segregation will jeopardize the military's autonomy in matters of manpower. At a later stage, the scarcity of military manpower is likely to convince these officers to permit entry of the first ethnic youth into the armed forces as noncombatant and "second-class" soldiers. Then, inspired by new military doctrines and foreign military training that emphasize the need for a tightly integrated force to withstand a broad gamut of military challenges, from conventional wars to low-intensity guerrilla campaigns, the senior commanders begin to integrate the military ethnically. Thus, the impetus for change often comes from senior staff even though politicians take credit. In addition, I propose that ethnic leaders who condition their support for ethnic recruitment on the opening of more military doors to their groups can be very effective in accelerating military integration.

Chapter 1 discusses the roles professional officers and ethnic leaders play in making ethnic military manpower policy. Chapter 2 illustrates the process of ethnic integration within a professional military organization by analyzing the history of black, colored, and Indian soldiers in the white-dominated South African Defence Forces. It highlights the role played by a rising group of young western-educated officers who taught their senior commanders about the importance of an ethnically integrated force. This group reformed and then used the military's educational system to inculcate the officer corps with a new kind of thinking on ethnic issues. The chapter then focuses on the trial-and-error experiments that arose from this new thinking, and demonstrates how these experiments gradually paved the way for ethnic integration. It also argues that the pace of integration is likely to be much faster under battle conditions, as exemplified by the history of the SADF during the war years in South West Africa (1974–1988).

Chapter 3 studies the evolution of a policy that gradually abolished an existing integration within the armed forces and ultimately resulted in the virtual exclusion of members of a particular ethnic group. The chapter explains how politicians afraid of having a disloyal ethnic group within the armed forces can staff the military's senior ranks with civil servants who share their fear of ethnic Trojan horses. These civil servants in uniform work relentlessly to exclude allegedly disloyal ethnic groups, even at the cost of reducing overall fighting capability. The history of Malay Muslim soldiers in the Chinese-dominated Singaporean military shows what can happen to ethnic minorities in militaries where professional officers lack the autonomy to organize their troops according to combat needs.

Chapter 4 examines the impact of military professionalism on ethnic integration in armed forces in transition from semi-political underground organizations to full-fledged professional military organizations. The history of non-Jewish soldiers in the Israeli Armed Forces demonstrates the positive impact of increased military professionalism: professional officers use the combat records of their ethnic troops to justify opening more doors to them. Chapter 4 also argues that senior ethnic officers who retire from the military can become effective leaders for their communities (as compared to traditional or religious leaders), and successfully exert pressure on the military to speed up ethnic integration.

Chapter 5 offers several recommendations for the militaries of the new republics in Eastern Europe and the former territories of the Soviet Union. It provides guidelines for politicians, military commanders, ethnic leaders, and ethnic soldiers to promote integration. Through discussion of a dramatic trial which ended in 1996 in South Africa, the epilogue raises another tough question: are soldiers with kin across the border mere marionettes manipulated by the state to divide and rule weak ethnic groups from within? The answer to this question is far from conclusive.

Napoleon once boasted that a man like himself cared little about the fate of a million soldiers. Today more than ever, the number of soldiers recruited or lost on the battlefield remains a poor indication of the military's overall quality and expected performance in wartime. A hastily assembled multitude of soldiers from various ethnic groups may be called a military, albeit a poor one. In this age of technological warfare, the fate of armies is determined by the military's internal cohesiveness and the dedication of all its soldiers. This book examines one neglected—

yet vital—component in making a military organization internally cohesive: the recruitment, training, promotion, and deployment of soldiers
from ethnic groups that the state and the general public mistrust.

The idea for this book was born during my conversations with the late
Judith N. "Dita" Shklar. Dita's devotion to her students, relentless skep-
ticism, and scholarly work will continue to inspire me throughout my
academic career. I am also greatly indebted to Samuel P. Huntington,
who read endless drafts of my chapters, corrected them, and provided
me with contacts, resources, and ideas. Stephen Rosen, Steve Walt, and
Michael Sandel also offered many insights, comments, and suggestions
that contributed much to the final product. I am also very grateful to
Roger Haydon of Cornell University Press for his patience and advice
on how to make the ideas and research of this manuscript more acces-
sible.

My deepest gratitude and eternal love are reserved for my wife, Alisa,
without whom this book would not have been completed. Alisa read all
the chapters, corrected them, debated the book's ideas with me, and
supported me even during the most difficult hours. Her superb analytical
thinking and skills as a historian were, and remain, the true inspiration
for my work. My parents, Arye and Sylvia, and my brother, Amir, had
to endure long years during which I was far away from home, research-
ing and writing this manuscript. The geographical separation of our family was very difficult for all of us. Their love and confidence in me gave
me the necessary energy to finish the book.

I am also indebted to the Mellon, Kennedy-Sinclair, and MacArthur
foundations as well as the Olin Institute for Strategic Studies at Harvard
University. The grants I received from these institutions enabled me to
conduct field research in South Africa, Singapore, and Israel. During my
field research in these countries, I located numerous sources that I could
not have obtained otherwise. Thus, the contribution of these foundations
to the completion of this manuscript was critical.

Last but not least, I met numerous people in South Africa, Singapore,
and Israel who went out of their way to facilitate my research. It would
be impossible to mention all of their names, but their assistance was
essential to the completion of the work.

ALON PELED

Jerusalem

[1]

The "Trojan Horse" Dilemma

Will ethnic soldiers who have kin across the border in an enemy country fight for their country if the enemy invades? Or will they turn their guns against their fellow soldiers? Can members of ethnic groups whose loyalty to the state is questioned by the government and the general public be recruited, trained, integrated, and promoted within the armed forces? Why do some armies humiliate, starve, and brutalize their ethnic soldiers, whereas other military organizations promote such soldiers in rank, allow them into elite units, and treat them as first-class soldiers? Together these questions constitute the Trojan horse dilemma.

This dilemma exists in the minds of politicians, military commanders, and the general public in multiethnic states where one or more ethnic groups have kin in an enemy country. In such countries, the dilemma is always on the public agenda. The topic is so sensitive that even the slightest change in the military status of the allegedly disloyal ethnic group can result in great political turmoil. In South Africa, sixteen black soldiers were recruited in 1973—the first to serve in infantry positions since 1945—and were armed and trained with automatic rifles. Anxious South African newspapers reported the story under headlines such as, "Will They Turn Their Guns on Us?" Israel's second president, Yitzhak Ben-Zvi, argued that Israel's Arab enemies were plotting to install Israeli Arab citizens as a fifth column in the Israeli Defence Force (IDF). Touching a sensitive nerve in the newly established Jewish state, Ben-Zvi claimed that Israeli Arab soldiers would play the same role as the Sudeten Germans had done in Czechoslovakia, aiding the invaders. Such incidents exemplify how deeply embedded is suspicion in states where one or more ethnic groups may have dual loyalties. The Trojan horse dilemma can be summarized in a simple question: If recruited, trained, and armed, will ethnic soldiers become loyal soldiers or dangerous saboteurs?

In this book I suggest that, given a chance, ethnic soldiers will serve loyally. But they are more likely to get a fair chance of becoming first-class soldiers in professional military organizations than they are in politicized armed forces. The principal argument is that ethnic soldiers are likely to be promoted within one generation (twenty years) to the status of first-class soldiers in professional military organizations where officers—not politicians—make manpower policy. In contrast, ethnic soldiers are usually doomed to segregation, exclusion, even ongoing humiliation and brutalization, in armed forces where politicians formulate manpower policy based on political considerations rather than combat needs.

The initial recruitment of soldiers from ethnic groups with kin across the border typically is a measure adopted by politicians and military officers desperate for additional manpower. Once in the military, however, ethnic soldiers will fare differently in professional than in politicized military organizations. In professional military organizations they will be promoted in rank, be given a chance to command, assume combat positions, and become equal members of the defense forces. In politicized armed forces where the senior command is composed of "politicians in uniform," or where the professional autonomy of the military's commanders is curtailed by the politicians (as in the Iraqi military), ethnic soldiers will be doomed to serve—generation after generation—in service-oriented and poorly equipped units, with no chance of becoming first-class soldiers. Politicized armies also may opt to exclude allegedly disloyal ethnic groups from the armed forces. Ethnic integration within the armed forces, I believe, depends more on the military itself than on external pressures on the military to integrate.

ALTERNATIVE EXPLANATIONS OF ETHNIC MILITARY INTEGRATION

Why might ethnic soldiers be integrated into, or excluded from, the armed forces? Observers have promoted three alternative explanations: external threat, strong political leader, and national ideology. According to the proponents of external threat, a simple "last-in-first-out" manpower formula has been used time and again by governments in multiethnic societies: when external threat increases, ethnic groups are called to the flag, and when external threat fades, ethnic soldiers are the first to be demobilized.[1] Moreover, according to this line of argument, ethnic soldiers whose loyalty the state questions usually fare poorly in the armed forces. They frequently are used in menial service positions or segregated into poorly equipped and ill trained "cannon fodder" units.

Yet the argument in favor of external threat fails to answer some important questions. Why do some militaries treat their ethnic soldiers better than others facing similar threats? Why do some armies discharge ethnic soldiers immediately after the war whereas others continue to promote, deploy, and equalize the status of such soldiers? Why do some states opt to recruit ethnic soldiers, whereas others adopt alternative solutions, such as enlisting women or foreign mercenaries, or acquiring improved military technology (which in turn can reduce the demand for military manpower)? What accounts for ethnic soldiers' promotion in rank and status during peacetime?

The histories of the armed forces in Singapore, Israel, and South Africa support these doubts concerning the validity of the external-threat argument. All three states have had to cope with potent military threats during the past four decades. Since 1948, Israel has fought five large-scale wars and has been involved in numerous military operations against its Arab neighbors. Singapore was born and developed in conflict with its powerful and much larger Muslim neighbors, particularly Malaysia.[2] South Africa was involved in a protracted war with Angola and other neighboring countries between 1974 and 1988. Still, despite similar strong external threats, the ethnic military manpower policies of these three states were remarkably different, ranging from integration (South Africa) to semi-integration (Israel) to exclusion (Singapore). The external-threat argument fails to account for these important differences.

The choices made by Israel, Singapore, and South Africa also cast

1. Cynthia H. Enloe, *Ethnic Soldiers: State Security in Divided Societies* (Athens: University of Georgia Press, 1980), pp. 52–53.

2. To this day, Singapore's leaders express fears of an Islamist Malaysia under the control of a fundamentalist Muslim movement. One scholar claims that Singapore will execute a "brutal and fearless preemptive strike" if Malaysia displays signs of imminent attack. This strategy includes destroying Malay airports and having the army cross the causeway connecting Singapore to Malaysia and advance into Peninsular Malaysia. See Tim Huxley, "Singapore and Malaysia: A Precarious Balance?" *Pacific Review* 4, no. 3 (1991): 208.

doubt on the strong-leader explanation for ethnic integration within the military. According to the proponents of this argument, conservative military organizations will always be reluctant to recruit or integrate ethnic troops. Only a strong statesman, this argument continues, will be able to overcome conservative political forces and generals and compel the military to move in the direction of ethnic integration. But I focus on a historical era when these three countries were dominated by cunning, strong, and internationally acclaimed political figures (David Ben-Gurion in Israel, Lee Kuan Yew in Singapore, and Hendrik Verwoerd and Pieter Willem Botha in South Africa). The book demonstrates that with a strong political leader ruling the state, ethnic integration within the military will still vary greatly among states. The mere existence of a strong political leader cannot explain why one military chose to integrate its ranks while another opted to expel ethnic groups.

Proponents of the strong political leader thesis also argue that a strong and conservative statesman is likely both to curtail the degree of autonomy of professional military officers and to exclude ethnic groups from military service. Thus, they argue, there is no reason to focus on the relationship between military professionalism and ethnic integration. Instead, according to this line of argument, one is better off examining the impact of strong leaders on several military domains, including ethnic integration and military professionalism. But as the chapter on ethnic integration within the South African military demonstrates, even strong and conservative political leaders will not alter the well-established standards and long-standing traditions of a professional military inherited from their predecessors. Chapter 2 also shows that strong statesmen may temporarily change existing ethnic recruitment policies, but not the fundamental processes of learning and transformation within the military. Eventually, as the South African case shows, even strong political leaders will yield to the pressure of military officers to open the door to ethnic soldiers in order to improve combat readiness.

The histories of South Africa, Singapore, and Israel exemplify the weakness of the national ideology thesis. According to this line of argument, the state of ethnic integration in the military depends on how exclusive or inclusive the national ideology is. Thus, states with a pluralistic national ideology or a strong nation-building ethos will integrate members of subordinated ethnic groups in the military; on the other hand, in states where racial division and ethnic stratification characterize the national ideology, ethnic soldiers will suffer from exclusion, segregation, and humiliation. I find, however, that there is no relationship between national ideology and ethnic military integration. In South Africa, which adopted a highly racially divisive national ideology (apartheid) between 1948 and 1992, the military had an impressive history of progress toward ethnic integration at the height of apartheid. In contrast, Singapore, which adopted an all-inclusive national ideology (multiculturalism) after 1965, gradually pushed Malay officers, NCOs, and soldiers out of the military.

This book therefore proposes a fresh line of argument, focusing on the military itself rather than on the politics, enemy, or ideology of the state. The next section in this chapter explains how the changing nature of war and the military vocation in the twentieth century created a new class of professional officers, and why ethnic soldiers are likely to fare much better in militaries commanded by such professional officers than in those led by "politicians in uniform."

FROM MILITARY PROFESSIONALISM TO ETHNIC INTEGRATION

Before 1914, military commanders had little incentive to integrate their ethnic troops because of the relatively benign destructive power of military technology, the limited mobility of large troops, the constrained logistical systems of armies on the march, and the socioeconomic structure of aristocratic and feudal societies. The carnage of World War I compelled military commanders to adapt quickly to new military doctrines. Because of its increased destructiveness, the new military technology offered commanders the opportunity to fight faster and more decisive battles, provided they reorganized and retrained their troops.[3] In addition, the rise of the conscripted nation-in-arms model compelled military officers to find a way to fight shorter and more decisive wars, since they could no longer depend on long-term standing armies.

The modern theory of blitzkrieg (lightning war), which emerged from the ashes of World War I, highlighted the need to abolish arcane ethnic distinctions between divisions and brigades. It required the attacker to hit the points where the enemy was weak and least expected to be at-

3. Observing the destruction on the battlefields of World War I, one distinguished military scholar wrote that "the battle has annihilated itself." See John Keegan, *The Face of Battle* (London: J. Cape, 1976).

tacked. The attacker therefore had to use special break-in forces to secure a foothold in the enemy's lines, and then pour in large break-through forces to expand the foothold. The blitzkrieg doctrine demanded the creation of well-trained army groups equipped with independent artillery, armor, mechanized infantry, engineering, air support, and logistical elements led by independent-minded commanders who knew how to pursue relentlessly the weakest spot in the enemy's lines. Nonmilitary factors, such as the traditional ethnic division of the military, had to make way for a new type of manpower organization. Now troops from all groups (including ethnic groups) were to be trained jointly, and their leaders chosen according to their ability to lead on the battlefield, not their ethnic origin.[4]

The emergence of guerrilla warfare and counterguerrilla doctrine after World War II highlighted from a different perspective the need to integrate ethnic troops. Officers who sought to capture "the hearts and minds" of the local population in a foreign terrain quickly discovered that intimate knowledge of the local religion, culture, and language was vital to the success of the campaign. Since ethnic soldiers possessed these crucial skills, their combat deployment, integration, and promotion became an important topic on the agenda of military staff planners. Thus two of the most important doctrinal contributions of the twentieth century (i.e., blitzkrieg and counterguerrilla theory) indirectly pushed military commanders to integrate fully their ethnic troops.

A new class of officers, educated in foreign schools, dispersed these new doctrines across borders. The twentieth century has superseded any other era in the global dissemination and sharing of new military knowledge. Visiting foreign officers, foreign military advisors and attachés, international military organizations, joint national war games, and media coverage of highly publicized wars such as Vietnam have turned the professional modern officer into a perpetual international student. Gradually, officers schooled in the military academies of other countries came to staff the higher echelons of most militaries, and they were eager to implement reform at home in light of the doctrines they had learned and their experiences abroad.

Foreign-educated officers challenged their colleagues to rethink traditional military policies, including ethnic military manpower, in military staff courses and, later on, in all military schools. New textbooks and

4. Bryan Perrett, *A History of Blitzkrieg* (New York: Jove Books, 1983), pp. 12–13.

war games encouraged officers to explore the new military doctrines and determine how to adopt them successfully. These investigations led to manpower experiments—the recruitment of previously excluded ethnic groups, the promotion of ethnically segregated units to the status of combat units, and the incorporation of ethnic soldiers into courses, units, and assignments previously closed to them. The success of the first experiments quickly led to new, more daring ones.[5]

Successful ethnic experiments resulted first in horizontal ethnic change, defined as a set of reforms of traditional ethnic manpower policies for the promotion and integration of the rank and file. This set is usually the subtotal of many incremental changes in the service terms of ethnic soldiers: incorporating previously excluded ethnic groups into the military, training ethnic soldiers with weapons and live ammunition for the first time, upgrading ethnic units from auxiliary and service-oriented to fully fledged combat units. External observers not privy to classified military manpower and training information still can collect a host of minor—and less classified—signs that the military has begun changing its traditional ethnic manpower policy. These signs may include the introduction of a cadet system in minority high schools, the provision of service symbols (uniforms, insignias, serial numbers) and pay (salaries, benefits, veteran status) equal to those of soldiers from the dominant ethnic group, and establishment of special staff departments to study the unique problems and needs of ethnic soldiers to further their status. Horizontal ethnic change intensifies when the military begins incorporating the first ethnic soldiers into specialized corps (mechanized fighting units, intelligence, commandos, the air force) and deploying ethnic soldiers and units in sensitive missions and in combat. It culminates in the complete integration of these soldiers and units into the general military schooling system, the abolishment of separate military schools, and, ultimately, the opening up of all regular and reserve units and corps to ethnic soldiers.

Horizontal ethnic change then leads to vertical ethnic change—a set of reforms of traditional ethnic manpower policies on the commissioning and promotion of ethnic NCOs and officers. Unlike horizontal change, which can commence in different ways in different armies, vertical ethnic

---

5. This pattern of ethnic innovation is not restricted to ethnic military manpower policy. Rosen argues that military innovation, in general, results from a new promotion pathway created by senior officers for junior officers practicing a new way of war. See Stephen Peter Rosen, *Winning the Next War: Innovation and the Modern Military* (Ithaca: Cornell University Press, 1991), p. 252.

change begins the same way in every military organization, with the commissioning of the first ethnic officers. This kind of change intensifies as the military opens up more academies, colleges, and advanced courses for ethnic officers and NCOs, and as it equalizes the service status and benefits of ethnic and nonethnic officers. Other signs include the assignment of the first ethnic squad, platoon, and company leaders to combat missions and the commissioning of the first officers to command formations outside their segregated units. Vertical ethnic change culminates in the promotion of a significant group of junior ethnic officers (lieutenants and captains) to mid-career ranks (major and lieutenant colonel) and, later on, to senior ranks (colonel and general), and the assignment of officers to command large-scale, nonethnic combat formations.

Even despite military secrecy, the researcher can piece together sufficient information to determine if a military organization is integrating its troops or if it is moving away from integration. It is important to note, however, that the progress of military ethnic integration is not linear. Occasionally, even a professional military organization on course to integrate its ranks may succumb to external pressures and temporarily scale back its integration experiments. For example, in 1986 the South African navy was forced to terminate abruptly a new racially integrated course for female cadets when news about this course leaked to the conservative white media and all hell broke loose. But I will show that such setbacks are rare, and that they stand in complete contrast to the general and long-term efforts of the military to improve the status of ethnic troops. Six months after the course was canceled, the South African navy renewed the racially integrated course—this time under a tighter veil of secrecy.

To uncover a military's true stand on ethnic integration, we need to study both the horizontal and vertical dimensions of ethnic change. Vertical change alone could be mere tokenism. Military organizations intent on an ethnic status quo might promote a few ethnic officers to senior positions in order to mask the lot of the vast majority. Similarly, horizontal change, in and of itself, is an insufficient indication of overall integration. Military organizations may reform minor policies (by, for example, providing ethnic soldiers with better salaries) in order to reduce dissatisfaction in segregated units. A military organization that refuses to commission ethnic officers is, in fact, admitting its ongoing suspicion of ethnic soldiers and its unwillingness to provide them with equal opportunities. In short, neither vertical nor horizontal change alone is sufficient to support a claim that a military organization is moving toward—or away from—ethnic integration.

Horizontal and vertical change affect each other. For example, an increase in the size, number, and military specialization of ethnically segregated units may convince senior officers to commission the first ethnic officers so that they can assume greater responsibilities within their units. And the first contingent of ethnic officers may convince military planners that it is now possible to recruit larger numbers of ethnic youth and form new ethnic formations. This dynamic relationship between vertical and horizontal ethnic change ultimately leads the military to abandon most of its traditional ethnic manpower policies.

Manpower planners should carefully coordinate the pace of horizontal and vertical ethnic change. They often find themselves trapped between ethnic soldiers who desire equality and political leaders who, fearing ethnic Trojan horses, wish to slow down the pace of military integration. A rapid pace of horizontal, but insufficient vertical, change will frustrate ethnic soldiers who feel deprived of a fair chance of promotion. On the other hand, hasty vertical change will alarm security-minded politicians who want to see ethnic soldiers bearing arms for the state but not commanding. One type of ethnic change, therefore, ought not supersede the other. For these reasons, the integration (or exclusion) of ethnic troops usually is a sensitive topic kept far from the public eye.

If successful, horizontal and vertical ethnic change modifies the military's corporate culture. The military will scrap discriminatory statutes, and its courts will discipline unruly behavior toward ethnic soldiers. In the final stage, the military will integrate ethnic and nonethnic soldiers in the same schools, units, and missions. The combat experience of ethnic soldiers will become too valuable to be restricted to segregated units alone. Figure 1 illustrates the road map for ethnic integration in professional military organizations.

Armies also can move in the opposite direction: from integration of various ethnic groups to degradation of the service status of some uniformed ethnic groups and the exclusion of others from the military. Protracted status degradation ultimately leads to change in the military's regulations and esprit de corps. The dominant ethnic groups create new military statutes—for example, a compulsory language test, based on the ethnic language of the dominant group, for officers seeking promotion—to institutionalize their monopoly of the military. Brutalization of, and discrimination against, ethnic soldiers become the new norm. Ultimately,

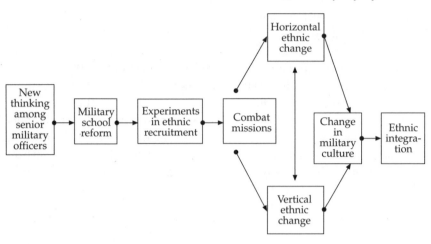

Figure 1. Road map to ethnic military manpower integration

these servicemen will leave (or desert) the military en masse, and the military history books will scrap any mention of their legacy, as happened with the Malay soldiers in the Singapore Armed Forces (SAF) between 1965 and 1977 (see Chapter 3).

The theory proposed in this section is ambitious, as it affirms a causal relationship between two factors that at first appear to be completely unrelated—military professionalism and ethnic integration. The next section explains how the examples of South Africa, Singapore, and Israel, which I selected as my principal case studies after surveying the ethnic histories of more than 150 armed forces, support a causal relationship between military professionalism and ethnic integration.

ETHNIC HISTORIES OF THREE ARMED FORCES

South Africa, Singapore, and Israel are multiethnic states in which society is ethnically stratified and ethnic groups are hierarchically ranked. The dominant ethnic groups are the Jews in Israel, the Chinese in Singapore, and the whites in South Africa (until 1992); they command virtually all the political and military power, economic wealth, and social prestige. Since the creation of these countries, conflicts among their dom-

Table 1. Subordinated ethnic groups in South Africa, Israel, and Singapore

Country	Dominant ethnic group	Subordinated ethnic group	Subethnic group
Israel	Jews	Arabs	Muslims Christians Bedouins Druze Circassians
Singapore	Chinese	Malays Indians Eurasians	
South Africa	Whites	Blacks Coloreds Indians	

inant and subordinated ethnic groups have dominated the political agenda. The subordinated ethnic groups, which vary greatly in their relative power vis-à-vis the state, are presented in Table 1.

I will focus on the ethnic histories of the armed forces in Israel (1948–1982), Singapore (1965–1977), and South Africa (1948–1985) in Chapters 2, 3, and 4. My extensive field research in these countries uncovered much new information concerning the lot of Israeli Arab; Singaporean Malay Muslim; and South African black, colored, and Indian soldiers. The fascinating historical narratives that emerged from piecing together this information differ, in many cases, from the formal histories of the armed forces in these countries.

There is a tension between my goal of providing a new general ethnic history of the three nations' armies and my attempt to substantiate the theory that professional military organizations are more likely than nonprofessional ones to integrate their ranks ethnically. Such a tension, though not new, becomes especially strong when both tasks—a new historical narrative and a new theoretical argument based on this narrative—are pursued simultaneously. On the one hand, a good historical narrative needs to focus on one country at a time and on the flow of chronological events. On the other hand, a scientific study requires structured comparisons between case studies and a thematic discussion that often violates chronological order. Thus, my main methodological concern was to substantiate a comparative theoretical argument while preserving the flow of a historical narrative.

[11]

My solution was to embed the focus and chronological order of a good historical narrative in the structure of a chapter, but break the new ethnic history into multiple "stories" (known as "observations" among social scientists) and compare these with each other.[6] The story—defined as a chain of decisions and activities directly linked to each other and limited in time, place, and scope of actors—is the smallest building block of the general historical narrative. For example, the decision-making processes involved in recruiting coloreds (1963), Indians (1973), and blacks (1973) into the South African Defence Forces constitute three distinct stories that can be compared because each involved different actors, time spans, and concerns (Indians were recruited by naval officers to the navy; coloreds, by the army, into their own distinct unit; and blacks, by the army, into a training center that became an independent army unit a year later).

Three techniques are used to identify, recount, and compare such stories. First, I highlight cases where similar ethnic military manpower policy changes took place under different conditions in the three countries. I then show how the differences in the outcomes of these changes are related to the differences in the level of military professionalism. For example, decisions to begin recruiting an ethnic group previously excluded from military service in Israel (the recruitment of non-Jews after the War of Independence) and South Africa (the re-enlistment of non-whites into the SADF after 1963) are compared. I then argue that the recruitment was faster and smoother in South Africa than Israel because of the SADFs' long-standing professional standards and the lack of such standards in the IDF, which, during its first years, underwent a transition from a guerrilla to a military organization. In another example, the impact of the Soweto riots (1976) on the SADF's policy toward its new nonwhite soldiers is compared to the impact of the riots in Malaysia (1967 and 1969) on the policy of the SAF toward its Malay Muslim soldiers. I then argue that in South Africa the riots only temporarily halted the integration of nonwhites into the SADF, while in Singapore the riots accelerated the removal of Malay Muslims from the military. In both cases, the riots had little or no independent impact on the military, and

6. Gary King, Robert O. Keohane, and Sidney Verba, *Designing Social Inquiry: Scientific Inference in Qualitative Research* (Princeton: Princeton University Press, 1994), p. 117, state that countries (such as Israel, Singapore, and South Africa) are "mere boundaries within which a large number of observations are made."

shortly afterwards politicians and military commanders resumed the ethnic manpower policy they had adopted before the riots.

Second, I always try to break one ethnic manpower decision (such as
a decision to commission the first ethnic officers) into multiple stories
about the ethnic groups and units affected by the decision. The history
of the SADF is rich with such examples. On numerous occasions, decisions to recruit, promote, and deploy members of a given ethnic group
were discussed, debated, and eventually executed by the South African
navy, the army, and the air force—each corps making up its mind in-
dependently of the others and implementing decisions in its own way.
For example, the decision to send nonwhite units to combat for the first
time since World War II was broken into three stories because the army
and navy adopted this policy separately, at different times and under
different circumstances for the respective ethnic groups (the navy decided to deploy Indians on battleships in 1973; the army decided to deploy coloreds in battle in 1975, and blacks in 1977). Similarly, the military
followed three distinct and separate decision-making processes to determine when to promote the first colored cadets to officership (1975), Indian sailors to midshipmen (1978), and black servicemen to officers
(1984). Singapore's decision to segregate Malay Muslim servicemen was
implemented in radically different ways before and after 1969 (before
1969, Malay Muslim soldiers were "controlled" within existing units;
after 1969, Malay Muslim-dominated units were "controlled" by new
Chinese-dominated units). Similarly, Israel's decision to take some non-
Jewish groups into the military was carried out differently for different
groups (Druze and Circassians were conscripted; Bedouins were permitted and encouraged to volunteer to serve; Muslims and Christian
Arabs were left outside the military's gates).

The "snowball" phenomenon (for example, when one corps decides
to commission its first ethnic officers because it feels pressure from another corps that has already done so) does not necessarily mean that two
stories constitute a single story. To the contrary, snowballing frequently
does not work, and an ethnic change that may appear to be similar across
units and corps can actually be quite different. The South African air
force never followed the pace of the navy and the army in promoting
ethnic officers. Moreover, when the air force finally did promote its first
ethnic officers, it offered them only service, not combat, positions. And
although the SADF was successful in a clandestine initial experiment to
establish its first black unit (Battalion 21) between 1973 and 1974, it was

unable to use Battalion 21 as a model for creating additional black units because the battalion included blacks from different ethnic groups. The composition of this unit violated the official apartheid policy of building ethnically separate black homelands (one homeland per one ethnic black group). The SADF therefore spent almost a year (1976) studying the problem of recruiting additional black servicemen before launching a campaign to build ten new black battalions (1976–1984), each consisting of members of one—and only one—black ethnic group. The case of Israeli Druze servicemen in the IDF illustrates that, in fact, organizational inertia is more likely to overcome the snowball phenomenon. After their exemplary performance against guerrilla infiltrators in the Jordan Valley (1968–1970), Druze servicemen expected to be rewarded with the opportunity to break out of their ethnically segregated unit. But the IDF was slow to remove traditional barriers, and it took a considerable amount of pressure from Druze servicemen before they finally were posted outside the Minority Unit (also known as Unit 300).

Finally, in this study I sometimes trace multiple stories even within one corps in the armed forces of one country. For example, the decision to elevate one army brigade from a service to a combat unit does not guarantee that the same decision will be adopted for a different unit. If riots erupted across the nation shortly after the army elevated the first ethnic brigade to a combat unit and if, despite these riots, it decided to elevate a second ethnic unit, then the first and the second decisions really are two distinct stories, each taking place in its own time, space, and circumstances. Indeed, in this example, the conditions under which the first and second stories occurred are so radically different that the second story presents an excellent opportunity to test whether a professional military organization is committed to its experimental ethnic integration policy despite changing socioethnic conditions. In South Africa, the decision and efforts to recruit blacks into Battalion 21 occurred long before the Soweto riots (1976). Thus, the SADF's decision to press on with the recruitment of blacks, and even to establish newer black units after 1976, provided a chance to examine the military's determination to change its internal ethnic composition. In another example, the decision to post a limited number of non-Jewish servicemen outside the Minority Unit (1972) was very different from that of spreading Druze infantrymen throughout the military after the 1973 War, during which the IDF learned that it was short of manpower, particularly of infantry soldiers.

[14]

This book not only carefully documents and scrutinizes stories that confirm its theoretical argument, but analyzes and discusses the failures and setbacks of military organizations that, in general, successfully integrated their ranks. Although the SADF is an exemplary professional military organization, which successfully achieved ethnic integration despite the dictates of apartheid, I also discuss incidents such as the failure of General Magnus Malan, the former chief of the SADF and minister of defence, to absorb blacks into the all-white commandos (1976), and the long—and poorly justified—delay in commissioning the first black officers in the South African military (1978–1984). Similarly, even though the Israeli military moved toward a greater degree of internal ethnic integration as it became more professional, I discuss the IDF's decision to continue to segregate non-Jewish soldiers under Jewish commanders in the Minority Unit (1954). And in the case of Singapore, where the military was set on a decade-long course of excluding Malay Muslim soldiers from its ranks, I discuss the failure of senior Defence Manpower planners to stop the recruitment of new Malay soldiers—and the price one key official had to pay for this failure.

The ethnic histories of South Africa, Singapore, and Israel, therefore, are rich in stories that can be compared as I examine the fate of ethnic soldiers in professional versus nonprofessional military organizations. The reader can focus on either the historical narrative or the scientific argument of this book. Those more interested in history will learn how nonwhites, including blacks, entered the white South African military after 1963, how Malay Muslims were removed from the Singaporean military after 1965, and how some Arab youths found a home in the IDF after 1948. The more theory-oriented can focus on the structured comparisons between the stories, and on my conclusion that professional militaries are more likely to integrate ethnic soldiers.

Before turning our attention to these fascinating histories, we must consider briefly two questions. First, why is the Trojan horse dilemma an important topic deserving our attention? And second, what do *military professionalism, ethnicity,* and *ethnic military manpower policy* mean in this study? The next section explains how the Trojan horse dilemma has emerged from an obscure topic in history to become a dominant issue shaping the politics, culture, and sometime survival of multiethnic states. The last section in this chapter presents a brief explanation of this book's key concepts.

[15]

The Historical Roots of the Trojan Horse Dilemma

Group membership, defined in terms of ethnicity, race, religion, and language, has been a common criterion used by military commanders to decide who to recruit and who to exempt from military service. Ethnic recruitment arrangements have characterized the armed forces of both ancient and modern empires and states.[7] Presently, in many countries, only weak and powerless ethnic groups are compelled to serve in the military. In Guatemala, for example, it has always been the practice to conscript soldiers from the ranks of the impoverished Indian and Latino-speaking populations. One scholar, noting this phenomenon, commented that, "to be liable for conscription is a good index of one's lack of power to avoid it."[8] In the vast majority of countries that conscript from the ranks of weak ethnic groups, members of the dominant ethnic group continue to monopolize senior officer positions while members of sub-ordinated ethnic groups staff the rank-and-file positions. In Jordan, Bedouins dominate the officer corps while many soldiers are of Palestinian origin. In Syria, the ruling Alawite ethnic group holds a virtual monopoly over all combat command positions.

Ethnic recruitment is not limited to developing nations. Black American soldiers served in segregated units until 1948. Nor is it a vanishing phenomenon. Every one of the seventeen new republics of the former Soviet Union has adopted a draft bill with special clauses exempting citizens of Russian origin from military duty. But despite the importance of this phenomenon, which has affected the lives of millions of youth, we know relatively little about the historical roots of ethnic military manpower policies.

Virtually every large military organization until the French Revolution was organized along ethnic lines, and ethnic armies were simply accepted as a fact of life with which officers had to make do. Emperors often empowered ethnic leaders with the authority to fill quotas of military recruits from among the members of their groups. Frequently, subject peoples entered the armies of the great empires with their own weapons and formed corps ancillary to the army's main fighting force.

7. Cynthia H. Enloe, *Police, Military, and Ethnicity: Foundations of State Power* (New Brunswick, N.J.: Transaction Books, 1980), p. 15.

8. Richard N. Adams, "The Development of the Guatemalan Military," *Studies in Comparative International Development* 4, no. 1 (1968–1969): 95.

When Darius met Alexander at Gaugamela (331 BC), his Persian military was composed of no less than twenty-four different subject or mercenary nationalities. Similarly, Assyrian, Roman, and Ottoman militaries recruited troops without ethnic discrimination. Muslim rulers in the middle of the ninth century extended ethnic recruitment beyond ancillary forces; they enslaved non-Muslim youth from central Asia to be raised as Muslims and trained as soldiers.[9]

The great military commanders of antiquity used the division of the troops along ethnic lines to their advantage. Hannibal used Spanish light troops to lure the Roman center into his collapsing center at Canne. Other military leaders capitalized on the ethnic divisions of the enemy's army to find and strike at its most unmotivated and demoralized troops. For example, in 1211, Genghis Khan's conquest of the Chinese empire was aided by the fact that the Great Wall was in the hands of barbarian (i.e., non-Han) people, and that another non-Han group occupied the western flank of the empire.[10]

Emperors, fearing that their own people would betray them, even staffed the high command of their militaries with ethnic groups, as did Ivan the Terrible (1547–1584) with the Tatars from Kazan, Astrakhan, and the Crimea. Ivan also appointed Tatar nobles free from association with Russian aristocratic cliques to senior command positions over purely Russian battalions. Similarly, Tso Tsung-t'ang, a leading and experienced Han Chinese general, relied on Mongols, Tibetans, and Monguors as soldiers in his anti-Muslim campaign in northwest China in 1866.[11] Indeed, emperors staffed their militaries with so many ethnic groups that historians, taking it for granted, rarely touched upon the polyethnic nature of these armies.[12]

Such long-standing agreements between emperors and ethnic leaders came to an end with the French Revolution. In revolutionary France, the new ideas of nation, freedom, citizenship, and patriotism ended the tradition of military ethnic quotas and military manpower contracts be-

9. John Keegan, *A History of Warfare* (New York: Alfred A. Knopf, 1994), pp. 34, 172, 261.
10. Keegan, *History of Warfare*, pp. 203–204.
11. Lanny Brice Fields, "Ethnicity in Tso Tsung-t'ang's Armies: The Campaigns in Northwest China, 1867–1880," in *Ethnicity and the Military in Asia*, ed. DeWitt C. Ellinwood and Cynthia H. Enloe (Buffalo: State University of New York, 1980), pp. 29–47; Alexander R. Alexiev and S. Wimbush Enders, *Ethnic Minorities in the Red Army: Asset or Liability?* (Boulder, Colo.: Westview Press, 1988), p. 14.
12. N. F. Dreisziger, *Ethnic Armies: Polyethnic Armed Forces from the Time of the Habsburgs to the Age of the Superpowers* (Waterloo, Ont.: Wilfrid Laurier University Press, 1990), p. 3.

tween emperors and ethnic leaders. The ideological fervor of French citizen soldiers transformed the French military into "the school of the new nation."[13] The Prussian-German army in 1870 revitalized the spirit of the French Revolution—against the French. During the late nineteenth century, the popularity of military service increased enormously, unlike any other era in history. Most European nations established their draft systems during this period. French and Prussian officers aided nations around the globe in adopting the model of a universal citizen soldier army.[14] Even the critics of such armies had to acknowledge their strength. Engels, for example, argued that revolutions against these popular conscript-based military organizations were doomed to fail. Only after such armies collapsed and vanished from within could the Communist revolution take place.[15]

Emperors encountered great difficulties when they attempted to reverse the trend of nationalism by conscripting ethnic groups. Napoleon faced a series of national insurrections when he instituted conscription in Italy after Wagram (1809), and among his own French troops.[16] The Austrian administration had to tackle an uprising in Montenegro (especially in Krivosije) and riots in the Zillertaler Valley after the introduction of a new conscription bill in 1869. Desertion was rampant among the several dozen conscript-based Hungarian and Transylvanian infantry regiments in the Austro-Hungarian army after hostilities broke out in 1859.[17] And the Albanians experienced the beginnings of a national awakening in their struggle against conscription to the Ottoman Empire's military (1836–1839).

In the 60 percent of the world's nations using conscription, the citizen-soldier legacy of the French Revolution remains important in three respects.[18] First, a general consensus has developed that the military is a

13. Maury D. Feld, *The Structure of Violence: Armed Forces as Social Systems* (Beverly Hills, Calif.: Sage, 1977), p. 22; Stephen Wilson, "For a Socio-historical Approach to the Study of Western Military Culture," *Armed Forces and Society* 6, no. 4 (Summer 1980): 540–541.

14. Wilson, "For a Socio-historical Approach," pp. 527–552.

15. Martin Berger, "Engels' Theory of the Vanishing Army: A Key to the Development of Marxist Revolutionary Tactics," *Historian* 37, no. 3 (1975): 435.

16. Isser Woloch, "Napoleonic Conscription: State Power and Civil Society," *Past and Present* 111 (May 1986): 101; Sanford Kanter, "Sacrificing National Defense to Class Interest: The French Military Service Law of 1872," *Military Affairs* 49, no. 1 (1985): 5.

17. Peter Hidas, "The Army of Francis Joseph and Magyar Public Opinion, 1849–1859," *Hungarian Studies Review* 14, no. 2 (1987): 13.

18. Of 143 countries, 88 used universal or selective conscription in 1993. See *The Military Balance, 1992–93* (London: International Institute for Strategic Studies, 1993).

nation builder. Statesmen in developing nations have adopted the idea that the military can be used in an "architectural or mechanical" way to assimilate ethnic groups into a new, unified, and loyal nation.[19]

Second, the citizen-soldier legacy popularized the notion that the military is a character-building institution and the foremost school of good citizenship. According to this belief, military service enables individuals to recognize their own values under difficult conditions, and so it serves as a catalyst for improving their personality, willpower, and aspirations.

Finally, the French legacy has inspired people everywhere to believe that the military serves as the ultimate leveling ground among all social, ethnic, religious, and racial groups. A 1972 French white paper captured this popular notion in philosophical language rare for a defense document: "Military service is an opportunity to make lasting friendships which are not bound by social constraint. The comradeship which emerges from sharing the same existence every day, the quality and the unselfishness of human relations which develop there, the integration of men from different milieus, trades and geographic origins, and the possibility of judging men without bias are all factors which can contribute to the personal enrichment of the man who is willing to make his contribution generously to the reality and esprit de corps of the small community that his section, platoon, company, squadron or company represents."[20] Thus the citizen-soldier legacy can be summarized in three phrases: nation building, character building, and social leveling.

Such popular passionate sentiment about the educational role of the military has been matched only by the fervor of those who resist military service. The refusal of any group of citizens to bear arms in the name of the state has grown to signify a fundamental political and moral challenge to the central regime rather than merely a mark of the regime's weakness.[21] For example, the struggle of French citizens in Canada and Catholic citizens in Australia against conscription during the two world wars quickly evolved into severe constitutional crises.[22] Since the French

19. Karl W. Deutsch and William J. Foltz, *Nation-Building* (New York: Atherton Press, 1963), p. 3. Enloe, *Ethnic Soldiers*, p. 64.

20. France, Ministry of Defense, "Universal Military Service in France," vol. 1, chap. 3, a 1972 white paper on national defense, quoted in *Military Review* 53, no. 1 (January 1973): 57–58.

21. Alasdair MacIntyre, "U.S. Draft Resistance: Whose Moral Problem?" *New Society*, October 10, 1968, 517–518.

22. Michael McKernan, "Catholics, Conscription, and Archbishop Mannix," *Historical Studies* 17, no. 68 (1977): 299–314; Frances V. Harbour, "Conscription and Socialization:

Revolution, both proponents and opponents of the citizen-soldier have grown accustomed to viewing military service in absolute terms, or as a value in and of itself. One absolutist argument equates good citizenship and membership in the nation with the military. Another equally powerful absolutist argument equates refusal to serve in the military with a denial of the state's legitimacy and a rejection of its citizenship.

Modern ethnic groups have faced an acute dilemma in light of the debate between these two viewpoints. On the one hand, military service was not likely to provide their members with equality either during their military service or after their discharge. On the other hand, a refusal to bear arms signaled disloyalty and even betrayal to the rest of society. Special military arrangements between ethnic leaders and the state were no longer possible. In the age of national armies and universal conscription, one had to be either a citizen-soldier or neither soldier nor citizen.

For their part, governments discovered that only at a high cost could they coerce ethnic soldiers to serve in the military. Coercion, when employed, yielded mass armies, but their morale was often low and soldiers lacked the will to fight. Mass armies in which ethnic soldiers were brutalized, as in Iraq, ran the risk of speedily collapsing on the battlefield through mass desertion of ethnic soldiers. This should come as no surprise to those familiar with Hobbes's Leviathan: fear is a strong motive insofar as it is the gravest fear; if the fear of the enemy's sword outweighs the fear of your ruler's sword, desertion is to be expected and the army is doomed. In Hobbes's words, "For he that wants protection may seek it anywhere."[23]

In addition, governments attempting to coerce ethnic youth into the military ran the risk of invoking an armed rebellion that would be costly to suppress. Pressed by the manpower needs of World War I, the Russians declared conscription in Central Asia for the first time on June 25, 1916. There the Muslims rebelled against this sudden reversal of the long-standing status quo exempting them from bearing arms to defend the interests of their Russian conquerors. Significant Russian military intervention was required to put down this rebellion. The Bolsheviks repeated the folly of the Tsar in January 1919 during the civil war when

---

Four Canadian Ministers," *Armed Forces and Society* 15, no. 2 (Winter 1989): 227–247; G. Walker, "Race and Recruitment in World War I: Enlistment of Visible Minorities in the Canadian Expeditionary Force," *Canadian Historical Review* 70 (1989): 1–26.

23. Thomas Hobbes, *Leviathan*, part 2, chap. 29 (Harmondsworth: Penguin Books, 1968), p. 375.

they attempted to coerce men of German origin in Warenburg into the Red Army. Massacred to the last man, Warenburg males never served in the Red Army, and the Bolsheviks wasted many men, and much equipment, time, and energy to destroy an ethnic enclave that had little to do with the pressing war against the White armies.[24]

Coercion also can produce economic devastation for the families, villages, and regions of ethnic conscripts, resulting in more pressure on the national treasury. The British colonial rulers of Kenya recruited too many locals for military service during the two World Wars, and thus contributed to four major famines that afflicted Luoland in 1906–1907, 1917–1919, 1928–1929, and 1942–1943.[25] Politicians who pursued extremely harsh conscription campaigns risked losing their ethnic populations. For example, Russian conscription caused many Lithuanians and other emigrants from Eastern Europe to leave for America between 1890 and 1914.[26] Opposition to military conscription resulted in the mass migration of tribes from French West Africa into British-held territories between 1914 and 1945.[27] And three million Afghans escaped to Pakistan between 1973 and 1987 to avoid the conscription imposed on them by chieftains of other tribes.[28]

For the military and economic reasons mentioned above, modern politicians have become increasingly reluctant to employ coercion to recruit ethnic groups. Instead, they have opted to recruit on a voluntary basis. Voluntary recruitment, however, has opened yet another Pandora's box. Once ethnic youth were permitted into the military, securing their loyalty became a difficult and sensitive dilemma. The history of the Egyptian

24. Alexiev and Wimbush, *Ethnic Minorities in the Red Army*, pp. 20–22; Richard Kisling, "Uprising in Warenburg," *Journal of the American Historical Society of Germans from Russia* 8, no. 4 (Winter 1985): 13–16.

25. William R. Ochieng, "Colonial Famines in Luoland, Kenya, 1905–1945," *TransAfrican Journal of History* 17 (1988): 28, 30. Unlike the French, however, Britain used Africans only in the African campaigns and did not transfer them overseas to Europe's bloody battlefields.

26. Compulsory military conscription also caused the 1874 emigration of 18,000 Mennonites from Russia to the Central Prairie of the United States. Fred R. Belk, "Migration of Russian Mennonites," *Social Science* 50, no. 1 (1975): 17–21.

27. French methods of conscription were exceptionally coercive. Thus, escape into British-held territories was for many Africans "the lesser of two evils." A. I. Asiwaju, "Migrations as an Expression of Revolt: The Example of French West Africa up to 1945," *Tarikh* 5, no. 3 (1977): 36–37.

28. Mary Ellen Chatwin, "The Afghan Refugees in Pakistan: A Nation in Exile," *Current Sociology/La Sociologie Contemporaine* 36, no. 2 (Summer 1988): 75.

[21]

military after the assassination of Sadat by a group of Muslim fundamentalist soldiers is a case in point. Just days later, the military announced its plans to construct twenty-two military towns in the
following decade at a cost of $3.5 billion dollars. The goal of this cam-
paign was to remove the troops from camps near the poor urban areas
of Cairo, where the Islamist movement had its strongholds, and transfer
them to the Egyptian desert, where surveillance and control would be
more manageable.[29]

The Egyptian case palls in comparison with countries that require
military troops to put down domestic racial riots. There, the ethnic
makeup of the troops can determine whether the military will squelch
or inflame the riots. During the December 1992 riots, Indian newspapers reported that Hindu troops had sided with the rioters, especially
in Bombay, the state of Madhya Pradesh, and parts of Uttar Pradesh.
The sympathy of these soldiers for the Hindu rioters resulted in Muslims suffering the highest casualty rates in these regions.[30] In more extreme cases, such as civil wars, the army may simply fall apart or
become paralyzed due to its internal ethnic structure. In 1968, the
armed forces were officially disbanded in Cyprus because of the civil
war raging between the Turkish and Greek populations. Likewise, the
Lebanese military has not functioned as a national organization for almost two decades, partly because of its internal ethnic divisions. In addition, resolving protracted civil wars often depends on the ability of
the warring parties to reach an agreement on the future ethnic composition of the state's armed forces. The tribal warfare in Afghanistan
is a case in point.

In sum, during the last decade, the military recruitment of racial, religious, and linguistic groups has become one of the most sensitive and
difficult-to-resolve dilemmas in developing countries. It encompasses issues such as overrepresentation of dominant ethnic groups within the
officer corps, control of religiously fundamentalist soldiers, promotion of
ethnic officers, public sensitivity to the action of ethnic troops during
domestic riots, preservation of the unity of the military during a civil
war, and the provision of collective exemptions for alleged Trojan horse
ethnic groups.

29. Robert B. Satloff, *Army and Politics in Mubarak's Egypt* (Washington: Washington Institute for Near East Policy, 1988), p. 28.
30. *New York Times*, December 12, 1992, A6.

Military Professionalism, Ethnicity, and Manpower Policy

Three concepts frequently explored in this book require explanation: military professionalism, ethnicity, and ethnic military manpower policy. A professional military organization has a complex system of military schools providing continuous education to service personnel at all ranks. These schools expose officers to new ideas and concepts, even ones that are socially controversial. Officers in professional military organizations focus on the mission of defending the state against a conventional external threat rather than on participating in the state's internal politics. A professional military is reluctant to accept an internal defense mission, such as a counterguerrilla campaign, and will do so only to defend the state against an external force. Officers take much pride in their training, experience, and expertise and emphasize the difference between the professional standards of the military and those of other quasi-military security organizations (such as local militias). Most important, professional officers must have a high degree of autonomy in the training and deployment of their subordinates. For example, professional organizations frequently expose their officers to new military doctrines and combat challenges by sending them to train in foreign military academies where they can acquire vital new knowledge. In addition, professional officers must be allowed to organize the military schooling system and determine the curricula of these schools according to the challenges the military faces. Finally, they must have complete autonomy to build up, train, and deploy their soldiers along functional, rather than political, lines.

In contrast, a military with low professionalism is characterized by a weak schooling system that does not encourage independent thinking and the examination of new concepts. Officers in these organizations are immersed in politics rather than in the mission of defending the state from external threat. In extreme cases, these officers are politicians or civil servants appointed to senior ranks because of their political allegiance, not their military expertise. Highly ranked commanders in such militaries do not conceive of themselves as professional officers because their military careers frequently are a quick springboard to political careers. A variety of factors account for the erosion of military professionalism. They include external political intervention, which can destroy a class of professional officers (such as the officer purge in the Iranian military after the revolution in 1979); the political ambitions of senior officers, which drag their subordinates into nondefense activities and can

[23]

lead to coup d'etats and military regimes (as in the modern history of many Latin America and African states); a deteriorating domestic political situation that draws the military away from its mission on the border and into the state's domestic politics (as in Yugoslavia after 1992); a defeat on the battlefield from which the military corporate spirit fails to recover; and the creation of semipolitical militia institutions that compete with the military and hinder its professional autonomy in the defense of the state.

Sociologists define an ethnic group as a distinct category of the population with a culture different from that of the larger society. Members of such a group are, or consider themselves, or are thought to be, bound together by common ties of race, nationality, or culture.[31] Max Weber was the first sociologist to formulate the idea that members of a given ethnic group do not necessarily need to share objective blood ties in order to consider themselves part of the same ethnic group. The only essential characteristic of an ethnic group, Weber argued, is that its members "entertain a subjective belief in their common descent because of similarities of physical type or of customs or both, or because of memories of colonization and migration."[32] The individual's belief in his "common descent" with a subset of the general population, whether it be scientifically true or empirically false, accounts for the prevalence of ethnic groups around the globe. This belief includes features such as shared religion, similar physical attributes, common language, and similar geographic origin, and it highlights similarities in lifestyle among group members, such as shared traditions.[33] Members of ethnic groups often are bound to each other through formal rules (such as religious precepts), communal institutions, and, most important, informal codes of behavior, traditions, and customs. These groups often remain cohesive and endure for many years despite external assimilative pressures (e.g., modernization).[34]

Multiethnic states are characterized by the coexistence of several principal cohesive and enduring ethnic groups. More often than not, such states are ethnically stratified. The term *ethnically stratified society* refers

31. H. S. Morris, "Ethnic Groups," in *International Encyclopedia of the Social Sciences* (New York: Macmillan 1968), 5:167.
32. Max Weber, *Economy and Society* (1922; reprint, New York: Bedminster Press, 1968).
33. Richard D. Alba, "Ethnicity," in *Encyclopedia of Sociology* (New York: Macmillan 1992), 2:575.
34. Morris, "Ethnic Groups," p. 168.

to a state where individuals identify themselves exclusively with one ethnic group and where virtually every person is allocated to one of these ethnic groups. Most important, ethnic groups in ethnically stratified societies are hierarchically ranked according to their differential access to political and economic resources.[35] In other words, ethnic group affiliations heavily influence—and sometimes determine—the position of individuals on the social ladder of prestige, wealth, and political power. And conflicts among ethnic groups—usually between the politically dominant and the subordinated—rule the political agenda.

Throughout this study, the designation *ethnic group* describes politically and economically subordinated groups whose members are distinguished from the rest of society by either a (real or perceived) common language, race, religion, or ethnic origin, or by any combination of these primordial features. Accordingly, *ethnic leaders* refers to the indigenous political leadership of these groups. The terms *ethnic youth* and *ethnic soldiers* describe those young members of the groups, usually between eighteen and twenty-eight years of age, who are either liable for military service or are already serving in the military. Finally, *ethnic units* refers to military units where the vast majority of soldiers belong to politically and economically subordinated ethnic communities.

Ethnic military manpower policy refers to an array of political decisions concerning the integration of ethnic youth in the military: which ethnic groups to recruit, the terms of service, and the kinds of military missions in which ethnic soldiers will be employed. These decisions are usually published as defense act amendments, white papers, and executive orders. Ethnic military manpower policy is itself a subset of *military manpower policy*, which refers to the broader spectrum of manpower decisions, including issues such as medical and conscientious-objection exemptions from military service, changes in the service terms for soldiers from the dominant ethnic group, and the buildup, call-up, and training of reserve units.

At the end of this century, the Trojan horse dilemma has turned into a serious problem for leaders of multiethnic states—many of which are new states. With the end of the Cold War, ethnic and racial conflicts have erupted around the world, this time without superpowers to douse the ethnic flames. Especially among developing countries, the ethnic

---

35. Morris, "Ethnic Groups," p. 169.

structure of the military has exacerbated civil war among tribal factions. In Africa, for example, the military sometimes has appeared to be a mere arsenal for a given ethnic group, or, worse, a bloodthirsty tribal militia in an ethnic "search and destroy" mission. Elsewhere, local dictators have turned the military loose on frail ethnic groups, as in the onslaught of Saddam Hussein's military on the Iraqi Kurd community. Embroiled in an internal ethnic-cleansing campaign, the military in many a developing state has lost its credibility as the guardian of the nation. In Sri Lanka, atrocity and barbarity became a way of life for the military in its prolonged war with the Tamil rebels. In Yugoslavia, the once internationally acclaimed multiethnic army has degenerated into a host of inhumane ethnic militias that frequently target the only "enemy" unequipped for resistance: innocent women and children.

The deterioration of the military from a state institution into an ethnic militia could not have come at a worse time. With the end of the Cold War and the rise of ethnocentrism, the military's role as the great "supraethnic" state institution has become even more important. In the developing world, where ethnic strife always verges on erupting into a fully fledged civil war, the military alone has the potential to fulfill three functions: to be a powerful symbol of national unity, to serve as a meeting ground for youth from all ethnic groups, and to secure the peace on the state's borders. Alas, politicians, officers, and ethnic leaders in these states appear to be at a loss about how to bridge the gap of distrust between the state and its subjugated ethnic groups and how to create this great supraethnic military. Gleaning lessons from the ethnic histories of the armed forces of South Africa, Singapore, and Israel, this book aspires to offer some guidelines for bridging this gap.

[2]

South Africa: From Exclusion to Inclusion

THE EVOLUTION OF THE APARTHEID IDEOLOGY

The ideology of separation, commonly referred to as apartheid, was conceived, nurtured, and developed by senior Afrikaner leaders, including Daniel. F. Malan (prime minister, 1948–1954), J. G. Strijdom (prime minister, 1954–1958), Hendrik F. Verwoerd (minister of native affairs, 1950–1958; prime minister, 1958–1966), and B. J. Vorster (minister of justice, 1961–1966; prime minister, 1966–1978). Yet the origins of apartheid can be traced back to the turn of the century. In 1905 the Langden committee (also known as the South African Native Affairs Committee), appointed by Lord Milner, recommended the separation of the white and black residents of South Africa in all matters of politics, land ownership, and occupation. Though segregation was already a common practice, the committee elevated it to an official political doctrine.[1]

While the Langden committee officially authorized the principle of racial separation, economic conditions set it in motion. Attempting to alleviate the problems of impoverished Afrikaner farmers, the South African government launched a series of racial policies that sought to secure jobs for whites at the expense of blacks. The Mines and Works Act (1911) restricted black mine workers to the lowest quarry occupations. The Native Labor Regulation (1911) made strike action by blacks a criminal offense. After the great Afrikaner insurrection of 1922, when poor

---

1. Martin Meredith, *In the Name of Apartheid: South Africa in the Postwar Period* (London: Hamish Hamilton, 1988), pp. 33–34.

[27]

Afrikaners rebelled against the employment of cheap black labor in the mines, the government enacted the Apprenticeship Act (1922), which stipulated a minimum of eight years of education for apprenticeship—a requirement that, because virtually all blacks and many coloreds and Indians could not satisfy it, deprived them of just about their only opportunity to acquire a skill and a well-paying job. After Hertzog's government came to power in 1924, additional racially discriminatory economic measures were enforced. The Industrial Conciliation Act (1924) excluded blacks from collective-bargaining procedures; shortly after its promulgation, most black civil-service workers were replaced by whites.

The principles of enforced separation and discrimination against non-whites quickly spilled over from the economic sphere to land ownership and housing. The Native's Land Act (1913) prohibited Africans from purchasing or leasing land in white areas, permitting them to buy land only in native reserves, which constituted 8 percent of the country's territory. With the brief stroke of a pen, the Native's Land Act altered the legal status of millions of blacks who were leasing white-owned land, changing them from legal tenants to illegal squatters. This draconian law forced thousands of rural black farmers to immigrate to the white cities in search of employment. Thus, between 1921 and 1935, the urban African population grew by 95 percent. The government then enacted the urban version of the Native's Land Act—the Native (Urban Areas) Act (1923)—which permitted blacks to reside in white towns only as long as they were serving white needs.[2]

These racially discriminatory employment, land ownership, and housing acts were complemented by similar policies in the political sphere. No coloreds, blacks, or Indians attended the deliberations over the first constitution of the Union in 1910. Although nonwhites were allowed to vote only in the Cape Province, no black or colored ever set foot in the Cape Parliament. And in 1936, black voters were eliminated from the voting process in the Cape Province as well.[3]

In 1948, the Afrikaner-based National Party (NP) won the elections by a narrow margin of five seats; it ruled the country until 1994. Leaders of the first NP government, composed exclusively of Afrikaners, were committed to expanding and enforcing the apartheid ideology. During their first decade in power, they enacted a barrage of parliamentary bills

2. Meredith, *In the Name of Apartheid*, pp. 35–37.
3. Meredith, *In the Name of Apartheid*, pp. 33–34, 39.

that tightened the grip of apartheid over society in every sphere, including family and sexual behavior. For example, the Prohibition of Mixed Marriage Act (1949) outlawed marriage between Europeans and non-Europeans. In order to end the "prostitution of apartheid," the Immorality Act (1950) banned sexual intercourse between Europeans and coloreds.

NP leaders then decided to establish apartheid on scientific grounds. The Population Registration Act (1950) provided the means, institutions, and resources to assign each South African resident to one of three racial groups: whites, coloreds and Africans. Taking advantage of the campaign to classify scientifically and register the racial origin of each South African resident, parliament passed bills further widening the boundaries of apartheid. The Groups Areas Act (1950) demarcated separate residential areas for each racial group. The Natives Resettlement Act (1954) gave the government the power to "clean" so-called "black spots" in white residential areas. The Reservation of Separate Amenities Act (1952) compelled the use of racially separate facilities in all spheres of public life, including buses, trains, post offices, stations, restaurants, and theaters.

Among nonwhites, blacks bore the brunt of apartheid policies. The Natives Abolition of Passes and Coordination of Documents Act (1952) forced blacks to carry personal reference books that tracked their movements in the country. An amendment to the old Native (Urban Areas) Act in 1952 prohibited blacks from remaining in a white area more than seventy-two hours unless they had been living in the area for more than fifteen years or were employed by the same employer for more than ten years. This law divided numerous African families, separating husbands from wives, children from parents.

Apartheid was also relentlessly pursued in the economic and political domains. The Native Labor (Settlements of Disputes) Act (1953) outlawed all strikes by blacks and denied recognition to their trade unions. The Industrial Conciliation Act (1956) allowed the government to enforce racial separation in trade unions, and reserved jobs for whites in specified industries. The right of the Cape coloreds to vote was abolished after a long constitutional battle between the government and the Supreme Court (1951–1956). But the apex of the campaign to enforce apartheid undoubtedly was the plan to create ethnically segregated black homelands.[4]

4. Meredith, *In the Name of Apartheid*, p. 70.

Even before he became prime minister, Verwoerd began promoting the idea of total territorial separation between whites and blacks. The plan was to give each race mastery over its own area, thereby preventing one group from claiming rights based on numerical superiority. Verwoerd relied on black tribalism and traditional African chiefs to execute this plan. In 1951, he enacted the Bantu Authorities Act, which gave him the power to staff the administrations of native reserves with African chiefs loyal to him. Two years later, the government enacted the Bantu Education Act (1953), and appropriated responsibility for the education of blacks from missionary groups. The explicit goal of this act was to educate the Bantu from early childhood "to realize that equality with Europeans is not for them."[5]

After his appointment as prime minister in 1958, Verwoerd pushed the idea of a multinational South Africa one step further. The Promotion of Bantu Self-Government Act (1959) provided for eight black homelands, one for each major ethnic group: North Sotho, South Sotho, Swazi, Tsonga, Tswana, Venda, Xhosa, and Zulu. Not surprisingly, Verwoerd refused to invest public funds in developing the economies of these homelands. His goal was to separate whites and blacks physically and to slow down the immigration of blacks into white cities while allowing whites to continue to exploit cheap black labor.[6]

Through a series of draconian security measures—the Suppression of Communism Act (1950), the Criminal Law Amendment Act (1953), and the Public Safety Act (1953)—South African politicians endowed themselves with almost unlimited constitutional power to declare a state of emergency at will, abolish antiapartheid organizations, and imprison and punish persons for acts of civil disobedience. Against the protests of the UN and the West, Verwoerd declared his country a republic in 1961, exited the British Commonwealth, and advised his fellow NP leaders to stand by apartheid like "walls of granite." By 1960, the South African polity had developed into the "most elaborate racial edifice the world had ever witnessed."[7]

Thus, from the fairly crude and ad hoc political doctrine of the Langden committee, apartheid developed into a comprehensive state ideology implemented through numerous governmental policies and parliamen-

5. Meredith, *In the Name of Apartheid*, p. 73.
6. Meredith, *In the Name of Apartheid*, pp. 75–76.
7. Meredith, *In the Name of Apartheid*, pp. 54, 65, 89.

tary bills in all public domains. For many white South Africans, apartheid grew to be a religious doctrine, as the Dutch Reformed Church (the leading white church, counting among its members most of the state's leaders) used biblical texts to justify apartheid. By the 1960s, only a handful of whites dared to criticize the fundamental assumption of the apartheid ideology: the existence of separate South African races, nations, peoples, and tribes.

THE MILITARY AND APARTHEID IDEOLOGY

While economic exploitation of nonwhites was a constantly defining motive in the historical evolution and course of apartheid, a different motive, no less powerful, determined the fate of nonwhites in the armed forces. In South Africa, where the allegedly Trojan horse racial group remained the majority, the survival of whites, not security breaches, was the government's principal concern when dealing with nonwhite military service. Wherever whites had trusted blacks with rifles, National Party leaders argued, those guns had been turned against them. One parliament member, for example, suggested that in Kenya most of the Mau Mau leaders were ex-servicemen of the King's African Rifles.

South Africa therefore structured its military manpower policy along harsher lines than its racially discriminatory housing, economic, and political policies. Every effort was made to insure that whites had an absolute monopoly over all the means of violence in the state. Article 7 of the Union's Defence Act No. 13 (1912) exempted "persons not of European descent" from military service, but allowed for the "voluntary engagement" of nonwhites in the military.[8] When the National Party came to government in 1948, it immediately disbanded the last nonwhite units in the SADF. After independence in 1961, it constructed the SADF along the same racial guidelines as other state and social institutions. Official military papers and statements almost religiously adhered to the concept of "one South Africa, many South African nations." For example, after the first black soldiers were recruited in 1973, Dr. Riekert of the Bantu Administration Board in Potchetstroom wrote an eleven-page guide for white army personnel on how to treat these black soldiers, opening his work with the following: "In the defence of South Africa, united action

8. Union of South Africa, *Statutes*, 1912, act 13, clause 7.

of all the various nations (*volke*) is necessary."[9] A 1977 official Defence White Paper referred to nonwhite soldiers as "other nationals in the SADF."[10] And Major General E. A. C. Pienaar, inspector general of the air force, in 1979 described the SADF as a peoples' army, not a people's army (as in the cases of Israel and Singapore).[11]

When Botha presented the first universal-conscription bill to Parliament in 1967, he announced that only white males would be drafted. He hailed this bill as a nation-building act, but one clearly restricted to the white nation. When, after Botha's speech, Parliament members celebrated the first conscription bill, they used phrases such as "our army comes from the people" and "to bring our Defence Force to the people and the people to the Defence Force"—idioms analogous to those expressed in the Israeli and Singaporean Parliaments in the presentation of their first conscription bills. But unlike Israel and Singapore, which subjected all or most male citizens to conscription, only a small fraction of South Africa's residents (whites only) were included in "the people." When Botha promised that through universal conscription the military would contribute to the "nobility and character of our people" and to the "spiritual strength of the nation," he meant only of the character of the white people and the spiritual strength of the white nation.[12]

The argument of one South African Parliament member in favor of conscription was analogous to the idea of the military as a melting pot: "Our young men when they are called to do [compulsory] national service come from separate schools, and from different religious and social environments."[13] But here also the honorable member meant that national service would blend together separate white schools and the different white religious and social environments of English and Afrikaans-speaking males, not the rest of the population. The exclusive nature of this melting pot did not undermine the excitement of Parliament members from various parties. As one of them said: "[White] English and Afrikaans-speaking persons are being drawn together. The two offi-

9. *Sunday Times*, July 18, 1974.

10. South Africa, Ministry of Defence, *White Paper on Defence and Armaments Supply, 1977*, p. 21.

11. "The SADF—a Peoples' Defence Force—in the True Sense of the Word," *Rand Daily Mail*, March 28, 1979.

12. South Africa, *House of Assembly Debates* 30 (August 31, 1970), col. 2932; 37 (March 1, 1972), col. 2252.

13. South Africa, *House of Assembly Debates* 56 (April 23, 1975), col. 4619.

cial languages are used alternately, and there will be a wonderful opportunity to build a nation in this way. As a matter of fact, this is such a wonderful opportunity for building a nation that I want to plead—that once we have consolidated our efforts in this regard, we should also extend this system, in some or other modified form, to our young women."[14]

Even when W. V. Raw, the defense spokesman of the opposition United Party, praised the new conscription bill, saying, "They meet together as youth, they serve together as youth, and they learn to grow together into one nation," he was referring only to the unification of white native youth and white immigrant youth.[15] Other Parliament members who used the term "discrimination" were not worried about the exemption of colored, Indian, or black South Africans from military service; instead, they were concerned that *whites* exempted from military service on medical or immigrant grounds would be excluded from the new "spirit of unity among young people," which the military was instructed to instill in all of its white draftees.[16] Nonwhites clearly had no place in the new South African military.

THE MILITARY MANPOWER DILEMMA

The white-only conscription bill exacerbated the labor dilemma of white South Africa. Unlike the relatively stable population ratio among dominant and subjugated ethnic groups in Singapore and Israel, the demographic balance among the principal racial groups in South Africa was rapidly changing. Figure 2 highlights both the actual increase in the total black population (1960–1990) and the demographic projections for a continued increase well into the next century (1995–2010).[17]

The government clearly failed to curb the growth of the black population through political means. Between 1975 and 1985, it pushed four

14. South Africa, *House of Assembly Debates* 21 (June 8, 1967), col. 7456.
15. South Africa, *House of Assembly Debates* 21 (June 8, 1967), col. 7416.
16. South Africa, *House of Assembly Debates* 21 (June 2, 1967), col. 7164; 21 (June 8, 1967), col. 7424.
17. Data is based on the official estimates of the Central Statistical Services (CSS) as published in South African Institute of Race Relations, *A Survey of Race Relations in South Africa* (Johannesburg: Institute of Race Relations, 1963–1993). The demographic predictions are based on South Africa, *Statistics in Brief* (Pretoria: CSS, 1992), p. 1.

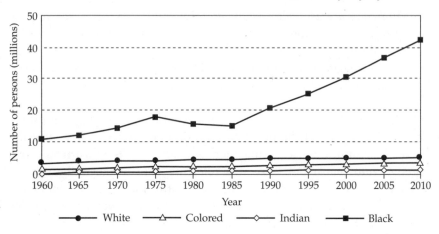

Figure 2. The population of South Africa by racial groups, 1960–2010

homelands (Transkei, Bophuthatswana, Venda, and Ciskei [TBVC]) to become independent. By excluding the roughly six million black citizens of the TBVC homelands, the South African Central Statistical Service was able to demonstrate a decrease in the total number of South African blacks during this period. After 1985, however, the trend of a rapidly growing black population, now excluding the TBVC homelands, resumed its natural course.

From the perspective of South African leaders, the truly alarming trend was that the ratio of blacks to whites within the total population was constantly growing because of an exceptionally high black birthrate (2.4 percent between 1970 and 1990) and a strikingly low white birthrate (1.32 percent for the same period).[18] Figure 3 compares the actual and predicted increase in the black population with the decrease in the white population.

During the early 1970s, therefore, South African politicians feared that the ever-shrinking pool of skilled white labor would not suffice for the future economic needs of this growing country. The 1967 conscription bill complicated this problem even further by pulling a large number of young whites from the labor force. Moreover, had a full-scale war broken

18. South Africa, *Statistics in Brief*, p. 1.

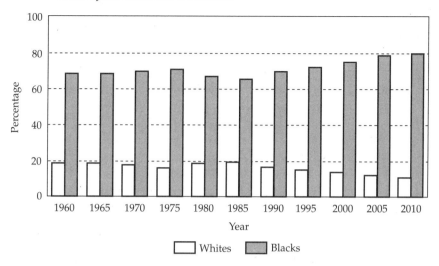

Figure 3. Black and white population ratio, South Africa, 1960–2010

out, total mobilization of the entire white population would have re-sulted in economic disaster.[19]

Several Parliament members began pressing the government to ex-pand the voluntary recruitment of nonwhite soldiers in lieu of whites. One member who advocated expanded nonwhite recruitment asked Bo-tha, "The Government fears to train them [nonwhites] for military serv-ice. Does it propose to send the White managers and technicians into battle while the Black people direct the economy at home?"[20] The logic behind this rhetorical question was compelling, and during the mid-1970s, the government steadily increased the enlistment of nonwhite vol-unteers. Botha, however, clarified that nonwhite servicemen would be rewarded with citizenship only in the future Bantu homelands. While white immigrants were becoming citizens by defending a nation and a country, Botha asserted that nonwhite soldiers were merely defending their temporary place of residence in South Africa and so deserved no special reward.[21]

19. Willem Steenkamp, "The SA Defense Force: Rogue Elephant, Slave of Circumstance, or Cyclops in the Land of the Blind?" *Leadership SA* 2, no. 4 (summer 1983): 55.
20. South Africa, *House of Assembly Debates* 47 (February 4, 1974), col. 23.
21. South Africa, *House of Assembly Debates* 43 (April 27, 1973), col. 5294.

Moreover, the enlistment of nonwhite soldiers did not imply that the government was willing to treat them on an equal footing with whites. In Parliament, Botha rejected such calls for racial equality among the rank and file.[22] He vowed to limit the service of Indians and coloreds to noncombatant positions and to employ blacks only in auxiliary and service-oriented jobs (such as drivers, cooks, clerks, orderlies, and laborers).[23]

For Botha's ethnic military manpower policy, the problem of black soldiers was the most vexing issue. He was committed to Verwoerd's plan of ethnically segregated black homelands: South African blacks were to become citizens of foreign countries. For example, after the Transkei was established in 1962, its citizenship was extended not only to blacks living within its territory but also to all blacks of Transkei origin, including those residing in white areas of South Africa.[24] Thus, many asked, how could black foreigners who owed no allegiance to South Africa be expected to serve in the SADF? Parliamentary opposition parties mercilessly exploited the contradiction between Botha's commitment to the homeland plan and his policy of employing blacks in auxiliary roles within the SADF.[25] He responded with assurances that indeed blacks would not be employed by the SADF: "If the Bantu wanted to build up a defence force, he should do so in his own eventually independent homeland. . . . As far as the Bantu are concerned, we say that we shall employ them only in certain auxiliary services as laborers. But we shall not employ them within the context of the South African Defence Forces in any fighting capacity."[26]

Fearing racial "agitations," Botha provided many details on exactly where and how the SADF was employing its nonwhite soldiers. On numerous occasions, he clarified that nonwhite soldiers were kept away from the conscript-based all-white "military melting pot."[27] For example, when the media reported about the training of the first black soldiers with weapons and live ammunition, Botha took great pains to assure his white audience that it was "so that they may protect themselves in time

22. South Africa, *House of Assembly Debates* 47 (February 7, 1974), cols. 295–296.
23. South Africa, *House of Assembly Debates* 30 (August 31, 1970), col. 2936.
24. Meredith, *In the Name of Apartheid*, pp. 94–95.
25. South Africa, *House of Assembly Debates* 30 (August 31, 1970), col. 2934.
26. South Africa, *House of Assembly Debates* 30 (August 31, 1970), cols. 2939, 2941.
27. South Africa, *House of Assembly Debates* 56 (April 22, 1975), col. 4582.

of war," and that nonwhite soldiers would not be used in infantry units.[28]

Throughout the 1970s, Botha argued for the conscription of whites into combat units and command positions, and voluntary recruitment of non-whites into noncombatant units and noncommand positions. Yet early on, foreign observers and military experts discovered that this formula and the reality of military life were at odds. The relatively quick promotion and integration of nonwhite soldiers within the apartheid military puzzled these observers. The following sections reveal, for the first time, the secret ethnic history of the South African military between 1963 and 1990, and the ethnic integration within the SADF that Botha labored so hard to conceal from the public.

IN THE BEGINNING: 1948–1963

South Africa employed nonwhite soldiers from the end of the eighteenth century to 1948. Colored troops, for example, served various Cape governments between 1793 and 1870. The shortage of military manpower compelled the government to deploy armed blacks overseas during World War I. But in January 1918, it withdrew its black soldiers from the European theater because "blacks in the French front were contaminated with foreign notions about race relations and other social grievances."[29] During World War II, the government mobilized almost three times the number of colored and Asian soldiers than in World War I, but a significantly smaller number of blacks.[30]

The nationalists declared their policy concerning armed nonwhites even before the NP electoral victory in 1948: "Africans should not be in a position, by virtue of military training and the possession of modern arms, to challenge effectively the asymmetrical balance of power between

---

28. South Africa, *House of Assembly Debates* 30 (August 31, 1970), col. 2939.

29. Kenneth W. Grundy, *Soldiers without Politics: Blacks in the South African Armed Forces* (Berkeley: University of California Press, 1983), p. 56.

30. During World War I, the South African military mobilized 146,897 whites; 15,744 coloreds, Malays, Indians, and Chinese; and 82,778 blacks. During World War II, it mobilized 211,193 whites; 45,892 coloreds, Malays, Indians, and Chinese; and only 77,239 blacks. No nonwhite soldiers participated in the Korean War, although 818 white South Africans saw battle. See South Africa, *House of Assembly Debates* 35 (March 26, 1971), cols. 615–616.

Africans and whites."[31] Indeed, fears of armed blacks ran so high that white employers refused to provide their black sentinels with even assegais or knobkerries.[32]

The colored unit (South Africa Cape Corps) and the black unit (Native Military Corps) that served in World War II epitomized everything the nationalists had been fighting against for decades. In April 1949, the new minister of defence disbanded these units. A small number of coloreds and, later on, several blacks were retained as part of the Auxiliary Force, which provided the military with cooks, drivers, and other menial workers. The disbandment of the Cape Corps, more than anything else, symbolized for coloreds the decline in their status during the first twenty-five years of the nationalist government. The 1957 Defence Bill preserved the right of the government to recruit voluntary "non-European" persons, but nationalist officials vowed that blacks would never again be armed.[33]

During the 1950s, the real ethnic struggle within the SADF was between two white groups, English speakers and Afrikaans speakers. Erasmus, the minister of defence, struggled throughout the first half of that decade to bring into the armed forces more Afrikaners who supported the NP. His efforts were successful, and by the first Independence Day, in 1961, the new SADF was already dominated by senior officers who were either supporters of the NP and its policies or politically neutral.[34] The bitter legacy of this struggle between English and Afrikaans speakers within the SADF cast its long shadow on the 1960s and the first half of the 1970s.[35] As a result, senior military commanders concluded that the

31. Richard Dale, "The Legacy of the Imperial-Commonwealth Connection," in *Defense Policy Formation: Towards Comparative Analysis*, ed. James M. Roherrty (Durham: Carolina Academic Press, 1980), p. 79.

32. *Weekend Post*, June 15, 1974.

33. Grundy, *Soldiers without Politics*, pp. 90, 91, 98–99; Chester Crocker, *South Africa's Defense Posture: Coping with Vulnerability* (Beverly Hills: Sage Publications, 1981), p. 34.

34. In 1948, supporters of the United Party dominated the military. Thus, Erasmus's efforts to bring new blood into the armed forces were prompted by political considerations, not ethnic calculations. Interview with Louise Jooste, researcher, SADF Archives, Pretoria, March 25, 1993. See also Grundy, *Soldiers without Politics*, p. 102.

35. The three principal corps of the SADF differed in ethnic white composition during the 1970s. In the navy, the ratio was 50:50 between Afrikaans speakers and English speakers; in the air force, 75:25. The army was heavily dominated by Afrikaans speakers, who accounted for 85 percent while English speakers were only 15 percent. At the time, the general white population was 60 percent Afrikaans-speaking and 40 percent English-speaking. See *Star*, August 8, 1974. Complaints of discrimination against English speakers within the SADF were often voiced in South Africa's Parliament. See South Africa, *House*

SADF ought to be as ethnically homogeneous as possible. The Afrikaner tradition of " 'n boer en sy roer' " ("a farmer and his rifle") decreed that national service was a "training ground" for citizenship;[36] thus, since only whites were citizens in South Africa, nonwhites had no place in the SADF.

THE SEEDS OF CHANGE: COUNTERGUERRILLAS, MILITARY SCHOOLING, AND NEW THINKING

During the 1960s and 1970s, two important trends complemented each other to reform SADF racial manpower policies. First, senior South African officers who received advanced training in Britain, France, and the United States introduced the lessons of guerrilla and counterrevolutionary warfare to the SADF. Second, during the early 1970s, the SADF built a self-sufficient military schooling system for its officers. The novel message of foreign-educated officers thus found a new medium. During the late 1960s, the lessons of counterrevolutionary warfare spread quickly in the military, as SADF officers learned how to win hearts and minds by using native soldiers who commanded local traditions, languages, and religions. This message, coupled with a manpower shortage, reopened the gates of the SADF to black soldiers.

The dangers of guerrilla warfare and the importance of a carefully designed counterguerrilla strategy were two lessons also hammered into the heads of South African officers who studied abroad between 1955 and 1965. The British experience in Malaya (1948, 1969), Kenya, and Cyprus, as well as the French campaigns in Indochina (1945–1954) and Algeria (1956–1962), illustrated how poorly equipped but popular guerrilla fighters could defeat well-trained militaries. In addition, South African officers who studied in American military academies during the early 1960s had the opportunity to follow the experiment of specially trained American advisory teams sent to Vietnam to counter Viet Cong guerrilla warfare.

South African officers could also observe the power of guerrilla warfare closer to home, in Angola and Mozambique in 1962 and in Rhodesia

---

of Assembly Debates 26 (May 5, 1969), cols. 5310, 5314–5316; 34 (May 5, 1971), cols. 6053–6054.

36. Crocker, *South Africa's Defense Posture*, p. 33.

after 1965. Even in their own country, they witnessed how the African National Congress (ANC) and the Pan Africanist Congress (PAC) had begun to think in terms of revolutionary warfare. For example, in June 1961, the ANC created a military wing, the Umkhonto We Sizwe ("The Spear of the Nation," known as the MK), and sent its first members to revolutionary warfare courses in Algeria, Cuba, Ghana, Ethiopia, Tanzania, and China. On December 16, 1961, the MK headquarters in Rivonia (a farmhouse north of Johannesburg) launched its first large-scale sabotage campaign. Even more alarming was the establishment of Poqo, the PAC's secret underground organization, which launched a campaign in 1962 to assassinate whites as well as black policemen and informers.[37]

A book published in 1962, *The Art of Counter-Revolutionary Warfare* by John J. McCuen, effectively summarized the new counterguerrilla theory taught to South African officers abroad.[38] McCuen's lessons, simple and influential as they were, defied traditional military thinking. The book taught that guerrilla wars were to be countered mainly with nonmilitary means; conquest of territory was just the beginning of the real campaign, to win the hearts and minds of the local population. To achieve this aim, military forces had to be equipped with a good working knowledge of such nonmilitary matters as foreign languages, local cultures, and the religious practices of the native population. Soldiers who mastered these subjects were vital for the success of these campaigns. McCuen also taught that military force should be a means of last resort, and that excessive use of military force would fail. Most important, counterrevolutionary theory suggested that a complete victory over guerrilla warfare is rarely achieved; the military, at best, can stabilize a deteriorating situation and thus buy time for politicians to resolve the conflict diplomatically.

South African officers abroad were present at the first trials of this counterguerrilla doctrine. Lieutenant General C. A. Fraser, the first chief of the army (1966–1967), witnessed firsthand the French struggle in Algeria during his service as a military attaché to France. He spent several weeks in Algeria on various occasions observing French attempts to squash the National Liberation Front (FLN). Fraser composed a textbook

---

37. Interview with Prof. Deon F. S. Fourie, University of South Africa, Naval Officer Mess, Pretoria, March 29, 1993; Meredith, *In the Name of Apartheid*, pp. 99–102.

38. John J. McCuen, *The Art of Counter-Revolutionary War: The Strategy of Counter Insurgency* (Harrisburg, Penn.: Stackpole Books, 1966).

on revolutionary warfare, based on his experiences, for the SADF military schools. Similarly, Lieutenant General Magnus Malan, who initiated many of the ethnic and racial reforms in the SADF during his tenure as chief of the army (1973–1976) and chief of the SADF (1976–1980), had studied at Fort Leavenworth, attending the U.S. Army Command and Staff Training Course, and later had undergone short stints with the 35th Armored Division in Colorado from 1962 to 1963. During his years at Fort Leavenworth, Malan was influenced by ideas about the role of military-sponsored political action as a vital component in the management of " 'communist-inspired' warfare."[39]

Counterguerrilla theory, foreign schooling, and personal experiences convinced Malan, Fraser, and a rising group of SADF commanders that white South Africa had to reform its attitude towards the nonwhite population in order to win the next war. Fraser and, later on, Malan were convinced that a conscript-based, all-white SADF could hold the ground for only so long. South Africa was running out of time, and the politicians had to reform the rigid racial structure of the South African polity. The slow pace of domestic change worried many of these generals throughout the first half of the 1970s. General R. C. Hiemstra (commandant general of the SADF, 1965–1972) aroused political wrath when he declared that the SADF was not, and could not be, strong enough to protect South Africa if political action did not help secure the home base. But, quietly and behind closed doors, Botha, the minister of defence, had already begun reading military papers and scholarly books, provided by Malan, concerning the need for change.[40]

One conclusion Botha drew from his readings and discussions with commanders was that the military needed to recruit nonwhite soldiers, and do so quickly. In addition to alleviating the problem of scarce white manpower, nonwhite soldiers were vital if the SADF were to fight a large-scale conventional war with one of its neighboring black countries, or if it had to confront a black uprising at home. Only nonwhite soldiers,

---

39. Interview with Rear Adm. Trainor, staff chief of naval support, Naval Headquarters, Pretoria, March 25, 1993; Philip Frankel, *Pretoria's Praetorians: Civil-Military Relations in South Africa* (Cambridge: Cambridge University Press, 1984); "The Tap of the Drum," *Inside SA*, May 1968, p. 12. Malan's military training in the United States was an "unusual posting" for an SADF officer back then. See *Paratus*, March 1993, p. 15.

40. Interview with Rear Adm. Trainor; interview with Prof. Deon F. S. Fourie; Deon Geldenhuys, *The Diplomacy of Isolation: South African Foreign Policy Making* (Johannesburg: MacMillan South Africa, 1984), p. 143.

particularly black soldiers, possessed the cultural and linguistic assets required to win such wars. The SADF at the time, however, was an all-white organization, and many among the rank and file and among the pool of junior and midcareer officers opposed the recruitment of non-white soldiers. It needed to prepare its own members for the recruitment of nonwhites and to find a channel through which young officers, the backbone of the military, could discover for themselves why traditional policies had to change.

Fortunately, such a channel of communication had already begun to develop: the self-sufficient SADF schooling system. During its early years (1912–1945), the SADF almost totally depended on Britain for its officer training, and the few South African officers who received staff training did so at British staff colleges. After World War II, the SADF launched a campaign to build its own staff colleges and provide some of its own staff training. The Military College introduced such training in 1949, and the air force began providing it for officers as early as 1951.[41]

Nonetheless, throughout the 1950s, most senior South African officers completed their military education abroad, usually in Britain. When Britain refused to admit these officers into its staff schools after 1961, the South African military devised two solutions to assist officers in completing their staff education. It sent several to military schools in France, Latin America, and the United States. More important, the SADF stepped up efforts to complete its own system of staff schools, colleges, and courses.[42]

The sanctions against South Africa that began in the mid-1960s left SADF officers with even fewer foreign military schools where they were permitted to study. In response, the SADF intensified its commitment to become more self-sufficient in all matters concerning training.[43] The Military Academy completely revised its officer-training program, launched courses open to officers from all branches, and opened a B.Mil. program

41. South Africa, Ministry of Defence, *White Paper on Defence and Armaments Supply, 1973,* pp. 15–16.

42. South Africa, *White Paper, 1973,* p. 15; South Africa, *Review of Defence and Armaments Production, 1960 to 1970* (Pretoria: Defence Headquarters, 1971), p. 10.

43. This "train-them-yourself" policy was similar to the "do-it-yourself" armaments policy. See South Africa, *Review of Defence, 1960 to 1970,* p. 26. Between 1960 and 1965, the defense budget experienced a large increase, triggered by the Sharpeville incident and the growing rift with Britain and other Western countries; the same happened between 1974 and 1977 because of Portugal's withdrawal from Angola and Mozambique; Crocker, *South Africa's Defense Posture,* pp. 12–14.

leading to B.A., B.Sc. or B.Com. degrees. The navy, which traditionally had sent most of its officers abroad for training, opened its first staff course at the Naval College in 1972. And in March 1973, the Defence College formally opened, offering a joint-staff course for midcareer army, air force, and navy officers.

The Defence College emphasized the study of broad topics, such as military strategy, joint operations, and all aspects of national security.[44] The establishment of this college, with its advanced staff course, was the jewel in the crown of the new educational system. The 1973 white paper proudly summarized the significance of this course: "Accordingly, we need no longer rely on overseas courses for this training."[45] In 1977 the military schooling system was completed, with the opening of the joint-staff course for senior officers from all four branches (army, navy, air force, medical corps), and for senior officers from the police, railway police, and Armscore (the national armaments-manufacturing conglomerate).[46]

Thus, toward the mid-1970s, the SADF had already achieved its goal: a self-sufficient training system for officers of all ranks. A longtime observer of the SADF summarized the system: "Both officers and other ranks punctuate their careers with a seemingly endless series of training, promotion and staff courses—even logistics specialists are required to qualify as combat team and battle-group commanders."[47]

The new system introduced officers of all ranks to the concept of guerrilla warfare and to its implications for the SADF. One senior officer recalled that, as a student in a staff course in 1978, he had to write three-thousand-word essays linking the geographical, demographic, economic, sociological, and political aspects of South Africa to theories of counterinsurgency strategy. Such assignments demonstrated to officers that parts of their country potentially were ideal hosts for insurgency. In 1985 this officer attended an advanced staff course where counterguerrilla theories were reintroduced, in an even more forceful fashion than in 1978.[48] This trend continued well into the 1980s. An instructor in one of these courses disclosed that in 1988 he divided his students into two groups:

44. Geldenhuys, *Diplomacy of Isolation*, p. 141.
45. South Africa, *White Paper*, 1973, p. 16.
46. This course was followed by two similar courses in 1978; South Africa, Ministry of Defence, *White Paper, 1979*, p. 20.
47. Steenkamp, "South African Defense Force," p. 65.
48. Interview with Rear Adm. Trainor.

one for the government and the other representing the ANC. Despite the negative reaction of a few cadets, the messages in 1988 were along the lines of the 1978 and 1985 staff courses, but more explicit: the SADF could not win the war by itself; the country needed to change, and the SADF needed to change as well.

New lessons reinforced the need to change. Al Venter, a distinguished South African journalist, argued in 1973 that the ten-year failure of the Portuguese military in Guinea was due to Portugal's failure to bid for the support of the black civilian population.[49] In addition, case studies suggested that black soldiers were likely to be very loyal once in uniform. In Rhodesia, for example, black soldiers prolonged the life of the regime after 1966.[50] One influential military analyst pointed out in 1974 that, provided with good training, blacks could be excellent soldiers, as exemplified in many African armies. The willingness of South African blacks to die for their country also was demonstrated by black policemen in South Africa who fought and died along the borders during the first half of the 1970s.[51] Opposition party members in Parliament highlighted these policemen's performance when demanding more and faster integration of blacks into the SADF.[52] The 1974 Lisbon coup, and the withdrawal of Portuguese forces from Southern Africa, only intensified the need to tap the black population for military service.

A major concern of SADF senior commanders was that the white rank and file would oppose recruiting nonwhites. Many soldiers, specifically the rural Afrikaner soldiers (many of whom served in the traditional commando units), strongly objected to the idea. Their opposition was well known to those trying to change the ethnic composition and racial policies of the SADF.[53]

49. *Argus*, May 7, 1973.

50. *Rand Daily Mail*, January 16, 1985.

51. *Paratus*, April 1974; *Evening Post*, June 17, 1974.

52. See, for example, South Africa, *House of Assembly Debates* 38 (April 26, 1972), col. 5858; 43 (April 27, 1973), col. 5289; 47 (February 7, 1974), col. 294.

53. In 1976, for example, Col. L. T. van Zyl, chief staff officer of the new Ethnology Section in Port Elizabeth, declared that it was time for all races to work as an integrated team in the Defence Force. He admitted, however, that there was a "profound reluctance on the part of whites to incorporate other races into the SADF." *Rand Daily Mail*, March 4, 1976. Senior officers also confessed that they were very sensitive to the reaction of white rank and file toward nonwhite recruits; interview with Rear Adm. P. van Z. Loedolff, deputy chief of staff personnel, Defence Headquarters, Pretoria, March 25, 1993. Grundy also admits that objection to racial integration was much more prevalent among the white

THE BEGINNING OF CHANGE: RECRUITING NONWHITES (1963–1975)

The first nonwhite recruitment experiment, launched in 1963, focused on the Cape colored community. Military manpower planners had good reason to believe that the largely conservative white public would accept a "coloreds first" experiment with relatively little opposition. The colored community had a long and rich history of military service, and, since 1949, its leaders had pressed persistently for the reestablishment of the Cape Corps. The military revived the unit under a new name similar to the old one, the South Africa Colored Corps (SACC), and military spokesmen pretended that there was nothing unusual about the new unit. Cursory readers of newspapers at that time could easily have been deceived into believing that colored soldiers who had been "on vacation" since 1950 were now being recalled for duty. Indeed, the parties involved in the reestablishment of the SACC employed considerable rhetoric to mask the daring ethnic experimentation within the SADF.

The SADF gleaned several valuable lessons from the SACC experiment: first, the military needed to recruit and train a small batch of ethnic soldiers to instruct the first intake; second, it needed to secure the support of influential ethnic leaders before launching the first recruitment drive among ethnic youth; and third, it needed to isolate the new ethnic soldiers from the larger ethnic community during their initial training. It is important to note that, in contrast to the policy of assigning "misfits from white units" to command nonwhite units during World War II, the SADF in the 1960s was careful to assign seasoned white officers to the colored experiment in order to secure its success.[54]

In early 1973, naval manpower planners launched a second experiment after the success of what the minister of defence called "the model organization of the SACC."[55] A new Indian naval unit followed in the footsteps of the earlier colored experiment. Senior military and naval commanders first discussed Indian recruitment with local Indian leaders, who in turn expressed in public their support for the new initiative. The navy then proceeded to the second stage of the experiment. In April 1973, a naval inspection party began examining Indian youth's aptitude

---

rank and file than among the military elite; Kenneth W. Grundy, "A Black Foreign Legion in South Africa?" *African Affairs* 80, no. 318 (June 1981): 111; *Soldiers without Politics*, p. 216.

54. Grundy, *Soldiers without Politics*, p. 89.

55. South Africa, *House of Assembly Debates* 47 (February 7, 1974), col. 304.

for technical skills. This stage ended in October 1973, when Rear Adm. Biermann and a special committee submitted their report on all aspects of the Indian Service Battalion.[56]

Protected from opposition by a thick veil of public promises that the new battalion would be no different than the SACC, Adm. Biermann sought to go beyond the original colored experiment. The committee headed by Biermann investigated topics such as Indian recruits' uniforms and the terms of their service. It determined that, as with colored soldiers, Indian recruits would serve their first year in the military as voluntary national servicemen, and then would be offered the option to join the Permanent Force, depending on how their first year of service was evaluated. In addition, the committee grappled with the sensitive issue of providing Indian recruits with firearms and firearm training. Its conclusions represent a careful attempt to walk a thin line. On the one hand, the committee wished to treat Indian sailors just like any other sailors; on the other hand, members did not wish to aggravate influential conservative politicians who were strongly opposed to the idea of arming nonwhite soldiers. Thus, the report proposed, "The [Indian] trainees will be given firearms training and sea training, but the emphasis will be on giving them a general background to enable them to join the Permanent Force if they wish as drivers, waiters, clerks, chefs, storekeepers and artisans."[57]

Following the SACC model, between August and December 1974 colored navy NCOs recruited and trained thirty-two Indians as instructors of the first Indian intake. The first two hundred Indian recruits finally began their training in January 1975. The name of the new unit, the Indian Service Battalion, also was carefully selected to suspend suspicions inside and outside the military about the purpose of the unit.[58]

But a vapid name like the Indian Service Battalion masked a very different reality. Like white sailors, Indian basic trainees were taught a wide range of subjects, including communications, land mines and booby traps, map reading, recognition (ships, aircraft, and weapons), and survival on land and sea. After their basic training, Indian sailors entered

56. *Natal Mercury*, April 11, 1973; April 14, 1973.
57. *Friend*, November 1, 1973.
58. *Star*, October 30, 1973; *Friend*, November 1, 1973; *Natal Mercury*, June 20, 1974; *Rand Daily Mail*, July 17, 1974; *Star*, October 4, 1974; *Paratus*, March 1980, p. 48; South African Institute of Race Relations, *Survey*, 1975, pp. 56–57.

a specialist training period, attending courses on topics such as advanced seamanship, leadership, and nuclear, biological, and chemical warfare. This curriculum suggests that, right from the outset, the navy planned to employ Indian recruits as real sailors, not merely drivers and chefs. There also were other indications that Indian recruits would be treated no differently than their white peers. The number of Indian instructors, for example, gradually increased, and by 1979 most instructors in the Indian base were Indians.[59]

The colored and Indian experiments paved the way for the third and politically most complicated experiment, the recruitment of blacks into the SADF. For many whites, such recruitment was a far-fetched idea. Although black men served in the Auxiliary Force, they were restricted to menial service positions, and none of them had received firearm training since 1949. Training black soldiers with live firearms and providing rifles to them simply was unacceptable to many whites, particularly those in the rural areas.[60]

Nonetheless, in November 1973 General Magnus Malan, chief of the army, authorized the establishment of the South African Army Bantu Training Center for black recruits. He was determined to bring blacks into the SADF as soon as possible, but in a manner and at a rate that would not antagonize whites in the SADF. The new unit's insipid name, and its first base in the Prison Services Bantu Training College at Baviaanspoort, were cunningly crafted to assure the white opposition that black recruits would serve merely as guards, similar to black prison guards. In addition, Botha guaranteed that black recruitment was merely an exercise in training unarmed sentinels.[61]

The army sought black applicants between the ages of eighteen and thirty-five who had passed at least seven grades of elementary school. Applicants had to be medically fit and have a clean police record with

59. *Paratus*, March 1977, p. 25; March 1980, p. 48.

60. In 1968, Parliament passed the Dangerous Weapons Act 43, aimed at depriving blacks of weapon ownership. Grundy, *Soldiers without Politics*, p. 42.

61. South Africa, *House of Assembly Debates* 47 (February 7, 1974), col. 304. Maj. C. J. Nothling, "Blacks, Coloreds, and Indians in the SA Defense Forces," *South Africa International* 11, no. 1 (July 1980): 26. The Prison Services Bantu Training College had been training black prison guards for many years. Military manpower planners therefore hoped that the college and its black instructors would be able to help the first black recruits adjust to the military's culture and discipline code. Interview with Maj. Gen. Pretorius, director of manpower provision, Defence Headquarters, Armscore, Pretoria, March 27, 1993.

no previous court sentences. Finally, applicants from all of the South African Bantu tribes were encouraged to join the new guard unit.[62] Few, if any, considered this open invitation to be a violation of apartheid policy, with its vision of ethnically segregated black homelands. It was not unusual to train Zulu, Xhosa, and Sothu black men together, since they were to be dispersed at the end of their training among various white units as guards. After all, even during World War II, blacks nominally had belonged to the Native Military Corps, although in fact they had served as laborers in numerous white units.

Yet the military's true intentions for this new unit were different from the start.[63] Numerous signs indicated that the unit would serve other than its stated purpose. Among themselves, senior military manpower planners referred to the new unit as "the project."[64] The army assigned an unusually large number of instructors to a project allegedly involving the training of a few guards. Major M. W. Pretorius, an experienced white officer who mastered the Zulu language and participated in the formation of the SACC, was assigned as the unit's first commander, supervising a staff of no less than ten Permanent Force white instructors appointed to oversee the training of only sixteen black "guards."[65] In addition, military officers carefully selected sixteen applicants who were Venda, Xhosa, Tswana, and Zulu speakers but also could handle the army's two official languages (English and Afrikaans). Many of the new recruits came from the Auxiliary Force, and thus were intimately familiar with the army's lifestyle. Moreover, many possessed educational certificates above the required level, even high school diplomas. In addition, in 1974, Botha finally yielded to a long-standing demand of the South African Legion's Black Welfare Liaison to grant black World War II veterans official status and partial veterans' benefits. By doing so, Botha revealed his intention to treat their successors as professional fighting soldiers.[66]

62. *Evening Post*, March 18, 1975.

63. The SADF's official line is that the decision to turn the Bantu Center into an army battalion was made only in August 1974, after a second intake of thirty-eight blacks began their training. See Cmdt. C. J. Nothling, "The Role of Non-whites in the South African Defense Forces," *Militaria* 16, no. 2 (1986), p. 53. The evidence above, however, suggests that the "black guard" cover story was just that.

64. Interview with Maj. Gen. Pretorius.

65. Nothling, "Blacks, Coloreds, and Indians," p. 26.

66. Between October 1974 and July 1976, allowances for disabled black veterans were set at 2.5 rand per veteran, compared to 10 rand for white veterans; South African Institute

In March 1974, the first sixteen blacks began their training. In April 1974, *Paratus*, the official military journal, published an unusual article in which the author advised South African officers to observe the qualities of black soldiers in other African armies. It praised African soldiers across the continent for qualities such as "good leadership, good training, and strong personal motivation," so vital for battlefield success.[67] In June 1974, only a few months after training started, readers of the *World*, a Transvaal-based African newspaper with a black audience, were invited to apply for military service. One newspaper even reported that black "guards" would be armed.[68] In August 1974 a second intake of thirty-eight blacks began its training in Baviaanspoort.[69] Observers who paid close attention to the early stages of the SACC and Indian Service Battalion experiments probably understood that the Bantu center was following a familiar pattern.

The military unveiled its true intentions shortly before the first black "guards" were scheduled to complete their training. In December 1974, Major General John Raymond "Jack" Dutton, acting chief of the army, held a press conference in which he confirmed that the unit would follow the model of the SACC. Dutton also declared that the newly recruited African soldiers would be allowed to carry arms and would receive the same pay and service benefits as white soldiers. As usual, he made every effort to calm opposition from within and without the military. Dutton explained that blacks could become officers one day but would never be permitted to give orders to white servicemen. He explained that, among the rank and file, it would take up to nine years before the new black soldiers could attain the rank of sergeant major. Finally, the general assured his audience that the new black unit was "well within the framework of government policy" and that no integrated units were contemplated.[70] Nonetheless, his statements were completely at odds with the traditional policy against arming blacks. Newspaper stories with headlines such as "Won't They Turn the Guns on Us?" analyzed the general's

---

of Race Relations, *Survey, 1986*, p. 805. Allowances were equalized, however, toward the end of the 1970s as more black recruits joined the force. See also *Cape Times*, April 12, 1975; *Sunday Express*, June 23, 1974.

67. *Paratus*, April 1974.

68. *Cape Times*, June 15, 1974.

69. Nothling, "Role of Non-whites," p. 53.

70. *Star*, December 9, 1974; *Rand Daily Mail*, December 10 and 11, 1974; *Cape Times*, December 10, 1974; Grundy, "Black Foreign Legion," p. 102.

statements. Several newspapers even described at length the types of rifle the military planned to supply to black soldiers.[71]

Between 1973 and 1975, the army relentlessly pursued its black experiment in order to turn the original guard unit into a self-sufficient military school for future generations of black recruits. In April 1975, a first group of thirty-six black servicemen completed basic training and an instructor course. The military absorbed most of the new instructors into the Permanent Force and immediately began training a second batch. In December 1975, the army announced that the South African Bantu Training Center had achieved self-sufficiency. The unit was renamed 21 Battalion, since its formal establishment date coincided with the twenty-first anniversary of the Infantry Corps. The battalion's base was moved to a new camp in Lenz, north of Johannesburg, and the first black instructors were promoted to the rank of corporal.[72] The establishment of 21 Battalion marked the end of the experimental stage in the recruitment of non-whites. Convinced that these experiments were a success, the SADF was now ready to increase the number of its black soldiers.

The desire to recruit more blacks, however, had to be reconciled with the government's grand vision of Bantu homelands. Simply put, how could the SADF recruit blacks if they were to become citizens of other countries? "As far as the Bantu are concerned," Botha said on one occasion, "one cannot decide today that one is going to use Bantu in the Defence Force and find tomorrow that one no longer has them."[73] Moreover, in 21 Battalion, soldiers from different black ethnic groups trained and lived together as brothers in arms. Its multiethnic composition therefore contradicted the dictates of apartheid, which assigned each "black nation" to its own segregated "homeland."

In 1974, therefore, without much long-term planning, Botha proposed a new experimental strategy: the SADF would assist the homelands in building their own armed forces.[74] A first experiment along these lines was launched between January and April 1976 after discussions between Admiral Biermann and General Malan and the government of Transkei. Black instructors and white officers from the SACC and 21 Battalion trained 151 black soldiers of the First Transkei Battalion. After

---

71. *Star*, June 14, 1974; *Sunday Express*, June 16, 1974; *Natal Mercury*, June 15, 1974.
72. Nothling, "Blacks, Coloreds, and Indians," p. 27.
73. South Africa, *House of Assembly Debates* 56 (April 22, 1975), col. 4583.
74. South Africa, *House of Assembly Debates* 51 (September 9, 1974), col. 2491.

Transkei's first Independence Day (October 26, 1976), the new soldiers became the core of Transkei Defence Force.[75] Then Chief Lucas Mangope, the leader of Bophuthatswana, requested and received SADF assistance in preparing his homeland army for Bophuthatswana's first Independence Day in December 1977.[76] A year later, soldiers of the future Venda Defence Force began their training in Lenz. The Ministry of Defence summarized the role of the SADF vis-à-vis the homeland armies: "Assistance and support to independent Black homelands, if requested, in developing their own defence forces, for the security of their territories, the maintenance of law and order and the assurance of their independence."[77]

Despite these new experiments, or rather because of them, the Ministry of Defence was forced to admit that a "general policy of employing other nationals in the South African Army" was yet to be formulated and approved. Botha promised that the new homeland armies would "occupy a position within the military milieu of the Republic of South Africa," but he could not say what this position would be.[78] Thus, as Botha himself acknowledged, the SADF was at a crossroads in the mid-1970s. Answers were needed to questions such as: Which and how many blacks would be recruited, and to what units? How and where would they be trained during their first few months in the military? Who would command these units, the SADF or the various homeland governments? These questions naturally transgressed the boundaries of the military, and Parliament members demanded answers to them, as the SADF was already involved in an escalating war in South West Africa.[79]

At the beginning of 1978, the army performed its first comprehensive study of the black soldiers issue. To make use of the experience gained from training 21 Battalion, it transferred that unit's first commander, Major Pretorius, to Army Headquarters, where he assumed the new title of "Senior Staff Officer—Other Race Groups." His new role was to de-

75. South Africa, *House of Assembly Debates* 56 (April 22, 1975), cols. 4583–4584. Ministry of Defence, *White Paper, 1977*, p. 21. At first, the small Transkei military comprised a ceremonial company and a rifle company, the latter composed of soldiers who had completed their basic training in Lenz; *Daily Dispatch*, April 13, 1976.

76. Nothling, "Blacks, Coloreds, and Indians," p. 27. See also Ministry of Defence, *White Paper, 1977*, p. 21.

77. Ministry of Defence, *White Paper, 1977*, p. 9.

78. Ministry of Defence, *White Paper, 1977*, p. 21; South Africa, *House of Assembly Debates* 56 (April 21, 1975), col. 4495; 56 (April 22, 1975), col. 4584.

79. South Africa, *House of Assembly Debates* 56 (April 17, 1975), cols. 4361–4362.

vise a long-term philosophy for the use of black manpower in the SADF. Instead of the trial-and-error approach characterizing previous ethnic experiments, Pretorius was instructed to take a long, close look at all aspects of the issue.

Pretorius offered the army three basic options for building new black units. The first was to establish on a regional basis several new black battalions similar to 21 Battalion. The second was to abolish 21 Battalion and send its soldiers to the various homeland armies. With this option, the SADF would have no black soldiers of its own. Whenever the SADF needed black soldiers for operational missions, the homeland leaders would supply them. The third was to integrate black soldiers into white infantry units. According to this option, segregated black platoons would be attached to white companies; 21 Battalion would become the training school for these platoons.

The second option was dismissed because of the uncertain future of the homelands. Even if the homelands achieved independence, their leaders were not considered reliable enough to be trusted with the entire pool of black soldiers needed by the SADF.[80] Senior military manpower planners rejected the third option because they feared that white units were not ready to absorb black soldiers. Malan made the final decision: the army would train its own black soldiers under a scheme of regional units.

The plan to form ethnically segregated black units was an ingenious solution to the problem of integrating black recruits into the SADF without alarming the right-wing opposition. Unlike the multiethnic 21 Battalion, the new battalions would be ethnically segregated (Zulu battalion, Venda battalion, etc.). As such, these units indeed had the potential to serve as the core for the future armies of various tribal homelands. This satisfied and even pleased almost everyone in the government, the conservative opposition, and the military. Influential conservative groups that had feared the creation of additional SADF black armed formations were now confident that the SADF was merely assisting "foreign countries" with building "their armies."[81]

---

80. In April 1978, Chief Matanzima of the Transkei announced that he was breaking off diplomatic relations with South Africa. In response, the South African government terminated its involvement in the training of the Transkei Defence Forces. The event exemplified that, indeed, the SADF could not have relied on the fickle homeland governments for the supply of well-trained and experienced black soldiers.

81. South Africa, Ministry of Defence, *White Paper, 1982*, p. 4.

In practice, senior SADF commanders built the new regional black battalions to remain part of the SADF. Some SADF internal papers confirm that the military never viewed its new battalions as foreign forces in the making. The SADF, for example, officially explained the political and military future of one of these units (111 Battalion) to its white personnel this way: "Should Ka-Ngwane become fully independent, these Swazi-unit members will form the core of a future Ka-Ngwane Defence Force. Ka-Ngwane will, however, not reach full independence within the foreseeable future, and the unit is utilized as a command COIN-force (Counter Insurgency Units). Currently, interesting and exciting new possibilities for the utilization of the unit are being considered on a high level."[82]

The history of these new battalions provides additional indications that the SADF built them to remain SADF units. They were built and trained according to the 21 Battalion model. In 1980, several of these units already were operational and patrolling the border, sometimes in cooperation with other black units, an arrangement that broke the allegedly rigid ethnic and regional barriers between them. Moreover, black instructors from 21 Battalion were routinely transferred to serve in these regional units irrespective of their tribal origins.[83]

SADF officers correctly assessed in 1978 that many of the homelands would not declare independence. Except for one battalion, all the new regional black battalions have remained part of the SADF (see Table 2).

Ironically, even one unsuccessful ethnic experiment resulted in a greater number of full-time black soldiers. After his appointment as chief of staff in 1976, Malan launched a campaign to integrate blacks into the commandos,[84] regional units of part-time soldiers who were called for duty upon need and served only within the boundaries of their regions. In South Africa, the commandos are popularly known as rural, all-white units usually manned by conservative soldiers; these units were thus the least likely to accept black recruits. For their part, black soldiers were

82. SADF, "111 Battalion in Amsterdam," Unit File, SADF Archives.

83. A team of experienced NCOs and soldiers from 113 Battalion, for example, assisted the young 116 Battalion in its first operational mission; *Paratus*, March 1986, p. 38.

84. Malan used every weapon at his disposal to promote his plan: newspapers, meetings with white commando units, white papers published by the Ministry of Defence, and, after 1980, in his capacity as minister of defence, parliamentary speeches. See *Cape Times*, August 16, 1976; Ministry of Defence, *White Paper, 1977*, p. 30; South African Institute of Race Relations, *Survey, 1983*, p. 580.

Table 2. SADF ethnic battalions, 1963–1993

Unit	Location	Ethnic Group
SA Cape Corps (before 1972 known as the "South African Colored Corps"). Created 1963. Renamed 9 SAI after 1990.	Faure (Cape Town)	Coloreds
SAS Jalsena (before 1979 known as the "Indian Service Battalion"). Created 1974. Closed down March 1993.	Durban	Indians
21st Battalion (before 1975 known as the "Army Bantu Service Corps"). Created 1975.	Lenz	Multiethnic blacks
111th Battalion. Created 1977.	Amsterdam (East Transvaal)	Swazis
112th Battalion. Created 1978. Soldiers transferred to the Venda Homeland Army in 1982.	Madumo (Northern Transvaal)	Vendas
113th Battalion. Created 1979. Renamed 7 SAI March 1992.	Impala (Northern Transvaal)	Shangans
114th battalion. Planned but never established.		
115th Battalion. Created 1984.	Sustershoek (Central Transvaal)	Ndebeles
116th Battalion. Created 1984.	Messina (Northern Transvaal)	Northern Suthos
117th Battalion. Planned.	Northern Transvaal	
118th Battalion. Planned.		
121st Battalion. Created 1978.	Dukuduku (Northern Natal)	Zulus
151st Battalion. Renamed 1 SAI after January 1993.	Orange Free Area	Southern Suthos
31st Battalion (imported 1988 from the SWATF). Created 1976. Disbanded March 1992.	Western Caprivi	Bushman
32nd Battalion (also known as the "Buffalo Battalion," imported 1988 from the SWATF). Created 1976. Disbanded March 1993.	Pomfret (Northern Cape)	Black FNLA members

SOURCES: *White Paper 1984*, p. 13; *Paratus* (July 1982): 50, and (July 1986): 13, 18; *African Defence* (November 1989): 30; Nothling, "Blacks, Coloureds and Indians in the SA Defense Forces"; Baynham, "Towards a National Defence," 121st. Unit Files, SADF Archives; Col. Claasen, head Army Formal Training, Army Headquarters, Pretoria, March 29, 1993; Maj. R. Khoza, public relations officer, Defence Headquarters, Pretoria, March 25, 1993; Brig. Gen. Pretorius, director of manpower provision, Defence Headquarters, Pretoria, March 27, 1993.

not very keen to serve part-time; most wished to become full-time in order to earn a full-time soldier's salary.[85]

Whatever his reasons, Malan's efforts to recruit blacks into the commandos were in vain.[86] With the exception of black commandos in South West Africa, the number of blacks in the SADF commandos remained very marginal. For example, in 1985, 431 black commando soldiers constituted a minuscule 1.73 percent of the total Commando Force. In 1988, only 4.1 percent of the commandos were black (9.2 percent of the commandos were colored, 2.1 percent Indian, and 84.6 percent white).[87] Thus, with the "back door" options (serving as part-time soldiers in the commandos and the Citizen Force service systems) closed, the SADF had only one choice: to let black recruits into the military through the "main gate" (serving as full-time soldiers in the Permanent Force or the Auxiliary Force service systems).

By 1979, the SADF had successfully completed a series of ethnic-recruitment experiments, and its doors were open to nonwhite soldiers. One observer wrote that he was puzzled by "the SADF and its tendency to proliferate small [ethnic] entities with big names."[88] But such proliferation was neither a bizarre phenomena nor an anomaly. Rather, each ethnic unit was an experiment that expanded on the previous one. The new units were just the first wave in a sea of change. It was the war in South West Africa that forced the SADF to continue its internal ethnic evolution.

INTERNAL ETHNIC EVOLUTION: THE WAR IN SOUTH WEST AFRICA (1974–1985)

During the first decade of ethnic recruitment, nonwhite servicemen witnessed the SADF's preparations for total war. In 1965, the SADF launched a ten-year plan to upgrade its combat readiness and strike ca-

85. Interview with Maj. Gen. Pretorius.

86. In 1983 Malan himself admitted his failure, declaring at a National Party Congress that although white commandos did not need other race groups, men of other race groups were still an essential manpower source for the commando service system; South African Institute of Race Relations, *Survey, 1983*, p. 580.

87. South African Institute of Race Relations, *Survey, 1985*, p. 417; *Business Day*, February 13, 1986; South African Institute of Race Relations, *Survey, 1988*, p. 522.

88. Crocker, *South Africa's Defense Posture*, p. 16.

pacity, and in 1968, it intensified field preparations for an antiguerrilla campaign. The SADF launched its first large-scale military exercise, Operation Sibasa, which dealt with a force of mock terrorists entering the Transvaal from Mozambique. In addition, the military established five special antiguerrilla training camps where soldiers learned to camouflage themselves, to track infiltrators, to protect convoys, and to execute antiguerrilla ambushes. The air force also was reorganized to make it more mobile and integrate it with other antiguerrilla forces. A 1971–1973 review of the army's tactical doctrine highlighted the "ever-increasing need for mobility and striking power, and more extensive training at a higher standard," which were required in order to meet nonconventional challenges. Clearly, antiguerrilla warfare was now a real eventuality for which the SADF was preparing; it was no longer a merely theoretical chapter in military textbooks.[89]

The SADF became involved in the war in Namibia at a relatively late stage. In March 1974, the SADF formally took over responsibility from the South African police for patrolling the borders, and relatively few soldiers saw action in South West Africa between 1974 and 1976. But the arrival in Angola of Soviet and Cuban forces, with their heavy weapons, in 1977 finally compelled the SADF to prepare for a large-scale conventional war. In September 1977, therefore, the SADF launched its largest ever conventional military maneuver, with the objective of testing a full mechanized combat group in conventional warfare. In addition, the conscription period for white men was raised from one year to two years in January 1978.[90]

Thus, after 1977, the SADF had to prepare for a worst-case scenario: a blitzkrieg-style invasion by Warsaw Pact soldiers arriving unexpectedly by air and using pools of waiting vehicles and weapons to launch an attack on South Africa with neighboring states' armies as backup. According to this scenario, widespread ANC-organized internal unrest would accompany a large-scale conventional attack. Botha called on South Afri-

89. Robert S. Jaster, "South African Defense Strategy and the Growing Influence of the Military," in *Arms and the African: Military Influences on Africa's International Relations*, ed. William J. Foltz and Henry S. Bienen (New Haven: Yale University Press, 1985), p. 126; South Africa, *White Paper, 1973*, pp. 4, 8; South Africa, *Review of Defence, 1960 to 1970*, p. 26.

90. Deon Fourie, "The Evolving Experience," in Roherrty, *Defense Policy Formation*, pp. 103–105; Jaster, "South African Defense Strategy," pp. 131–132; *Natal Mercury*, August 3, 1974.

1. The South African Coloured Corps Company displays weapons before departing for South West Africa, 1975. The company, established as a service unit in 1963, was upgraded to a combat unit at the beginning of the 1970s. Photo courtesy of the SA National Defence Force, Directorate of Documentation Service, Pretoria

cans to formulate a "total national strategy at the highest level." Since the SADF's role was to develop the manpower, plans, and doctrine to fight a total war,[91] more and better-trained soldiers were needed. It was time to move forward to the second phase of ethnic experimentation: promoting

91. Ministry of Defence, *White Paper, 1977*, p. 4; *White Paper, 1982*, p. 1; Steenkamp, "SA Defense Force," pp. 56, 66.

[57]

2. Musketry lesson for South African troops in South West Africa, unknown area, 1975–85 Border War period. Photo courtesy of the SA National Defence Force, Directorate of Documentation Service, Pretoria

nonwhite servicemen to the status of first-class combat soldiers and sending them to the escalating war in South West Africa.

Sending nonwhite soldiers to combat against a black enemy in foreign territory was a mission that touched a sensitive nerve in South African politics. Since the formation of the Union in 1910, South Africa had suffered from political turmoil whenever its government attempted to send soldiers to missions abroad. During World War I, Prime Minister Louis Botha had to overcome serious constitutional obstacles and suppress an armed rebellion in South West Africa in order to mobilize volunteers to assist the British war effort. Some of the German-speaking population viewed Botha as a traitor and refused to assist what they saw as a British imperial war against their German kin. And during World War II, many

3. Guard Tower, Border Area. Photo courtesy of the SA National Defence Force, Director-ate of Documentation Service, Pretoria

Afrikaners argued that Afrikaner blood ought not be shed in the service of the British Empire. This historical legacy forced SADF commanders to be very cautious, and to secure in advance the loyal service of non-white soldiers in South West Africa.

To do this, the SADF chose once again the "coloreds first" experimen-tal approach. The SACC was to be the first nonwhite unit tested under combat conditions. There were demands in the South African Parliament as early as 1967 that colored troops be assigned as "fighting troops", but only in 1972 did military planners begin the process of converting the SACC from a second-class to a full-fledged combat unit.[92] Within one

92. South Africa, *House of Assembly Debates* 21 (June 8, 1967), col. 7453. As late as 1971 the Ministry of Defence continued to insist that "it is important to note that members of

4. 81 mm mortar pit in the Border Area, 1975–85 Border War period. Photo courtesy of the SA National Defence Force, Directorate of Documentation Service, Pretoria

year, the SACC was reorganized almost from scratch. It was declared a Permanent Force unit, salaries were improved, and the unit was increased to two thousand men. Most of the recruits joined the SACC through a new voluntary national service track similar to the compulsory one for whites. A new center at Faure opened to train the new colored soldiers and to develop the SACC's first full-fledged infantry battalion. Finally, the name of the unit was changed to the S.A. Cape Corps. This last change was a clear indication of the military's plans for the unit, since S.A. Cape Corps was the historical name of the colored unit that saw combat during World War II.[93] *Paratus*, the military journal, highlighted the parallels between the fighting spirit of the World War II S.A.

---

the Colored Corps serve in noncombatant capacities"; South Africa, "Questions and Replies," in *House of Assembly Debates* 35 (February 9, 1971), col. 101.

93. *Argus*, August 1, 1974; May 12, 1973; *Cape Times*, January 15, 1975; *Uniform*, March 11, 1985; South Africa, *White Paper, 1973*, p. 11; *Pretoria News*, August 2, 1973.

Cape Corps soldiers and their modern successors.[94] Other newspapers accentuated the fact that, "for the first time in 60 years," coloreds were being trained as full-fledged infantry men.[95] To demand a quicker pace of racial reform, several newspapers referred to the military record of nonwhite policemen killed in action on the borders with South West Africa. One wrote in its editorial, "Won't someone please tell our Government that when a soldier has died for his country, his skin color makes no difference."[96] Experienced observers could clearly see that the SADF was preparing the colored unit for something entirely new.

The navy preempted the army in being the first to deploy coloreds in combat positions when, in June 1973, it stationed a small number of S.A. Cape Corps national servicemen on the survey vessel *Pretoria* and the defense vessel *Somerset*. Shortly after, twenty-six more colored sailors, some in specialist positions, joined the crew of the supply ship SAS *Tafelberg*. In 1975, the navy advanced further, staffing one of its minesweepers with a crew of colored sailors. These naval deployment decisions were historically important for two reasons. First, these were the first assignments of nonwhite soldiers to combat roles since World War II. Second, they broke the traditional segregation order. Aboard various naval vessels, nonwhite and white servicemen had separate sleeping and dining facilities but worked shoulder to shoulder. In 1977, even the separate facilities were quietly removed.[97] The decision to deploy a small number of colored sailors on naval vessels, however, was less sensitive than that to deploy a large number of colored infantrymen against a black enemy. The army remained the ultimate testing ground for the SADF's willingness to expose a large number of nonwhites to combat.

In January 1975, the army followed the navy and officially declared the S.A. Cape Corps a combat unit. Colored soldiers began preparations for their first combat assignments.[98] While newspapers were still analyzing the types of service rifle for the first SADF black "guards," colored soldiers quietly began to familiarize themselves with mortars, mines, ar-

---

94. *Paratus*, August 1972, pp. 32–33, 61.

95. *Cape Times*, March 28, 1975; *Rand Daily Mail*, March 28, 1975.

96. *Rand Daily Mail*, December 11, 1974.

97. *Argus*, June 12, 1973; South Africa, *House of Assembly Debates* 56 (April 22, 1975), col. 4582; South African Institute of Race Relations, *Survey, 1975*, p. 42; Ministry of Defence, *White Paper, 1977*, p. 31; *Star*, May 20, 1975; *Daily Dispatch*, May 20, 1975.

98. Interview with Brigadier Jacobs, director of army personnel maintenance, Army Headquarters, Pretoria, April 2, 1993; *Cape Times*, March 28, 1975.

tillery, air support, and company-level maneuvers. In November 1975, the first S.A. Cape Corps unit, consisting of one hundred and ninety soldiers, left for South West Africa—the first occasion since World War II a nonwhite unit was assigned a ground combat mission of its own. Two months later, in January 1976, the first colored infantry battalion reached full strength.[99] In August 1976, a second and larger S.A. Cape Corps unit left for extended service on the border, and its soldiers, according to a report by the Ministry of Defence, "acquitted themselves well" under combat conditions.[100] By 1984, members of the S.A. Cape Corps had completed four hundred and twenty thousand man days in operational missions along the borders.[101]

Military officers relentlessly provided politicians with reports about the positive impact of military service on nonwhites in order to soothe ultraconservative politicians' fears about the swelling numbers of nonwhite soldiers. Behind closed doors, several military studies presented to the political leadership suggested that colored and Indian men who volunteered for national service often enjoyed more success after discharge than others in school and on the job market.[102] After the riots of 1976, these studies contained a powerful message from senior officers to ultraconservative politicians: nonwhite military service can allay despair within the ranks of unemployed nonwhite youth, so do not oppose our efforts to reform the ethnic military manpower policy of the SADF.

Since Indians served exclusively in the navy, it was now the black soldiers' turn to be sent to the borders. Although calls for this action had been voiced during the first half of 1976, the Soweto riots (June 16, 1976) slowed the pace of ethnic evolution, but not for long.[103] In September 1976, General Malan, the architect of both the SACC and 21 Battalion experiments, was appointed chief of the SADF. Determined to resume

99. South Africa, *House of Assembly Debates* 60 (January 26, 1976), col. 56; 62 (May 6, 1976), col. 6210; *Cape Times*, December 5, 1975; *White Paper, 1979*, p. 4; *Argus*, August 1, 1976; *Daily Dispatch*, January 17, 1976.

100. Ministry of Defence, *White Paper, 1977*, p. 21. In August, several newspapers drew the attention of their readers to a recent conference of colored veterans who fought in the great World War I battle of Square Hill. The implications were very clear: colored soldiers in South West Africa were merely continuing a great South African tradition. See *Star*, August 12, 1976; *Paratus*, August 1978, p. 43. Needless to say, these newspapers chose to ignore the official NP line of the 1950s that it was a great South African tradition not to arm nonwhites.

101. *Uniform*, March 11, 1985, p. 10.

102. Interview with Brig. Jacobs.

103. South Africa, *House of Assembly Debates* 62 (May 6, 1976), col. 6167.

the SADF's ethnic reforms, Malan ordered his successor as chief of the army to continue with ethnic experimentation. Shortly thereafter, the chief of the army instructed the commanders of 21 Battalion to prepare a black company for operational duty. The first-ever operational company in 21 Battalion was established in mid-1977 and began training for combat.[104]

The SADF was determined to provide its black soldiers with advanced training, not the poor training given to black police officers, many of whom had been killed in combat in previous years. Thus, soldiers of this first operational company were taught to set up an ambush, to establish temporary bases in the field, to attack enemy bases, to perform vehicle movements, to conduct road blocks, and to operate mortars—activities hardly characterizing a guard unit. In March 1978, the company's soldiers were sent to the border. The unit entered into combat three days after its deployment and performed well. Thereafter the combat deployment of 21 Battalion's units and other black battalions became a matter of routine.[105]

Throughout this period, the official statements and publications of the SADF and the Ministry of Defence remained one step behind the ongoing ethnic experimentation. Thus, when *Paratus* published a story on the SADF black "guards" and their weapons, those "guards" were already preparing for their first combat mission in South West Africa.[106] Likewise, the government's 1979 white paper officially acknowledged the deployment of colored soldiers along the border since 1975, but omitted the fact that two black companies had also completed successful missions in South West Africa.[107] The policy was to report only experiments that had become routine. Experiments in their infant stages, even if successful, were to be shielded from the media.

The success of colored and black units in operational missions convinced the SADF that it was now time to increase the number of non-white recruits. In 1980, it raised the service period for voluntary national

104. "The Black Soldier in the South African Army," SADF internal publication, SADF Archives.

105. "21 Battalion, Unit File, 1978," SADF Archives, p. A–7; *Evening Post*, June 17, 1974; *Paratus*, April 1978, p. 4; July 1982, p. 50; *Sunday Post*, July 21, 1978; October 7, 1979; February 29, 1980; *Uniform*, August 1978; *Daily Dispatch*, November 24, 1978; *DFA*, February 3, 1979; "Black Soldier in the South African Army"; Grundy, "Black Foreign Legion," p. 109.

106. *Paratus*, February 1977; Grundy, *Soldiers without Politics*, pp. 200–201.

107. *White Paper*, 1979, p. 4.

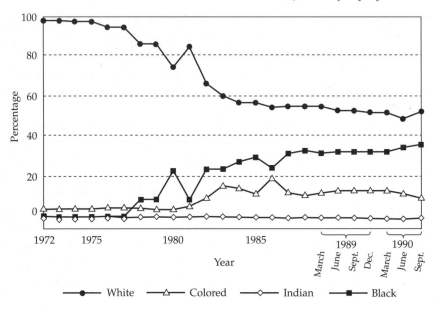

Figure 4. The internal evolution of the SADF.

serviceman (which included most of the new colored and Indian recruits) from twelve to twenty-four months. From the second half of the 1980s, the number of nonwhite Permanent Force and voluntary national servicemen increased dramatically (see Figure 4).[108] The graph's numbers represent the proportions—not the total numbers—of Indian, colored, black, and white full-time servicemen. Most important, it illustrates the ever-decreasing ratio of full-time white servicemen to full-time black servicemen.[109]

108. South African Institute of Race Relations, *Survey, 1979,* p. 83. The number of non-white applicants for military service increased even more dramatically. In 1986, 4,517 non-white applicants volunteered for national service; South African Institute of Race Relations, *Survey, 1986,* p. 516. In 1987, 3,437 nonwhite applicants volunteered for national service; South African Institute of Race Relations, *Survey, 1987–88,* p. 522. Figure 4 was provided to the author by Rear Adm. P. van Z. Loedolff, deputy chief of staff personnel, Defence Headquarters, Pretoria.

109. The proportion of colored servicemen increased between 1980 and 1986. Between 1986 and 1988, however, the army raised the educational qualifications for coloreds who wished to become full-time soldiers (the qualifications were equalized with those of white recruits). As a result, fewer coloreds were admitted to the Permanent Force. After 1990,

In light of this ethnic evolution, the SADF was forced to reorganize its ethnic units. In 1980, it restructured the S.A. Cape Corps as a full-scale corps with its own infantry school, a full-fledged infantry battalion, and a maintenance unit. In 1986, the SADF established a second S.A. Cape Corps Battalion, and in 1982, it reorganized 21 Battalion as a corps with five wings, including an Infantry Wing, a Regimental Wing, and a Counter-Insurgency Wing. Finally, SAS Jalsena, the Indian naval base, began taking two intakes of recruits in 1985.[110] Service units at their foundation, the SACC, and the various black battalions had now become first-class operational infantry units.

The reorganizations of both the S.A. Cape Corps and 21 Battalion exemplify the long road traveled by nonwhite SADF servicemen since 1963. But much was still left to be desired. For example, while South African Parliament members expressed fears that if a regional all-white unit were lost in battle, small white towns might suffer "heavy losses," they never raised such concerns about regional all-black units.[111] Nonetheless, by the end of the 1970s, remarkable progress in the status of nonwhite soldiers had been achieved. The time was ripe to begin the process of vertical ethnic change in the SADF.

FROM HORIZONTAL TO VERTICAL CHANGE: THE FIRST ETHNIC OFFICERS

Long before the first colored soldiers were sent to battle, senior defense officials admitted that the combat deployment of nonwhite servicemen would eventually lead to commissioning the first nonwhite officers.[112] Senior SADF manpower planners knew perfectly well that nonwhite combat soldiers would need nonwhite officers to command them. The large increase in nonwhite recruits created a great demand for—and an acute shortage of—NCOs and officer instructors.[113] The combat assign-

---

the ratio of colored soldiers began to drop again as the SADF launched a vigorous campaign to recruit more blacks. The ratio of full-time Indian servicemen remained steady because virtually all Indian recruits served in the small South African navy.

110. *East Province Herald*, December 28, 1979; "History of the Cape Regiment, 1986," SACC Unit File, SADF Archives; South African Institute of Race Relations, *Survey, 1986*, p. 806; "Black Soldier in the South African Army"; *Citizen*, May 17, 1986.

111. South Africa, *House of Assembly Debates* 21 (June 8, 1967), col. 7443.

112. South Africa, *House of Assembly Debates* 30 (August 31, 1970), col. 2935.

113. Ministry of Defence, *White Paper, 1977*, p. 4; *White Paper, 1979*, p. 5.

ments of the first nonwhite units compounded this problem. The first operational deployment of a black unit, for example, exhausted the cadre of black instructors in 21 Battalion.[114] More important, SADF commanders knew that nonwhite units performed better under nonwhite officers and NCOs; the third operational company of 21 Battalion leaving for the border already had black platoon sergeants.[115] The military therefore had to begin training a cadre of nonwhite NCOs and officers who would assist in building, training, and leading nonwhite units in combat.

Though nonwhite officers already were serving in the police, plans to commission nonwhite SADF officers were bound to encounter opposition. In 1972, Botha began laying the groundwork for the next stage in the SADF's ethnic evolution. He announced that in the future the government intended to allow colored servicemen to become officers and to work "side by side" with white colleagues in all three fighting branches.[116] While the audience assumed that the minister of defence was discussing a plan for the distant future academically, Botha moved quickly to implement the new idea. In July 1973, he instructed Comdt. Henry Kempen, the commanding officer of the S.A. Cape Corps, to invite colored servicemen to apply for officers' school.[117]

Seventy S.A. Cape Corps soldiers submitted applications; twenty-seven were admitted. Colored cadets were trained in the Military Academy for only four weeks, however, and spent the rest of their twenty-one-month officer course in the S.A. Cape Corps base. While the colored cadets were training, the Ministry of Defence was preparing the hearts and minds of white soldiers and the general public for the upcoming ethnic novelty. *Paratus*, for instance, published an essay arguing that blacks had been very successful as officers throughout Africa. Botha informed Parliament about the first colored officers only three weeks before their graduation ceremony.[118] Seven colored cadets successfully completed the course. In Capetown, with its large colored community,

114. Experienced black instructors served as soldiers in this company. It was one of the SADF's precautionary measures to insure the operational success of the unit. Grundy, "Black Foreign Legion," p. 109.

115. *Paratus*, 1978, p. 4; "Black Soldier in the South African Army"; Nothling, "Role of Non-whites," p. 53.

116. As usual, Botha artfully crafted his words as to allow each political group its own interpretation. "Side by side" was an ambiguous term that kept both opponents and proponents of integration within the SADF equally confused. See *Argus*, May 12, 1973.

117. Nothling, "Blacks, Coloreds, and Indians," p. 24; *Rand Daily Mail*, July 20, 1973.

118. *Paratus*, April 1974.

local newspapers called them "the Magnificent Seven" (named after the popular Steve McQueen movie of that time). Similarly, the first black cadets in the U.S. navy, who received their commissions during World War II, were publicly known as "the Golden Thirteen." Such names symbolized both the admiration of contemporary observers for the achievement of the first nonwhite officers and their understanding that something very important was happening in the military.[119] The May 1975 graduation day was celebrated as a national event. Shortly afterward, the first colored officers returned to the S.A. Cape Corps to train a new intake of colored infantrymen.[120]

The SADF experiment with colored officers quickly spilled over from the army to the navy. On November 1, 1973, only a short time after the first colored cadets had begun their officer course, Rear Admiral Biermann announced that Indians could eventually become naval officers. Indeed, in 1978, the first Indian sailors received commissions as midshipmen. The number of colored and Indian naval officers grew steadily during the 1980s, and today several dozen serve in the navy, in ranks ranging from midshipman to commander.[121]

Although previous ethnic experiments suggested that it was now time to send the first black soldiers to officers' school,[122] the SADF did not do so until 1984, and between 1984 and 1990, it commissioned only a small number of black officers.[123] SADF officers and scholars argued that a host of linguistic, educational, motivational, and institutional factors explained the paucity of black officers before 1990. One officer claimed that black serviceman needed many years to acquire proficiency in Afrikaans and English, and the educational levels required of officer cadets, and that by the time they did, they were usually too old for the officers'

119. Interview with Brig. Jacobs; *Rand Daily Mail*, November 2, 1973.

120. *Star*, May 15, 1975; *Rand Daily Mail*, May 16, 1975; *Cape Times*, May 16, 1978; March 28, 1975.

121. *Paratus*, March 1979, p. 4; Nothling, "Role of Non-whites," pp. 50–51; interview with Comdr. Yegan S. Moodley, former naval attaché, South Africa Embassy, Washington, D.C., June 12, 1992; interview with Comdr. Sagarem Pillay, former deputy commander, SAS Jalsena, Naval Mess, Pretoria, March 31, 1993.

122. *Rand Daily Mail*, April 18, 1975; January 16, 1985; Crocker, *South Africa's Defense Posture*, pp. 39–40.

123. South African Institute of Race Relations, *Survey, 1984*, p. 746; *Star*, October 5, 1984; *East Province Herald*, March 17, 1986. By 1985, only five black members of the SADF had completed an officers' course; Nothling, "Role of Non-whites," p. 54. Nine other black officers were commissioned in 32 ("Buffalo") Battalion that year; *Paratus*, July 1986. At the time, however, the battalion was still part of the South West Africa Territorial Force.

course. He also suggested that black men joined the military with lower expectations than their white peers. Fourie argued that the regional commanders responsible for recruiting promising black candidates for officers' school preferred to hold on to their best soldiers. Grundy suggested that the shortage of black cadets resulted from the more attractive civilian career alternatives available for such qualified blacks.[124]

None of these explanations is very convincing. Linguistic or educational skills could have been upgraded faster had the SADF deemed them a priority. For example, the SADF could have promoted a group of promising black NCOs through an intense schooling period to prepare them for officers' school.[125] Moreover, it could have recruited qualified civilian blacks directly to officers' school. This idea had a recent precedent: the navy had recruited a few Indian academics for midshipmen courses in 1978.[126] It is also hard to believe that among the thousands of black recruits who served in the SADF during the 1980s, such a small number wished to become officers. Finally, since senior officials such as Botha and Malan had closely supervised ethnic reforms within the SADF, it is doubtful that they left to the discretion of regional commanders an issue as sensitive as the commissioning of black officers.[127]

It seems clear, therefore, that the paucity of black officers before 1990 was due to political considerations. It was much easier for the politicians

124. Interview with Prof. Deon F. S. Fourie; interview with Col. W. Bernard, deputy director, Directorate Language Services, Defence Headquarters, Pretoria, March 25, 1993; Grundy, *Soldiers without Politics*, p. 189.

125. Indeed, in 1991 several programs were successfully launched to prepare black servicemen for NCO and officer courses. One of these programs provides officer cadets with an opportunity to earn a B.A. degree and an officer rank within three years. Black (or poorly educated white) cadets spend a full year before the beginning of their formal studies in the Military Academy improving their language, science, and technical skills. Later on, throughout their studies in the academy, black cadets are provided with mentors and tutors to assist them with their course work. Occasionally, black cadets are even permitted to drop their two best courses so they can focus on their weaker subjects. The program was very successful during its first year, and the only drop-outs were two white cadets. Interview with Col. M. Rutsch, Career Development of Personnel Division, Army Headquarters, Pretoria, March 25, 1993. In 1993, 5 SAI (an army field battalion) launched a program to prepare black soldiers for courses in the Infantry School; interview with Col. Claasen, head, Army Formal Training, Army Headquarters, Pretoria, March 29, 1993.

126. For example, Comdr. Moodley was recruited for officer course directly from teachers college; interview with Comdr. Yegan S. Moodley. See also *Paratus*, March 1979, p. 4; South African Institute of Race Relations, *Survey, 1978*, p. 55.

127. The 1982 white paper explicitly argued that the involvement of other population groups in the SADF follows "programmed manpower development plans which extend to 1990." See *White Paper, 1982*, p. 11.

to justify publicly the commissioning of homeland officers than to explain that of SADF blacks. Homeland officers, commissioned shortly before the first Independence Day of their homelands, became foreign officers immediately upon graduation. Being of "foreign stock," these black officers were not subject to South Africa's apartheid policies and therefore were permitted to attend all military courses and to eat, sleep, and train together with white SADF officers. Such integration was not possible for South African black soldiers under the apartheid policy. The politicians "solved" the dilemma by delaying the commissioning of the first SADF black officers and by holding their numbers down. It is quite possible that officers and politicians did not see eye to eye on the issue of commissioning black officers, especially after 1984, when the military needed additional black officers to lead new units in support of police activities in the townships.[128]

The scarcity of black officers remains, however, an anomaly within the general context of the SADF's internal ethnic evolution. After 1975, the military intensified its efforts to promote Indian and colored servicemen to officer courses, and after 1979, it permitted nonwhite officers to specialize for the first time (e.g., in personnel, infantry, and logistics) and to join a specialized corps outside their ethnic units.[129] In 1981, all the salaries and service benefits of colored and Indian officers at the rank of lieutenant and above, as well as those of NCOs at the rank of sergeant and above, were made equal to those of their white counterparts. The assignments of most of the first nonwhite officers followed a familiar

---

128. In 1979, the army had to decline more than six hundred colored applicants; *Argus,* August 22, 1979. In August 1982, Cmdt. Johann Beyers of the SADF Media Liaison Office reported that only a fifth of the nonwhite applicants could be recruited because of the scarcity of leaders and segregated facilities to train them; *Natal Mercury,* August 26, 1982. In July 1984, Rev. Allen Hendrickse, the leader of the (colored) LP party, said that six thousand men were on a waiting list to join the S.A. Cape Corps alone; South African Institute of Race Relations, *Survey, 1984,* p. 745. The number of colored applicants to voluntary national service increased by 30 percent in 1985; see *Cape Times,* February 14, 1985; *Uniform,* March 11, 1985; *East Province Herald,* December 1985. In one instance, the S.A. Colored Corps turned away six hundred young coloreds in one day; *Star,* January 11, 1985; April 26, 1985. Petitions were submitted to create a second S.A. Cape Corps battalion, and preparations to establish it began in 1985; South African Institute of Race Relations, *Survey, 1985,* p. 417; *East Province Herald,* December 16, 1985. A second South African Corps battalion and a colored infantry Citizen Force unit were finally established in January 1986. The new units finally allowed the military to recruit 2,338 new colored volunteers. See South African Institute of Race Relations, *Survey, 1986,* p. 806.

129. Interview with Brig. Jacobs.

pattern: back to segregated units, then up the chain of command, usually to a personnel or public-relations position, and, finally, to field command or senior staff positions within regular SADF groups, units, and head-quarters. For example, Brigadier General Jacobs, the most senior non-white officer in the SADF until 1992, served as a platoon and company commander within the S.A. Cape Corps for the first five years after his graduation from officers' school in 1975. He then specialized in the personnel track for the next five years. In 1986, he became the first colored commander of the S.A. Cape Corps School. Finally, in 1989, he was transferred to the Army Headquarters, where he became director of army personnel maintenance, commanding a staff of two hundred (90 percent of them white civilians and officers).[130]

APPROACHING THE FINAL PHASE: THE EFFECTS OF CHANGE

As horizontal and vertical change increased, the SADF corporate spirit (or military culture) began to change as well. Motivated by the growing number of ethnic officers and soldiers and the combat performance of ethnic units, the SADF began uprooting petty discrimination from its statute books. It is important to note that the change in military culture was the result, not the cause, of ethnic integration.

The first indications of a change in the military culture appeared in 1975, when the first colored cadets launched a campaign to abolish an old discriminatory Defence Amendment. Passed in Parliament in March 1963, this amendment to the Defence Code excluded "persons of color" from the definition of a "Superior Officer." Anticipating the revival of the SACC, it ensured that nonwhite servicemen would never be in a position of authority over whites. Its implication was that neither the rank nor the position of a nonwhite serviceman placed him above white servicemen. A nonwhite NCO or officer was not to be saluted by white soldiers, even when the latter held lower ranks then the former. Thus, among SADF's rank and file, the amendment was known as the "non-salute" clause,[131] and it was often used to calm the worst fears of conservative whites during the first half of the 1970s. Botha, for example, declared in August 1970, "I would commission them [colored service-

---

130. Interview with Brig. Jacobs; *Paratus*, March 1980.
131. *Natal Mercury*, April 17, 1975.

men], in as far as they would have command over their own people, but I would not allow them to be in command of white soldiers. . . . We say that under our system we shall allow only white officers to be in charge of white soldiers."[132] And only five months before the graduation of the first colored cadets, General Dutton, chief of the army, declared that nonwhite officers would never give orders to white soldiers.[133]

The first seven colored officer cadets, who had experienced the humiliating consequences of the "non-salute" clause as soldiers in the SACC, decided to challenge the clause. A month before graduation, they entered the office of the officer commander in charge of their training and informed him that they were determined to decline their commissions unless the "non-salute" clause was abolished. Usually, such behavior is deemed unacceptable in military organizations and could easily be interpreted as an act of mutiny. Cadets may not submit to their superior officers ultimatums concerning the amendment of the Defence Code. Nonetheless, these cadets had a powerful weapon on their side: time. The graduation ceremony had been planned months in advance as a major political event, to which top political and military leaders and foreign observers had been invited. The media had already announced the event, and it had been one of the leading stories around Cape Town for months. The government therefore could not cancel it without suffering serious embarrassment. Furthermore, future ethnic experiments depended on the success of this one. The navy, for instance, had already used the precedent of these future colored officers to convince Indian leaders in Durban that members of the new Indian Service Battalion also could become officers.[134]

Faced with little choice, Botha passed an amendment in Parliament abolishing the "non-salute" clause, and redefining the term "Superior Officer" in the Defence Code as "any officer, warrant officer or noncommissioned officer subject to this Code who holds a higher rank than such person, or who holds the same or an equivalent rank but is in a position of authority over such person."[135] This amendment, which passed in a few minutes, went even further than the original request of the colored cadets: it obliged all whites to salute and to obey the au-

---

132. South Africa, *House of Assembly Debates* 30 (August 31, 1970), cols. 2939, 2941.

133. *Star*, December 9, 1974; *Rand Daily Mail*, December 10–11, 1974; *Cape Times*, December 10, 1974.

134. Interview with Brig. Jacobs.

135. *Natal Mercury*, April 16, 1975; *Daily Dispatch*, April 17, 1975.

thority of both nonwhite officers and NCOs on the basis of either their rank or their position. Newspapers highlighted the effects of this change on the SADF military culture in stories bearing headlines such as "Rank, Not Culture," and "A Salute to Progress."[136] Even more important, these articles provided ample evidence that the SADF military culture itself was changing. One newspaper reminded its readers that a salute to black officers and NCOs really meant a salute to "the authority of the State President."[137] Another newspaper explained that white SADF NCOs on instruction missions to various homelands would have to salute the black officers of these "foreign" armies. If so, the journalist asked, why not do the same at home?[138] A third newspaper argued that since the training of black officers and NCOs was identical to that of their white peers, they were entitled to the same "respect and obedience" from their soldiers.[139]

In early 1978, the SADF submitted a classified study to the minister of defence recommending the elimination of all legal vestiges of segregation based on sex and race, effective April 1, 1978. During the next decade, inequalities and petty discriminations were abolished one by one. The army and the air force scrapped orders prohibiting personnel from accepting rides from blacks. Uniforms, symbols of rank, and serial numbers were equalized among servicemen.[140] The navy changed the name of its segregated Indian unit to a standard naval title—SAS Jalsena—in 1979. In 1978, coloreds were admitted for the first time to the paratroops, the Permanent Force, and the Citizen Force/commandos. The latter two openings were particularly important, since they allowed the SADF to offer lifelong careers to the more experienced S.A. Cape Corps soldiers and to continue employing experienced colored veterans as part-time soldiers after their discharge. By 1987, 10.6 percent of the part-time soldiers were coloreds.[141] The progress of coloreds and Indians in the navy

136. *Natal Mercury*, April 17, 1975; *Rand Daily Mail*, April 18, 1975.

137. *Cape Times*, April 16, 1975. One of the first black officers in the U.S. navy forced a white sailor to salute him by sticking his navy hat in front of the sailor and saying, "Now salute the insignia of the United States Navy." See Paul Stillwell, ed., *The Golden Thirteen: Recollections of the First Black Naval Officers* (Annapolis: Naval Institute Press, 1993), p. 24.

138. *Rand Daily Mail*, April 18, 1975.

139. *Natal Mercury*, April 17, 1975.

140. The suffixes of serial numbers for black soldiers, however, remained different from those of white soldiers.

141. Grundy, "Black Foreign Legion," p. 110; *Friend*, November 1, 1973; *Sunday Express*,

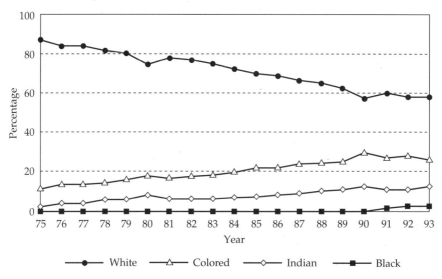

Figure 5. Racial composition of the South African navy

was even more impressive than in the army, as more of these sailors were being absorbed into the Permanent Force (see Figure 5).[142]

After 1976, the SADF also intensified its efforts to provide special assistance to ethnic soldiers. It created a new core of two hundred black instructors to facilitate communication between white and black personnel, and language instructors were dispersed among the various commands, groups, and units. This marked the first time white officers and NCOs attended classes led by black instructors. In addition, the SADF created a new network of Adult Education Centers to promote the educational standards of full-time black soldiers.[143]

June 16, 1974; *Cape Times*, April 12, 1975; *White Paper, 1979*, p. 6; Nothling, "Blacks, Coloreds, and Indians," pp. 25–26; *Paratus*, March 1980, p. 48; South African Institute of Race Relations, *Survey, 1988–89*, p. 522.

142. Until 1990 the navy did not recruit blacks because of a ministerial decree limiting the service of blacks to the army. In 1987, the army admitted 2,232 of 2,260 blacks (98.76 percent), but only 122 of 460 coloreds (26.52 percent) and 18 of 31 Indians (58.06 percent); South African Institute of Race Relations, *Survey, 1987–88*, p. 522.

143. Interview with Col. D. P. Stoffberg, former director, Ethnology, SA Army, Military Archives, Pretoria, March 24, 1993; interview with Col. W. Bernard; *Paratus*, August 1980,

THE CULMINATION OF A PROCESS: MIXING WHITE AND BLACK

The final stage of the SADF's internal ethnic evolution—the mixing of white and black servicemen—began along the borders of South West Africa, where strict segregation codes could not be maintained. White and black units fought together, ate together, and shared quarters. By 1979, military bases in combat zones were completely integrated.[144] But even in noncombat zones, orders instructing units to maintain strict segregation were not always enforceable. In one instance, officers from 21 Battalion reported that white soldiers from a poorly equipped ammunition depot unit nearby came every night to use the sport and recreational facilities at Lenz.[145]

More important, rigid segregation in the 1980s was nonsensical from a purely military standpoint. Such rigidity would have resulted in rejecting many nonwhite applicants due to a shortage of segregated facilities precisely when more soldiers were needed. Indeed, during the early 1980s, the army repeatedly complained that it was losing good nonwhite applicants because of "accommodation problems."[146] The navy, on the other hand, did not even bother to conceal the fact that in SAS Jalsena, rank messed with rank (i.e., there were no segregated dining facilities for white and Indian NCOs, officers, and base personnel).[147] In 1987, Malan disclosed that the S.A. Cape Corps School would be closed down because most of its members were serving in other corps and taking their promotion courses in other units.

Even more compelling reasons speeded up the integration of white and black soldiers. In 1988, the SADF completed a study of the war years in South West Africa (1974–1988). Comparing the operational performance, discipline, and morale of black and white soldiers, it confirmed

---

p. 39. In 1986, the SADF launched a new series of African language courses, attended by fifteen hundred Permanent Force members; *Eastern Province Herald*, July 10, 1986.

144. Deon Fourie, "Universal Service: A Military View," in *Conscientious Objection*, 2d ed., Occasional Papers no. 8 (1989), p. 43; *Evening Post*, June 17, 1974; Grundy, "Black Foreign Legion," p. 111; Jaster, "South African Defense Strategy," p. 135.

145. "21 Battalion: 1976 Training Report," Unit File, SADF Archives, p. A–7.

146. In February 1980, a military spokesman admitted that the army had a "waiting list" of fifteen hundred black applicants for which the military had no accommodations; *Sunday Post*, February 29, 1980. See also South African Institute of Race Relations, *Survey, 1985,* p. 417.

147. *Daily Dispatch*, May 17, 1985.

what commanders had known for quite some time: black infantrymen were excellent combat soldiers.[148] Thus, the policy restricting black servicemen to ethnic units meant that white units were being deprived of the best and most experienced manpower pool.

The commanders of the Citizen Force already had noted the combat experience and high training standards of the S.A. Cape Corps soldiers, and in September 1978, the all-white Kimberely Regiment admitted colored veterans for the first time. A month later, the first two colored officers were commissioned as Citizen Force officers.[149] Quietly and gradually, military schools began mixing black and white servicemen after 1976. After 1976, nonwhite servicemen began taking courses at the Infantry School, which had been "a closed shop" for them. After 1980, the school quietly began admitting colored junior leaders (NCOs and officers), thereby abolishing an old segregation practice that limited the training of colored officers and NCOs to the S.A. Cape Corps School.[150] Shortly thereafter, the army launched its first series of studies comparing black and white trainees in the Infantry School; they revealed that white servicemen performed well in theoretical studies while black servicemen excelled in practical training. Thus, the 1988 report suggested, cooperation among white and black soldiers often resulted in the higher performance of both groups. The navy quietly desegregated its NCO and officers' schools after 1978.[151]

The general public occasionally noted these small changes, and sometimes political crises ensued. All hell broke loose when naval officers invited journalists to cover the opening day of a new racially integrated course for females, South African Women Attested for Naval Services (SWANS, a unit of the South African Auxiliary Naval Services).[152] With only four months remaining before the elections, right-wing opposition groups protested, and the government sought a solution to appease them. Vice Admiral Glen Syndercombe ordered the disbanding of the

148. Interview with Maj. Gen. Pretorius.

149. *Cape Herald*, October 14, 1978.

150. Interview with Brig. Jacobs. One white officer recalled black soldiers in his platoon while he was attending a course in the Infantry School in 1979; interview with Lt. Col. Van Rooyan, deputy commander, 21 Battalion, Lenz, March 30, 1993.

151. Interview with Col. Claasen; interview with Comdr. Yegan S. Moodley.

152. Twenty-two white, colored, and Indian women were recruited for this eleven-week basic training course, after which they were supposed to take up administrative positions in the navy.

course only a week after it had begun. But following the elections, and only six months after the disbanding of the first course, a second racially integrated course was quietly launched. This time journalists were not invited.[153]

Incidents like the SWANS affair were rare, since the SADF disguised integration behind a veil of denials, ambiguous terms, and meaningless statements such as that "everything is done within the framework of government policy." Malan, for example, after his appointment as minister of defence, announced that the SADF attempted to maintain separate training facilities for different race groups but that "operational requirements" and "limited training space" sometimes required mixed facilities. He assured his audience that such mixing was the exception.[154] In fact, by 1980, the integration of whites and nonwhites in the SADF was more a growing trend than an exception.

Integration did not occur everywhere. Air force and Citizen Force units remained exclusively white. A statement by Admiral Biermann, former chief of the navy, that declared "the sky is the limit" for nonwhite sailors meant just that. The air force remained almost hermetically sealed from nonwhite servicemen until very recently.[155] And in 1987, 98.8 percent of the soldiers in Citizen Force units were reported to be whites, and 1.2 percent coloreds; in 1988, 96.3 percent were whites, and 3.7 percent coloreds.[156] One can speculate that the air force and the Citizen Force were deliberately kept as all-white units in order to serve as the ultimate insurance policy for whites in South Africa under a black government.[157]

153. South African Institute of Race Relations, *Survey, 1987–88*, p. 518; interview with Rear Adm. Trainor.

154. South African Institute of Race Relations, *Survey, 1981*, p. 59.

155. *Paratus*, March 1980. In January 1977, 25 colored soldiers were transferred from the S.A. Cape Corps to the air force to be trained and to serve as ground personnel. See Nothling, "Role of Non-whites," p. 50. And in June 1980, the first two Indian Permanent Force members were admitted to the air force; *Rand Daily Mail*, June 23, 1978. The total number of nonwhite soldiers in the air force, however, remained minuscule until very recently. In 1987, for example, only 6 of 95 blacks, 27 of 198 coloreds, and 6 of 102 Indians were admitted to serve in the air force. See South African Institute of Race Relations, *Survey, 1987–88*, p. 522.

156. South African Institute of Race Relations, *Survey, 1988–89*, p. 522; *Survey, 1989–90*, p. 141.

157. Simon Baynham, "Towards a National Defense Force in South Africa: Problems and Prospects," *Africa Insight* 20, no. 2 (1990): 120.

NONWHITE LEADERS AND THE SADF'S ETHNIC MANPOWER POLICY

The issue of military service caught the leaders of the Indian, colored, and black communities on the horns of a difficult dilemma. They knew that the military could not guarantee that its nonwhite soldiers would be treated with greater equity in society at large. More important, these leaders feared that the specter of their cooperation with the military in recruiting nonwhite soldiers would undermine their opposition to the government's apartheid policies. Chief Lucas Mangope, the chief minister of Bophuthatswana, explained, "We do not want anyone to get the impression that we are prepared to defend the country for the privileged position of other groups and the disabilities and inequalities that we are subjected to."[158]

Nonwhite leaders also feared that employing nonwhite soldiers in military missions against nonwhite populations might trigger rage, riots, and destruction. "People simply will not accept those, especially from their own people, who are seen to be used to keep them subjugated," Grundy wrote.[159] The leaders also feared that recruitment of their youth might result in division and conflict within their communities between proponents and opponents of nonwhite service. Ethnic youth who volunteer for the military usually encounter accusations of sellout and betrayal from members of their communities. The first colored soldiers, for example, were depicted as "Uncle Toms" by coloreds who resisted negotiation with the military.[160] During the June 1976 riots, the SADF had to evacuate black soldiers' family members from Soweto as the raging mob attempted to lynch relatives of those who allegedly sold their souls to the white military.[161]

At the same time, the leaders of the nonwhite communities admitted that they could not provide jobs for their youth, while the military had good jobs to offer.[162] Ethnic groups are often impoverished communities, and, as the old Chinese proverb argues, "one cannot irrigate a dry land-

---

158. *Rand Daily Mail*, June 20, 1974.
159. Grundy, *Soldiers without Politics*, p. 150.
160. Interview with Brig. Jacobs.
161. Interview with Maj. Gen. Pretorius.
162. Similar arguments were made by the Barisan Sosialis opposition party in Singapore. See, for example, its antidraft publications: *Plebeian*, December 19, 1966, p. 12; June 13, 1968, p. 2.

scape better by closing the gates of the dam." Total resistance to military service amounted to closing the dam gates in communities where unemployment ran high, and there was no guarantee for impoverished parents that their children would have a better future. Thus, when young men from subjugated ethnic groups decided to join the military, they often received the quiet blessing of their parents, who hoped that military service would be the way out of a cycle of economic misery, poverty, and crime. Many South African township residents considered a black man in a uniform—military, police, MK, or even the African People Liberation Army (APLA)—to be a success. A successful man was defined as one who refuses to give up and ultimately gets a job. The uniform symbolized both the attempt to help oneself and the ultimate reward— a job. Under such conditions, even the most influential ethnic leaders were not able to oppose unconditionally the military's plans to recruit their youth.[163]

Astute and politically experienced nonwhite leaders understood that the best strategy lay somewhere between unconditional submission to every new military manpower initiative and complete resistance to cooperation with the military (a strategy advocated by nonwhite extreme organizations). According to them, the best strategy was to negotiate iteratively with the military every new manpower initiative and to adopt a "tit-for-tat" policy every time the military attempted to mobilize their goodwill in the recruitment of new soldiers.

Leaders with personal military experience were the first to comprehend the value for their communities of such bargaining games. They knew that the dilemma was not whether they should support or resist plans to recruit their groups' youth. The real question was what price they should extract from the state in return for supporting the state's recruitment plans.[164] They also understood that ethnic integration within a professional military organization was a protracted process, and that

163. Interview with Maj. R. Khoza, public relations officer, Defence Headquarters, Pretoria, March 25, 1993.

164. Many demobilized African soldiers who fought under British and French command in World War II returned home to find neither honor nor economic security. Some of these veterans translated their disappointment into political activism and joined the postwar nationalist movements. Tunisian veterans who had fought with the French, for example, played an important role in the development of the Tunisian nationalist movement. See Wendell P. Holbrook, "Oral History and the Nascent Historiography for West Africa and World War II: A Focus on Ghana," *International Journal of Oral History* 3, no. 3 (1982): 158; Francois Arnoulet, "Les Tunisiens et la premiére guerre mondiale (1914–1918)" (The Tu-

professional officers would likely resent new soldiers from groups that previously refused to serve. A senior colored officer explained in 1993 why colored soldiers might have an advantage over the new ethnic groups about to join the SADF: "If a year from today the doors are opened for any other groups who are not yet in the Defence Forces, then they are going to come to a Defence Forces whose traditions, standards, norms, expertise, esprit-de-corps and feeling to each other are unknown to them. They will feel out of place in this Defence Forces. I would have felt the same way if I had suddenly asked to be part of a team that is not shaped overnight."[165]

The veteran ethnic leaders also benefited from a nonpolitical and widely acclaimed source of power—their experience in the military during World War II. Presenting themselves as citizens who had already proven their loyalty to the state on the battlefield, they played the bargaining games with great skill and equanimity. The most impressive example of such a leader was Sonny Leon, the first colored man commissioned as a sergeant major during World War II.

Sonny Leon, Nic Kearns, and other colored World War II veterans established the Colored Ex-Servicemen Legion immediately after the war, and lobbied the South African government to reestablish a colored voluntary unit within the military.[166] After the unit was reopened in 1963, Leon and other Legion leaders bargained for almost two decades with much skill and wit. On numerous occasions, Leon and Kearns used the SADF's need for their support to press the military for quicker ethnic reforms. In 1976, for instance, when the SADF proudly announced that the first colored infantry battalion had reached full manpower strength, Leon responded, "If our men are being trained to fight on our borders, they must have something meaningful to look forward to when they return." Leon then elaborated on his definition of "something meaningful": "South Africa cannot afford half-price soldiers." He demanded equal status, equal service facilities, and the same pay for colored and white soldiers who served together in South West Africa. Kearns, then the president of the Ex-Servicemen Legion, also demanded that the dependents of colored soldiers be provided for should these soldiers lose

nisians and World War I, 1914–18), *Revue de l'Occident Musulman et de la Méditerranée* 38 (1984): 47–61.

165. Interview with Brig. Jacobs; interview with Comdr. Sagarem Pillay.

166. Interview with Brig. Jacobs.

their lives in the defense of their country.[167] The government partially accepted these demands shortly after.[168]

After 1972, Leon based his iterated bargaining game on the gradually growing number of colored soldiers. On occasion, he threatened to withdraw his cooperation for the recruitment of colored volunteers when he felt that the military was not moving fast enough to integrate them among its ranks. He then would mobilize white Parliament members to remind cabinet ministers that Sonny Leon was speaking on behalf of past and present generations of colored soldiers, and that his demands should be accommodated. In September 1974, for example, a Parliament member pleaded with the government to yield to Leon's demands: "Mr. Leon is a colored ex-servicemen who served during the last war. These are people for whom I have the highest regard and there is many a White man today who owes his life to the Cape Corps stretcher bearers and to their service in the last war. There are many of the Cape Corps who lost their lives while serving in our defense forces. . . . Mr. Leon and I were associated for many years after the war in regard to ex-servicemen's matters, he with the South African Colored Ex-Servicemen Legion and myself with the South African Legion. . . . We must avoid conflict between his children and my children in solving the problems of South Africa."[169]

As the years passed, Leon's tactics turned into well-defined tacit understandings between the government and the colored community. For example, when Mr. Curry, a less moderate and pragmatic leader from the Colored Council, said that he would not offer South Africa the blood of his son unless there were full civil rights for everyone in the country, an NP Parliament member responded, "Sir, I think one has to make a distinction here. On the one hand there is the political aspect. We can discuss that. If there are bottlenecks, we can discuss them and try to eliminate them. But on the other hand, there is the defence of our beloved country, for which I believe we should take up arms together."[170] The message was simple: the government had to heed specific demands

---

167. *Daily Dispatch*, January 17, 1976.

168. On June 1, 1976 Parliament approved the Military Pension Act, which reduced the gap in military pensions between black, Indian, colored, and white veterans. The gap between white, colored, Indian, and black salaries was also reduced in July 1976. See Grundy, *Black Foreign Legion*, p. 110. Complete parity in salaries between white and nonwhite officers and NCOs was achieved only in 1981. See *White Paper, 1982*, p. 16.

169. South Africa, *House of Assembly Debates* 51 (September 9, 1974), cols. 2523–2524.

170. South Africa, *House of Assembly Debates* 51 (September 9, 1974), col. 2532.

raised by the Colored Council, and the colored institutions were not to rock the boat too hard by threatening resistance in defense matters. Played carefully, the parliament member suggested, the game would benefit both the government and the colored community.

Leon and other Ex-Servicemen Legion leaders relentlessly pursued and created new bargaining opportunities for the colored community by calling upon the service record of colored soldiers. Leon, for instance, never ceased campaigning to turn the SACC into a first-class infantry unit. Under his influence, Legion leaders gradually and shrewdly expanded their list of demands, from a request to replace the SACC's white instructors with colored instructors to a plea for promoting colored instructors to corporal and sergeant ranks, and, finally, to a call for converting the SACC into a combat unit.[171] The iterated bargaining game between colored leaders and government officials continued well into the 1980s, even after Leon's retirement from politics. Colored leaders successfully pressed their demand, for instance, that colored troops not be deployed in colored townships before the new multiethnic tricameral Parliament was approved.[172] One colored officer described how Leon's game affected the attitudes of senior SADF officers toward colored soldiers during the late 1970s and the 1980s: "Malan [chief of the SADF, 1976–1980], Vijoloen [chief of the SADF, 1980–1985], and Geldenhuys [Chief of the SADF, 1985–1990] promoted us [colored servicemen]. But General Meyer, who was the personnel boss of the Defence Force, also knew that he had a complement of people in the Defence Force and that if he did not take them along, they might just leave the military and *join the radicals*, and that was not in the interest of the state. So Meyer did all that he could to fight against all the remaining discrimination. It spilled over to the generals here today. I have not yet met one that does not think that way."[173]

Leon's simple tit-for-tat message and bargaining tactics strongly impressed senior military and political leaders. The successful integration of colored soldiers in the SADF after 1963 owes much to his pragmatic, conditional cooperation policy in all matters concerning their recruitment and integration. The leaders of the Indian minority in South Africa, however, were significantly less skilled than Leon in the art of tacit bargain-

---

171. South Africa, *House of Assembly Debates* 24 (May 24, 1968), col. 6003.
172. Interview with Brig. Jacobs.
173. Interview with Brig. Jacobs.

ing with the military. They concentrated all their efforts on demanding that Indian naval recruits be promoted in rank alongside their white peers, neglecting other important domains of integration within the military (such as the types of military training provided to uniformed Indians and their combat deployment). Indian leaders were fortunate, however, because their partner for negotiations was the navy, the most progressive arm of the SADF.

The navy attempted to mobilize the support of Indian leaders long before recruiting the first Indians. In 1973, Rear Admiral Biermann, chief of naval staff and chair of a special committee planning the recruitment of Indians to the navy, admitted that his committee had held discussions with the Executive Committee of the South African Indian Council, and therefore "expected good response."[174] Before completing their report, members of the Biermann committee met with leaders from the council to describe the progress of the new Indian naval unit and to discuss the details of its training programs.[175] Several years later, when the unit was up and running, Mr. J. N. Reddy, the chairman of the council, disclosed the nature of the 1973 discussions: "The South African Indian Council was consulted before the initiation of these training programs, and it was made very clear to us that there was no limit to the possibilities for the young Indian going into the Navy."[176] Mr. Chinsmay, another member of the council, claimed that the government had even promised that Indian sailors could become captains on all naval vessels.[177] The navy kept its word to the Indian community. In 1978, only three years after the establishment of the Indian Service Battalion, the first Indian servicemen were sent to the Naval Academy.

The Indian case study illustrates another interesting point: ethnic leaders wishing to cooperate with the military were challenged by proponents of submission within their communities who wanted to yield too much and too soon. At first, the Indian Council stated very clearly that its support for the voluntary recruitment of Indian youth should not be interpreted as implying support for the government's apartheid policies.[178] Yet, only a short while after the second voluntary intake of Indian

174. *Friend*, November 1, 1973.
175. *Natal Mercury*, June 20, 1974.
176. *Paratus*, March 1980, p. 50.
177. *Rand Daily Mail*, November 2, 1973; July 17, 1974; *Star*, October 4, 1974.
178. South Africa, *House of Assembly Debates* 60 (January 26, 1976), col. 87.

sailors was recruited, Salem-Abram Mayet and Amichand Rajbansi, two members of the Indian Council, introduced a motion calling on the government to conscript all Indians into the SADF on an equal footing with whites, provided it also granted full citizenship in the future. Such a proposal, if accepted by the council and approved by the government, could have submitted the entire pool of Indian youth to the discretion of the SADF, with minimal or no political leverage for Indian leaders.

Experienced Indian leaders sought ways to counter the motion without spoiling their good relationship with the government and the military. Thus, Y. S. Chinsamy and M. E. Sultan raised a counterproposal calling on the government to establish an Indian military corps on a voluntary basis, with parity and equality in service. Chinsamy even added a touch of rhetoric to this proposal: if South Africa ever were invaded, all South Africans, irrespective of race, should come to the defense of the country. The Indian Council approved the counterproposal, fifteen votes to eight. Rajbansi and Mayet argued that the defeat of their proposal was "a retrogressive step" for the Indian community, but one leader who had a good grasp of the rules of tacit bargaining disagreed. Aboo Abrahim of Pretoria said that Indians should not offer themselves to the military, but should wait to be called by the government. He added shrewdly, "Once we are called up, then we can make our demands."[179]

Leaders of the black communities were divided over the dilemma of whether to support or resist the military's efforts to recruit blacks. But, in 1980, even they began to adopt Leon's bargaining tactics, with some success. That year, for example, after units from the black 21 Battalion completed three successful tours of duty along the border in South West Africa, black leaders were invited to visit the battalion's camp in Lenz. During this visit, they proposed creating a network of military schools where black soldiers could upgrade their weak educational backgrounds.[180] The interests of black leaders (upgrading black education) and the military (improving the educational qualifications of black soldiers so they could attend advanced courses) coincided. During the early 1980s, therefore, the SADF established a network of Adult Education Centers in most of the SADF ethnic units, offering remedial education courses for both black soldiers and their family members. These courses

179. *Star*, February 20, 1976.
180. *Paratus*, November 1980, p. 34.

enabled many black servicemen to attain the required educational qualifications for NCO and officer courses.[181]

The tacit bargaining game between colored and Indian leaders and the SADF depended on continuing the voluntary recruitment of nonwhite soldiers. A unilateral move by the government to conscript nonwhite soldiers would threaten the very foundations of the bargaining process. After all, the SADF would have very little reason to cooperate with nonwhite leaders if it could recruit a sufficient number of nonwhite soldiers through regular conscription channels. But the twelve-year war of words between South African defense officials and colored and Indian leaders remains the most powerful example of how ethnic leaders can cooperate with the state in the voluntary recruitment of their youth, yet simultaneously resist its efforts to conscript unilaterally.

In 1977, encouraged by the success of tribal conscription in South West Africa and the combat performance of the colored S.A. Cape Corps and Indian sailors, Botha declared that the government accepted "the principle of conscription for colored and Indian citizens." He added that during the same year it would introduce into colored and Indian high schools a military cadet system similar to that in white high schools.[182] Many colored and Indian leaders considered Botha's statement a breach of a fourteen-year tacit agreement with the government over the voluntary recruitment of their youth. A new political climate in South Africa also inspired critiques of Botha's initiative. The nonwhite communities rapidly became more bellicose after the June 1976 Soweto riots. Botha also was condemned for making this statement precisely at a time when many coloreds were being forcefully evicted from townships around Cape Town. Sam Solomons, a Labour Party member on the Colored Representative Council, declared that coloreds and other blacks owed no allegiance to South Africa and could not be expected to go to the border and fight.[183] Solomons's statement implied a tit-for-tat strategy—if Botha

181. Interview with Col. M. Rutsch.

182. South African Institute of Race Relations, *Survey, 1978*, p. 56. In Parliament, only one member (Harry Schwarz of the Progressive Reform party) persistently argued throughout the 1970s for the recruitment of all citizens "irrespective of color." See South Africa, *House of Assembly Debates* 60 (February 2, 1976), col. 456; 62 (May 6, 1976), col. 6210. Yet even members of Schwarz's own Progressive Federal Party (PFP) and members of the United Party, the leading opposition party, argued that blacks could not be expected to fight on the borders of South Africa for rights that they themselves did not have. See *Rand Daily Mail*, June 20, 1974.

183. *Rand Daily Mail*, August 17, 1977.

dared to conscript colored youth, then colored leaders would withdraw their tacit endorsement of the military's new policy of sending nonwhite soldiers to fight in South West Africa (the first colored unit was sent to the border in 1975). This incident provided a clear reminder that both sides, the government and colored leaders, had something to lose if the rules of the bargaining game were changed unilaterally.

Botha decided to postpone the plan to conscript coloreds and Indians. Instead, he chose to alleviate the military's manpower shortage by increasing the service period of whites from twelve to twenty-four months, and by compelling more white immigrants to serve in the military. The issue of immigrant conscription was especially important, since Botha conditioned citizenship on the performance of military service. By doing so, Botha, in effect, acknowledged a linkage between the military service obligation and first-class citizenship (including the vote). Since coloreds and Indians were not eligible to vote, it seemed unfair to conscript them, even by his own standards.[184]

Nonetheless, Botha was under considerable political pressure to conscript blacks in order to free more white youth for the labor market. On several occasions, South African white politicians who represented large labor organizations proposed enacting a national civil service scheme for blacks, and demanded that only veterans of such a program be eligible for employment. The ultimate goal was to secure more jobs for low-skilled white workers at the expense of cheaper black labor.

Sometimes the cunning intentions behind these ethnic civil service plans became blatant. In 1979 the White Workers Union proposed, "The unions have asked the commission [the Wiehahn Commission] to recommend that the Apprenticeship Act be amended to make it compulsory for prospective apprentices to undergo military service, whether voluntary or compulsory."[185] In their desire to limit the pool of potential black apprentices, the authors of the proposal neglected to notice that, although military service for blacks could be either compulsory or voluntary, the stipulation that blacks be *compelled* to join a *voluntary* military service made no sense. When this proposal was rejected for obvious reasons, the all-white Artisan Staff Association (ASA) came up with yet another idea—that nonwhite apprentices be compelled to go through two years of national service in the railway police in lieu of

---

184. Grundy, *Soldiers without Politics*, p. 174.
185. *Rand Daily Mail*, December 4, 1979.

conscription. Botha did not fall into these traps: this idea, too, was re-jected.[186]

Nonetheless, in February 1982, Malan, the minister of defence, once again attempted to raise the specter of colored and Indian conscription when he declared in Parliament, "The writing is on the wall for a more comprehensive National Service System, the details of which will be announced shortly."[187] Botha, recalling his own experience with this issue in 1977, poured cold water on Malan's plans by reminding whites of the cost of nonwhite conscription. "Whites could not expect coloreds to do military service if the coloreds did not have any say in the government," Botha told a white audience one month after Malan's statement.[188] His audience understood perfectly well what the prime minister was implying: colored and Indian parliamentary representation would have to go hand in hand with increased military obligation. The only remaining question was to what degree political representation justified conscription. The government was still far from ready to grant such representation to nonwhites in 1982, and Malan's "more comprehensive National Service System" vaporized into thin air.

In 1984, amid political negotiations over the new tricameral Parliament, Malan declared that the president of the Cape Corps Ex-Servicemen Legion had asked him if colored men might face compulsory national service, like their white peers. Malan, recalling in turn his own experience with this issue two years earlier, responded that there was no need for colored and Indian conscription at present because of the large number of nonwhite applicants for voluntary national service.[189]

Leaders of the colored community were quick to join Malan's practical refusal to conscript members of their communities. Rev. Allen Hendrickse, the leader of the (colored) LP party, endorsed Malan's statement, noting that six thousand colored applicants had placed their names on a waiting list to join the Cape Corps alone. Thus, Rev. Hendrickse argued, if the SADF could not absorb all colored volunteers, why rock the boat by adopting an unnecessary colored and Indian conscription bill? And van der Merwe, the defense spokesman of the right-wing Conservative Party, asserted that premature governmental declarations about

186. *East Province Herald*, April 30, 1982.
187. *Star*, February 27, 1982.
188. *Cape Times*, March 26, 1982.
189. South African Institute of Race Relations, *Survey, 1984*, p. 745.

nonwhite conscription would force colored and Indians leaders to withdraw their support for the new tricameral Parliament.[190]

Other colored and Indian leaders used Malan's declaration as an opportunity to address more directly the relationship between representation and conscription. In May 1984, Philip Myburgh of the Progressive Federal Party demanded the establishment of a new defense council, with representation for all the parties in the new tricameral Parliament. He argued that only such a multiracial council should discuss colored and Indian conscription. Reddy, leader of the Indian Solidarity party, announced that his party was opposed to Indian conscription as long as Indians did not enjoy full equality with whites. The bottom line for these two speakers was one and the same: a tricameral system was not sufficient justification to launch a colored and Indian conscription campaign. If the white government wanted conscription, it had to provide colored and Indian leaders with a say—and a vote—in defense matters and speed up racial reforms in society at large. Malan, realizing he had opened a Pandora's box, attempted to subdue the turmoil by declaring that no decisions on this matter would be made before the new Parliament was in place.[191]

Between July 1985 and March 1986, the government announced a state of emergency in many parts of South Africa, and in June 1986, it declared an indefinite nationwide state of emergency. Fearing that these measures would increase the demand for soldiers (and therefore for nonwhite conscription), colored and Indian leaders attempted to preempt any calls for nonwhite conscription throughout 1985. Malan promised that the members of the two houses of Parliament should decide on the issue.[192] But there were signs that, like Botha in 1977, Malan already was retreating from whatever plan he might have had to conscript coloreds and Indians. He declared in Parliament that establishing cadet programs in high schools was the prerogative of each population group.[193] And he shelved one recommendation of the Geldenhuys report (November 1985)—to extend the principle of National Service to other ethnic groups—saying that colored conscription would remain an option for the future.[194] None-

190. South African Institute of Race Relations, *Survey, 1984*, p. 745.
191. South African Institute of Race Relations, *Survey, 1984*, p. 745.
192. South African Institute of Race Relations, *Survey, 1985*, p. 419.
193. South African Institute of Race Relations, *Survey, 1985*, p. 417.
194. South African Institute of Race Relations, *Survey, 1985*, p. 414; *Survey, 1986*, p. 804; *Citizen*, May 13, 1986.

[87]

theless, from the perspective of colored and Indian leaders, the danger of ethnic conscription was still clear and present. The war in South West Africa was escalating almost daily, and the SADF needed more soldiers.

To nip this danger in the bud, colored and Indian leaders intensified their campaign against conscription. In April 1987, only a month before the all-white elections, Ismael Omar, the new chairman of the Solidarity Party, warned that his party would withdraw from the tricameral system if any attempt was made to introduce conscription for Indians. He emphasized that it was the declared policy of all nonwhite parties in the Houses of Delegates and Representatives that there should be no conscription in the service of apartheid.[195] Such a withdrawal of colored and Indian parties from what the NP deemed to be its principal achievement, the tricameral system, would jeopardize the party's reelection campaign. But even after the elections, nonwhite leaders continued to foil any attempt to conscript their youth. When the Committee for Social Affairs of the President's Council again proposed to extend conscription to all racial groups, Frank Meintijies, the national public relations officer of the Congress of South African Trade Unions (COSATU), warned that any attempt to force blacks into military service would result in widespread conflict. Likewise, Albertina Sisulu of the United Democratic Front (UDF) declared that no conscription for blacks was acceptable.[196]

The explicit threat that a conscription bill for nonwhites might result in a renewed wave of riots finally convinced the government once and for all to put an end to the ongoing war of words between colored and Indian leaders and defense officials. So, when the Natal Provincial Congress of the NP called on the government to conscript coloreds, Indians, and selected urban blacks, Wynand Breytenbach, the deputy minister of defence, responded that conscription for nonwhites could develop in an evolutionary manner, following the model of white conscription between 1961 and 1967 (from voluntary service to a draft ballot to universal conscription). He also made the standard governmental excuse that the SADF did not have enough training facilities for a large intake of nonwhite conscripts.[197]

195. South African Institute of Race Relations, *Survey, 1987*, p. 513.
196. South African Institute of Race Relations, *Survey, 1987*, p. 513.
197. South African Institute of Race Relations, *Survey, 1987*, p. 513.

Breytenbach's statement, in effect, tolled the final death knell for an idea Botha had originally proposed in 1977. Victory belonged to colored and Indian leaders who had fought long and hard to scrap the plan for nonwhite conscription during the difficult war years (1984–1988). Between June and August 1988, peace talks were held in Cairo and Geneva, and a cease-fire agreement was established along the Namibian-Angolan border. On December 22, 1988, the Luanda accords were signed, establishing the new state of Namibia in the former South West Africa. The war was over; with it the demand for military manpower died and plans for nonwhite conscription vanished.[198]

The struggle over nonwhite conscription has an interesting epilogue. After F. W. de Klerk's extensive political and social reforms beginning in February 1990, Dr. Pieter Gous, the Conservative Party spokesman, said that conservative whites would resist conscription in the service of a future black government. He added that it was time to replace conscription with a voluntary-recruitment system for all South African citizens.[199] Gous's statement marked the closing of a cycle in the history of the debate over the relationship between conscription, representation, and citizenship. Presently, many white South Africans object to their conscription because they feel that the new political equality among racial groups should go hand in hand with a more egalitarian scheme to share the defense burden.

This argument against conscription for whites only reiterates and affirms what colored and Indian leaders said between 1977 and 1988. In ethnically and racially divided states, effective negotiation between leaders of subjugated ethnic groups and the military is best focused on voluntary-recruitment schemes. Ethnic conscription, especially if executed against the wishes of ethnic leaders, is likely to be counterproductive. Bargaining behind closed doors, and tacit understandings between military manpower planners and ethnic leaders, can be very effective in opening the military's doors to young members of subjugated ethnic groups if—and only if—the state does not unilaterally impose conscription on these groups.

---

198. At the beginning of 1990, the two years of service for white national servicemen was reduced again to the pre–1978 term of one year. In addition, defense budgets were severely slashed after 1989.

199. South African Institute of Race Relations, *Survey, 1992*, p. 136.

ETHNIC MILITARY INTEGRATION IN SOUTH AFRICA—A SUMMARY

In contrast to Singapore's national ideology (one multiethnic nation) and Israel's national ideology (one ethnic [Jewish] nation), South African leaders consistently denied the existence of a South African "nation" throughout the twentieth century. Instead, they declared that the South African landscape had been settled by many "nations" and "peoples," including the white nation (comprising the English and Afrikaans peoples), the colored people, the Indian people, and several Bantu nations (each of which was composed of various subtribes).[200] The policy of separating members of these nations already characterized all state institutions, including the military, before World War II. After the war, this separation policy grew into the apartheid ideology, which discriminated against the nonwhite population on allegedly scientific and empirical grounds.

Since this ideology dominated every state institution, many nonwhite soldiers were dismissed from the military. When the NP came to power in 1948, it abolished the S.A. Colored Corps and the Native Military Corps, the two leading nonwhite units in the SADF. During the 1950s, the military was consumed by the struggle between English and Afrikaans speakers. The emerging consensus was that the SADF ought to remain as homogeneous as possible, with no place for nonwhites. In the early 1960s, however, a group of officers educated in Western military schools, most notably Fraser in France and Malan in the United States, became convinced that the SADF should prepare itself for large-scale counterinsurgency campaigns. They brought back home the idea that, in order to win hearts and minds in counterguerrilla wars, the SADF ought to begin recruiting nonwhites. In the following years, the concepts and implications of counterinsurgency warfare, including the need for nonwhite soldiers, were introduced to SADF officers through the new self-sufficient military education system.

While officers were learning these new ideas, Fraser, Malan, and others launched a series of ethnic-recruitment experiments. First, coloreds were brought back into the military in 1963; then, Indians were recruited by the navy in 1973, and blacks by the army in 1975 (although a small black-recruitment experiment had been launched in 1973). These experiments

---

200. See, for example, South Africa, *Assembly Debates* 30 (August 31, 1970), col. 2940. Verwoerd coined the term "Bantu" to refer to all the black residents of South Africa.

were remarkably similar to one another, and each new one expanded on the success of earlier programs. The similarities among these experiments included the advance training of a small group of ethnic leaders to assist with the induction of the first class of ethnic soldiers; the isolation of ethnic soldiers for their first months of training; and the playing down of the importance of these experiments in public statements. Where politicians could not hide the experiments, they promised journalists that the military was merely training "guards" or more laborers for menial service vocations.

The war in South West Africa pushed the ethnic experiments one step further. Beginning in 1975, nonwhites were sent to the border, first as individual soldiers, then in nonwhite units under white command, and finally in nonwhite units under nonwhite command. Additional black battalions were built toward the end of the 1970s and sent to the border, where racial distinctions among soldiers and officers could not have been sustained. The mixing of whites and blacks in the field quietly spilled over into military schools toward the end of the 1970s. By mid-decade, SADF officers had begun pushing for more equality among white and black soldiers in every domain: uniforms, salaries, benefits, combat assignments, and military promotions.

The issue of promotion to officership was critical. After the first "Magnificent Seven" colored officers graduated in 1975, the navy trained its own Indian officers. Blacks had to wait much longer to be promoted to the ranks of officers, but in the so-called homeland armies, "foreign" black officers were permitted to study, work, and dine with white South African officers. In the 1970s and even in the mid-1980s, nonwhite soldiers and officers still were restricted from certain units, corps, and military vocations. Nonetheless, the SADF's achievement in integrating white and nonwhite servicemen during the apartheid era was remarkable.

The ethnic history of the SADF illuminates the potential contribution of a professionally autonomous group of senior officers in matters concerning ethnic integration within the armed forces. If professional officers become convinced that such integration can advance the cause of combat readiness, they will launch a series of ethnic experiments that, in time, may result in reform and integration. Thus, ethnic soldiers may do well in the military, even in countries with conservative politicians and weak ethnic leaders, if senior military officers begin to equate the promotion of these soldiers with an overall improvement in military capability. Under such conditions, ethnic soldiers may do even better in the military than in society at large.

The successful integration of nonwhite soldiers in the SADF since 1963 also illustrates the important contribution that ethnic leaders can make to improving the lot of their community's youth in the military. South African nonwhite leaders were not always successful in their tacit bargaining strategy vis-à-vis the military. Occasionally they failed to exploit bargaining opportunities given to them by new military manpower initiatives, as in 1980, when the government decided to increase the service period of colored and Indian voluntary national servicemen from twelve to twenty-four months. Colored and Indian leaders failed at that time to negotiate additional improvements in the status of colored soldiers, even though information on the government's plan was available at least eight months before the new policy was instituted. Nonetheless, in many instances, the nonwhite leaders—especially veterans—were successful. Generations of colored and Indian soldiers owe much to the tacit bargaining techniques of Leon and other colored and Indian leaders.

The success of the SADF in integrating nonwhite soldiers had its limits. A military organization does not exist in isolation from society, and though ethnic youth can be good soldiers, they can still be denied equal citizenship status. As Grundy points out, "In the end, even an enlightened military is called upon to interact with the very society it seeks to defend, yet escape."[201] Still, in the context of apartheid—the most complete and unconditional national racial ideology since World War II—the achievement of the SADF in integrating nonwhite soldiers is quite remarkable.

201. Kenneth W. Grundy, "Black Soldiers in a White Military: Political Change in South Africa" *The Journal of Strategic Studies* 4, no. 3 (September 1987): 301.

[3]

Singapore: From Inclusion to Exclusion

<small>THE ORIGINS AND EVOLUTION OF SINGAPORE'S MULTIRACIAL IDEOLOGY</small>

At its birth, Singapore's national ideology resembled the vision of the perfect polis in Plato's *Republic*: a philosopher-king running a tiny island state, assisted by a small and closed group of administrators (most of whom, in Singapore, had been educated at the finest British universities). Other characteristics of Plato's republic were also present in Singapore's national ideology: the instillation of new collective values through a highly developed public education system; the elevation of the principle of meritocracy above every other social value; the censorship of potential opposition through the control of the "arts" (i.e., the media); the demand that people adopt a Spartan lifestyle; the aspiration to create a rugged, resolute, highly-trained, and highly disciplined society; and, above all, the requirement that loyalty to the state resemble selfless devotion to one's family.

But while Plato's imaginary polis was akin to a family writ large, until very recently most Singaporeans considered their island a place to which one temporarily migrated in order to accumulate savings rather than an ideal state to which one owed ultimate allegiance.[1] Moreover, in 1965, the immigrant-citizens of newly independent Singapore considered themselves Indians, Chinese, or Malays rather than

---

1. Interview with Lt. Gen. Winston Choo, chief of general staff, SAF, Harvard Business School, April 1, 1992; interview with Col. (Ret.) James Aeria, former commander, Singapore navy, Singapore's Technologies Building, July 6, 1992.

Singaporeans. Dr. Goh Keng Swee, the first minister of defence (1965–1967, 1970–1979), argued that this personal, self-centered, antisocial migrant mentality was at odds with the vision of Singapore as a tightly knit community.[2]

Racial tensions further compounded the problem of self-interest versus national allegiance. The various ethnic groups have shared a long history of tensions, especially the Chinese majority (75 percent) and the Malay minority (15 percent). The tensions between these two groups have periodically exploded into racial riots, the most serious of which occurred in July 1964, only a year before Singapore exited the Malaysian federation. During the melee, twenty-one people were killed, 450 injured and 1,700 arrested.[3] There were also accusations that Malaysian parties intervened in the 1964 Singaporean elections on ethnic grounds.[4] Several commentators argued that the final ejection of Singapore from the Malaysian federation in August 1965 was propelled by Malaysian leaders' fear that Lee Kuan Yew's ambition to rule Malaysia would lead to renewed racial riots between the Malay majority and Chinese minority in Malaysia.[5]

In 1965, Singaporeans had very little in common except financial aspirations and a sorrowful history of racial riots. Singapore's leaders strongly believed that their citizens lacked a common loyalty, patriotism, history, or tradition. Without these common values, Lee argued, Singaporeans lacked "built-in reflexes" to face external and internal dangers. The new national ideology, therefore, was to create a closely knit community in which loyalty to Singapore would take precedence over all other racial or religious loyalties. According to Lee, the goal was to "reorient" and "re-shuffle" traditional individualistic values in order to create a state in which people "identify the future of the individual with

2. Singapore, *Legislative Assembly Debates* 25, no. 16 (March 13, 1967), col. 1179.

3. David W. Chang, "Nation-Building in Singapore," *Asian Survey* 8, no. 9 (September 1968): 766.

4. Interview with George Edwin Bogaars, former permanent secretary, Ministry of Interior and Defence, CPF Building, July 3, 1980 (oral history interview by Robert Chew, for the project "Political Development in Singapore, 1965–1975," file B000032/030, pp. 280–281). After the 1964 elections were over, Lee exchanged bitter words with the Malaysian UMNO Party secretary-general, Syed Ja'afar Albar, over racial issues. See Jean Grossholtz, "An Exploration of Malaysian Meanings," *Asian Survey* 6, no. 4 (April 1966): 228.

5. R. S. Milne, "Singapore's Exit from Malaysia: The Consequences of Ambiguity," *Asian Survey* 6, no. 3 (March 1966): 175–184.

the future of the community." Within one decade, he promised, Singapore would become a new society with "qualities of leadership at the top, and qualities of cohesion on the ground."[6]

According to this ideology, the very concept of distinct ethnic groups was at odds with the plan to transform "a rootless society of migrant stock" into a "closely knit community."[7] Speaking in Parliament, Lee defined the problem, which had been passed to the Constitutional Commission on Minority Rights: "The problem is how to create a situation where the minority, either in ethnic, linguistic or religious terms, was not conscious that it was a minority, and that the exercise of its rights as equal citizens with all the others was so natural and so accepted by society that it was not conscious of the fact that it was sharing equal rights with the others in dominant ethnic groups."[8] He thus set an additional integrative goal: that minority groups eventually lose their consciousness of being such.

To allow ethnic groups such as the Muslim Malays to become "unconscious of being a minority," Lee turned the concept of multiracialism into the very essence of Singapore's new national ideology. He prohibited all displays of Chinese chauvinism and ordered that everything in Singapore, including private publications, official policies, national symbols, and state institutions, reflect the multiracial character of the state.[9] On the other hand, he abolished the Malaysian practice of granting Malays "special privileges" (such as preference for jobs in the public sector) and "diluted" most of the recommendations of the Constitutional Commission on Minority Rights.[10] Lee declared that no ethnic discrimination or displays of ethnic chauvinism would be allowed and that all traces of preferential treatment for one ethnic community at the expense of others would be eliminated.

Between 1965 and 1975, Singaporean leaders pursued an aggressive "strategy of accommodation" in order to create a closely knit multiracial

6. Lee Kuan Yew, address to a Chinese rural community, October 30, 1966, quoted in *Singapore Year Book, 1966* (Singapore: Government Printing Office, 1967), p. 29.

7. Lee Kuan Yew, quoted in *Singapore Year Book, 1967* (Singapore: Government Printing Office, 1968), p. 9.

8. *See Singapore Year Book, 1967*, p. 3.

9. Interview with Prof. Lau Teik Soon, former head, Department of Political Science, and member of Parliament, National University of Singapore, July 16, 1992. See also Chang, "Nation-Building in Singapore," p. 767.

10. *Far Eastern Economic Review* 213 (January 26, 1967): 114–115.

community.[11] Even before independence, they launched a massive public-housing program (HDB) to mix members of the various racial groups within the same high-rise buildings and neighborhoods and eliminate ethnic ghettos. Between 1961 and 1965, the government built new high-rise units for five hundred thousand people (25 percent of the total population) at a rate of one new apartment every forty-five minutes. Residents were allowed and even encouraged to buy their new apartments.[12] The government further promoted the blending of hostile racial communities through the introduction of comprehensive social programs, such as low-cost maternity services and compulsory inoculation schemes, and through the massive development of a network of transportation, communication, and recreational services.

Singapore's leaders declared Malay, Mandarin, Tamil, and English the official state languages, and they took great pains to place them on equal footing. Lee himself delivered his speeches in three languages (Malay, Mandarin, and English).[13] In Parliament, members gave speeches in the four official languages, and they were obliged to command the Malay language even in cases where 70 percent of their constituencies were non-Malay. Legislation encouraged citizens to become bilingual: cab drivers had to take a basic test in other than their native language to obtain a taxi permit.[14]

The education system was restructured to ingrain multiracialism in students. Integrated elementary and high schools were established "to break down the racial and linguistic communication barrier."[15] Within these schools, reformed curricula were introduced to instill the values of multiculturalism and meritocracy in the younger generation. For example, Malay, previously the only official state language, became a compulsory subject in all primary schools, including those serving mainly non-Malay students. The local mass media (i.e., television and radio)

11. Interview with Prof. Chan Heng Chee, director, Singapore International Foundation, PUB Building, Singapore, June 26, 1992.

12. Chang, "Nation-Building in Singapore," p. 763. Currently, Singapore's ratio of home owners among the general population is the highest in the world. Close to 90 percent of Singaporeans own their own houses, which are fairly expensive in Western terms (on average, a three-bedroom apartment in a high-rise building costs between $100,000 and $150,000).

13. *Far Eastern Economic Review* 214 (February 2, 1967): 168.

14. Interview with Prof. Lau Teik Soon.

15. Chang, "Nation-Building in Singapore," p. 765.

broadcast programs in the four official languages to "create a multi-racial look."[16]

Nearly every sector, even sports, was redesigned to reflect and implement Lee's call for a closely knit multiracial state. Athletic subjects were taught in schools to inculcate values such as "initiative, perseverance, agility, endurance, courage and team-spirit" in the country's youth. Sport was also used as an official means to inculcate "a sense of dedication and loyalty to the nation" and "transcend religious, language and communal barriers."[17] Finally, Singapore established—and constantly expanded—an extensive network of parapolitical institutions, such as community centers and resident centers, to bring Chinese, Indians, Malays, and Eurasians together. The scope and intensity of Singapore's nation-building campaign during the past three decades is unmatched.

THE MULTIRACIAL IDEOLOGY AND THE MILITARY

Like everything else in Singapore, the state's first conscription bill was carefully designed to promote the twin goals of building a rugged and disciplined nation and transforming individuals into loyal and productive citizens.[18] Well-versed in classic texts, including the works of Thucydides and Plato, Dr. Goh was convinced that service in the Defence Forces often nurtured national consciousness.[19] Thus, when presenting the first conscription bill to Parliament, he declared, "This aspect of military service is at least as important as the purely defence consideration,"[20] and, "Nothing creates loyalty and national consciousness more

16. Singapore, *Legislative Assembly Debates* 27, no. 4 (May 13, 1968), col. 208.

17. Singapore, *Legislative Assembly Debates* 27, no. 6 (May 15, 1968), cols. 302–303.

18. *Singapore Year Book, 1966*, p. 176.

19. Dr. Goh referred to the works of Plato and Thucydides during the debate on Singapore's first conscription bill. See Singapore, *Legislative Assembly Debates* 25, no. 16 (March 13, 1967), col. 1161. In his interview with me, Dr. Goh admitted that after the declaration of Singapore's independence, he immersed himself in classic texts such as *The Peloponnesian War* in order to "discover what can go wrong" with small states surrounded by stronger enemies. These texts very much inspired his ideas on the relationship between military service and citizenship. Interview with Dr. Goh Keng Swee, former minister of defence, PSA Building, Singapore, July 3, 1992.

20. Singapore, *Legislative Assembly Debates* 25, no. 16 (March 13, 1967), col. 1179.

speedily and more thoroughly than participation in defence and membership of the armed forces."[21] Complementing the courses received in the civilian school system,[22] National Education programs in the new military were designed to instill in new draftees qualities such as valor, comradeship, discipline, diligence, common social purpose, and pride in oneself and one's community.[23]

Dr. Goh deemed discipline, loyalty, and leadership the most important values because veterans endowed with such qualities were invaluable for the productivity of the civil labor force.[24] In the years after the enactment of conscription, he relentlessly chastised the military for "taking over some of the soft migrant values of our civilian society."[25] To eradicate these "soft values" from the military, draftees were instructed to carry with them a little red book titled the *Code of Conduct*, which emphasized the positive values, and to memorize six rules contained therein.[26] The Ministry of Defence created a National Education Department to support educational programs, including civics education in every military unit (two hours weekly) and in military courses.[27]

In addition to instilling such values in individual soldiers, the military was instructed to continue the national campaign to bridge racial, lin-

21. Singapore, *Legislative Assembly Debates* 25, no. 16 (March 13, 1967), col. 1160. Also quoted in *Singapore Year Book, 1967,* p. 6.

22. Singapore, *Legislative Assembly Debates* 25, no. 16 (March 13, 1967), col. 1161.

23. Lee Kuan Yew, during a send-off dinner for the new national servicemen in his parliamentary constituency. See *Singapore Year Book, 1967,* p. 9; Dr. Yeo Ning Hong, "The Buildup of Singapore Armed Forces," in S. Jayakumar, ed., *Our Heritage and Beyond: A Collection: of Essays on Singapore, Its Past, Present, and Future* (Singapore: Singapore National Trade Union Congress, 1982), p. 38 (Dr. Yeo was minister of state [defence]).

24. Lim Kim San, minister of the interior and defence, on the graduation day of the second class of national servicemen officers from SAFTI (December 1968). See *Singapore Year Book, 1968* (Singapore: Government Printing Office, 1969), p. 10. See also Singapore, *Legislative Assembly Debates* 25, no. 17 (March 14, 1967), col. 1224. Castro promoted a similar idea in Cuba after 1963. He vowed to instill the values of "work" and "battle" (i.e., fight to win everywhere) in Cuban society through his 1963 conscription bill. Duncan, "Development Roles of the Military in Cuba," pp. 103, 107.

25. Dr. Goh Keng Swee, *The Practice of Economic Growth* (Singapore: Federal Publications, 1977), p. 233.

26. Singapore, *The Code of Conduct for the Singapore Armed Forces* (Singapore: Ministry of the Interior and Defence, 1967); interview with Col. Menon, director of pubic relations, MINDEF, SAF Officer Club, June 25, 1992.

27. Interview with Samuel, former head, National Education Department, Central Manpower Base, Depot Road, July 10, 1992.

guistic, and religious barriers. The 1971 *Singapore Yearbook* clarified this goal: "Apart from fulfilling military requirements, National Service has the wider object of integrating a multi-racial, multi-lingual and multi-religious community committed to Singapore and to the well-being of its citizens. It follows the direction begun in schools, where an integrated community is educated together, where young people of all races study together, to forge a national identity."[28]

On numerous occasions during the debate over the first conscription bill, Singaporean politicians hailed this nation-building aspect of the new military. Compulsory national service, ministers and members of Parliament argued, would serve as a "firm foundation for a multiracial society," as the youth of various races would "have the opportunity to live together, understand one another, and get to know their habits of living and their respective strong and weak points."[29] All Singaporeans in 1967—politicians and laymen alike—shared the explicit understanding that every young Singaporean male citizen would be conscripted, irrespective of racial background.

THE MALAYSIAN THREAT AND SINGAPORE'S INTERNAL SECURITY

The commitment to establish an exemplary multiracial military force created an immediate dilemma, since 15 percent of Singapore's citizens were Malays who had kin in Malaysia, which posed the gravest invasion threat to Singapore after 1965. A tiny island surrounded by powerful neighbors, Singapore had a sorrowful history of foreign invasions, the most gruesome in December 1941, when the Japanese army conquered the island after a two-month campaign despite a strong defense force of one hundred thousand British troops. Between 1945 and its 1965 independence, Singapore suffered from guerrilla attacks with almost no respite.[30]

---

28. This quote opened the section on compulsory national service in Singapore in the newly edited yearbook of 1971. See *Singapore Year Book, 1971* (Singapore: Government Printing Office, 1972), p. 104.

29. Singapore, *Legislative Assembly Debates* 25, no. 16 (March 13, 1967), cols. 1160, 1165, 1171; 25, no. 17 (March 14, 1967), cols. 1212, 1225, 1227; 27, no. 4 (May 13, 1968), col. 206.

30. Singapore, *Legislative Assembly Debates* 24, no. 10 (December 23, 1965), col. 347. See also L. Allen, *Singapore, 1941–1942* (London: Davis-Poynter, 1977); C. N. Barclay, "The Fall of Singapore (Feb 15, 1942): A Reappraisal," *Army* 18 (April 1968): 44–53; K. Booth, "Sin-

Dr. Goh admitted that, in light of such a history, some experts considered Singapore "quite indefensible."[31]

Dependent on water and food supplies from Malaysia and having no defense shield of its own, Singapore appeared to be the perfect prey for any external aggressor. To complicate matters even further, all historical efforts to upgrade Singapore's defense had failed. When the British government attempted to introduce a scheme of national service in Singapore in the mid-1950s, riots broke out and the British were forced to abandon the plan. Likewise, in 1962, Lee demanded the creation of five additional infantry battalions, arguing that without these battalions he was doomed to remain "empty-handed" vis-à-vis Singapore's neighbors.[32] Yet he was still empty-handed in 1965: the small Singapore Armed Forces (SAF) consisted of two infantry battalions (1SIR and 2SIR) comprising approximately fifty officers, a thousand enlisted men, and fewer than two thousand rifles.[33] A few days after the separation from Malaysia, Lee lamented that Singapore "would be finished" if, for example, Indonesia decided to invade the island with only a tenth of its force.[34] Using a similar tone in Parliament, Dr. Toh Chin Chye, the deputy prime minister, reported that even ministers from relatively small African countries asked him, "How could you be an independent country—no Army, no Navy and no Air Force?"[35]

When the British government decided in 1968 to speed up the retreat of its forces east of the Suez Canal, Singapore was left virtually defenseless.[36] Lee then launched a "crash program to build a credible deterrent," but it was not enough. In January 1969, Lee admitted that Singapore might need to employ mercenaries to defend itself.[37] And S. Rajaratnam,

gapore 1942: Some Warnings," *Army Quarterly* 102 (January 1972): 191–200; Chan Khoon Lip, "The Capture of Singapore," *Pointer* 14, no. 2: 26–43.

31. Singapore, *Legislative Assembly Debates* 25, no. 16 (March 13, 1967), col. 1158. See also *Far Eastern Economic Review* 214 (January 2, 1967): 169.

32. Singapore, *Legislative Assembly Debates* 18 (June 28, 1962), col. 174; Chang, "Nation-Building in Singapore," p. 770.

33. Yeo, "Buildup of Singapore Armed Forces," p. 37.

34. Lee Kuan Yew, press conference with Malay journalists, T. V. Singapura, August 11, 1965; interview by Neville Peterson of the Australian Broadcasting Commission, T. V. Singapura, August 12, 1965.

35. Singapore, *Legislative Assembly Debates* 24, no. 7 (December 20, 1965), col. 368.

36. See, for example, the annual speech of the Singaporean president in 1968; Singapore, *Legislative Assembly Debates* 27, no. 1 (May 6, 1968), col. 12–13.

37. Jerome R. Bass, "Malaysia and Singapore: Moving Apart?" *Asian Survey* 9, no. 2 (February 1969): 123.

the minister of foreign affairs, publicly admitted that the defense of Singapore had to "remain the concern of big powers."[38]

Malaysian politicians mercilessly exploited the military vulnerability of Singapore between 1965 and 1969. In 1965, they prohibited Singapore from trading with Indonesia.[39] Malaysian leaders were, on occasion, ruthless toward their Chinese citizens, whose political hero was Lee. In 1966, for example, Lee watched helplessly as the Malaysian government "resettled" the Sarawak Chinese community (Sarawak was an island member of the Malaysian federation), accusing it of cooperating with the predominantly Chinese Clandestine Communist organization (CCO). The Sarawak United People's Party, traditionally an ally of Lee's People's Action Party (PAP), asked him to protest the Malaysian decision, but he was too weak to defend even his own island, Singapore.[40]

Lee remained silent on the issue of the Sarawak Chinese community, mainly because he did not wish to provide Malaysian leaders with a pretext to invade Singapore. Fears about such an impending invasion ran high in Singapore between 1965 and 1969.[41] Lacking a reliable defense force of his own, Lee worked hard to defuse every conflict—especially racial—that might trigger a Malaysian invasion.[42] When the Malay newspaper *Utusan Melayu* published allegations that Singaporean Christian missionaries were forcing Malay Muslims to convert, Lee

38. *Far Eastern Economic Review* 238 (July 20, 1967): 152.

39. Harvey Stockwin, "Singapore: Likely Election," *Far Eastern Economic Review* 141, no. 11 (September 9, 1965): 491; "Malaysia: Ever Wider?" *Far Eastern Economic Review* 147, no. 3 (October 21, 1965): 110; "Divided Stand," *Far Eastern Economic Review* 148, no. 4 (October 28, 1965): 162–169.

40. Jean Grossholtz, "An Exploration of Malaysian Meanings," *Asian Survey* 6, no. 4 (April 1966): 235.

41. Interview with Encik Othman Bin Wok, former minister of social affairs and ambassador to Indonesia, Singapore Tourist Promotion Board, May 4, 1987 (oral history interview by Irene Lim, for the project "Political Development in Singapore, 1965–1975"), p. 5. Fundamentalist Islamist Mullahs attempted to convince the Malaysian government to invade Singapore while it was still weak. Interview with Lim Kim San, former minister of defence, PSA Building, Singapore, July 9, 1992.

42. Lee Kuan Yew, "Interview to Four Correspondents on August 14, 1965 at the Studios of Television Singapore" (University of Singapore, Singapore, 1976, photocopy). See also Lee Kuan Yew, "Press Conference at City Hall," August 26, 1965 (University of Singapore, Singapore, 1976, photocopy). Lee also feared that Malaysia would drive its Chinese population to immigrate to Singapore en masse, thereby inundating the island with millions of unemployed and frustrated refugees; Lee Kuan Yew, "A Speech To The Liquor Retail Traders Association 28th Anniversary Celebration," October 3, 1965 (University of Singapore, Singapore, 1976, photocopy).

spared no effort to prove them false.[43] And he ordered the closing of several newspapers, including the *Nanyang Siang* and the *Eastern Sun*, after they published stories on governmental discrimination against "certain people."[44]

Malaysian politicians also manipulated their military forces in Singapore, as well as the separation agreement, in order to limit Singapore's efforts to build its own credible defense force. The separation treaty had been carefully tailored to provide politicians on both sides with sufficient defense flexibility if Indonesia ever decided to attack Singapore[45] (although by 1966, Indonesia was ready to normalize its relationship with Singapore). Nonetheless, Malaysian politicians were determined to prevent Singapore from building a strong military that might endanger their own security and reduce their influence in the region.[46] They argued that Lee did not need to build a strong defense force, since Malaysia was responsible for the defense of Singapore. Naturally, Lee resented such an interpretation of the separation treaty, but being militarily "empty-handed," he had to play his cards with great canniness. Using a Themistoclean strategy, he deliberately played up the imaginary "survival" threat from Indonesia in order to buy time for quietly building up his military to face the real survival threat—a Malaysian invasion.[47] Even as the relationship with Malaysia warmed up during the early 1970s, Singapore's leaders did not lose sight of the Malaysian threat even briefly.

43. Interview with Encik Othman Bin Wok, pp. 38–40. See also "Prime-Minister Lee Kuan Yew at the 1st Anniversary Celebrations of the Upper Serangoon Community Center," September 26, 1965 (University of Singapore, Singapore, 1976, photocopy); "Statement to Religious Representatives and Members of the Inter-religious Council at Mr. Lee's Office in City Hall," September 30, 1965 (University of Singapore, Singapore, 1976, photocopy).

44. Interview with Encik Othman Bin Wok, pp. 38–40; Singapore, *Legislative Assembly Debates* 24, no. 7 (December 20, 1965), col. 365.

45. Singapore, *Legislative Assembly Debates* 25, no. 1 (February 23, 1966), col. 24.

46. Milne, "Singapore's Exit from Malaysia," p. 183.

47. See Singapore, *Legislative Assembly Debates* 25, no. 1 (February 23, 1966), col. 18. Before 1967, Singapore recruited men for its new army using quiet methods such as the distribution of pamphlets in community centers (rather than mass media recruitment campaigns) in order not to attract Malaysian attention. Interview with H. R. Hochstadt, former director of manpower, MINDEF, PSA Building, Singapore, July 2, 1992. Lee's strategy of buying time to build Singapore's own defensive shield resembled Themistocles' foreign policy as described by Thucydides. Themistocles deliberately prolonged his negotiations with the Spartans, thus providing Athens with crucial time to build its long walls. See Thucydides, *The Peloponnesian War*, 1.90–91, 138, trans. Crawley (New York: Modern Library, 1982), pp. 52–53, 79.

"We must remember," said Rajaratnam, "that a crocodile is dangerous even when it is friendly."[48]

SINGAPORE'S INTERNAL-SECURITY DILEMMA

The Malaysian threat complicated the SAP's quiet buildup on three fronts: the presence of Malaysian military forces in Singapore, the refusal to discharge Singaporean officers and soldiers serving in Malaysian units outside Singapore, and, most important, the domination of Singapore's own police and military forces by Singaporean Malays.

Between 1965 and 1967, Malaysia refused to evacuate its Fourth Brigade and one of its infantry regiments from Singapore. Justifying such unusual behavior, its leaders argued that the separation agreement allowed them to maintain "bases and facilities" in Singapore for military purposes.[49] The presence of these forces led to a full-scale diplomatic crisis between the two countries when, in February 1966, the 2SIR (2nd Singaporean Infantry Regiment) returned home from a long and arduous mission in Sabah, only to find its camp occupied by the Malaysian Fourth Brigade.[50] The Fourth Brigade also refused to hand back military signal and transport equipment vital to the new SAF.[51] Under heavy British pressure, Malaysia finally removed the brigade and other units from Singapore on September 31, 1967.[52]

The buildup of the SAF was further complicated because much of its manpower nucleus consisted of officers and soldiers who had been serving in the Malaysian defense forces at the time of separation. For their part, Singaporean manpower planners were delighted to release back to Malaysia several hundred Malaysian citizens serving in 1SIR and 2SIR. The Malaysians, however, were less eager to release Singaporean officers and soldiers back to Singapore. The Singaporean Defence Forces' first director of manpower recalled that he and his officers devoted most of

48. S. Rajaratnam, "Non-Communist Subversion in Singapore," in *Trends in Singapore: Proceedings and Background Paper*, ed. Chee Meow Seah (Singapore: Singapore University Press, 1975), p. 112.

. 49. Singapore, *Legislative Assembly Debates* 25, no. 1 (February 23, 1966), col. 24.

50. Singapore, *Legislative Assembly Debates* 25, no. 1 (February 23, 1966), col. 23; interview with Lt. Gen. Winston Choo; interview with George E. Bogaars; interview with Encik Othman Bin Wok, p. 15.

51. Singapore, *Legislative Assembly Debates* 25, no. 1 (February 23, 1966), cols. 19–20.

52. Singapore, *Legislative Assembly Debates* 26, no. 16 (January 24, 1968), col. 1105.

their time and effort in 1966 to preparing lists of Singaporean citizens in the Malaysian military in order to assist Singaporean politicians bargaining with senior Malaysian leaders over the release of these men. Lim Kim San, Singapore's second minister of defence (1967–1969), admitted in December 1968 that his ministry did not even know exactly how many Singaporeans were serving in the Malaysian defense forces as of August 9, 1965 (Singapore's first Independence Day).[53]

For all the difficulties, manpower problems involving Malaysian soldiers in Singapore or Singaporean soldiers in Malaysia were susceptible to solution through interstate negotiations. In contrast, the issue of the significant number of Singaporean Malays serving in the police and the military was much more complicated because Singapore did not have the option of exporting these men to Malaysia: they were Singaporean citizens and wished to remain such. The police force had an overwhelming number of Singaporean Malays (seven-eighths of the force, according to one source).[54] Malays dominated the police to such an extent that, during the 1964 riots, the multiethnic Singapore Voluntary Corps (SVC) had to be mobilized because many Singaporean Chinese citizens perceived that the police force took a "biased approach" toward them.[55]

Like the police, the rank and file of the new Singaporean military was also predominantly Malay. The British colonial rulers had regarded Malays, both in Singapore and in Malaysia, as a "martial race" and had encouraged them to volunteer for military service during that era. As a result, the hard core of the new Singaporean military (1SIR and 2SIR) contained many professional Malay soldiers and NCOs. Estimates of how many of Singapore's first soldiers were Malay range between 50 and 80 percent.[56] The presence of Malay soldiers in the SAF was so prev-

---

53. Singapore, *Legislative Assembly Debates* 25, no. 1 (February 23, 1966), col. 20; Singapore, "Oral Answers to Questions," in *Legislative Assembly Debates* 28, no. 6 (December 17, 1968), cols. 430–431; interview with H. R. Hochstadt; interview with Col. Armugam, former SAF officer (oral history interview, for the project "Political Development in Singapore, 1965–1975").

54. *Singapore Year Book, 1971*, p. 108.

55. Interview with Kirpa Ram Vij, former SAF chief of staff, NOL Building, June 29, 1992; interview with Col. Armugam.

56. Aeria, the first commander of the Singaporean navy, estimates that 40–50 percent of Singapore soldiers were Malay (compared with only 15 percent Malays within the general population). Senior officers who were closer than Aeria to 1SIR and 2SIR, however, estimate that the percentage of Malay soldiers was much higher. Winston Choo, who in 1965 was an infantry captain and deputy commander of one of the companies of 1SIR, estimates that 60 percent of the new Singaporean military were Malays. Col. Syed Ibrahim bin Syed

alent that one Parliament member complained it was virtually impossible to find a Chinese newspaper in the new military, as there was very little demand for a paper that most soldiers could not read.[57]

Even before independence, Singapore's leaders questioned the loyalty of their Malay soldiers. Only five days before declaring the country independent, Lee invited George Edwin Bogaars, the permanent secretary to the Ministry of Interior and Defence, for a private conversation during which they discussed the loyalty of the police and the military. Lee even interrogated Bogaars about whether five Malay officers (named by Lee) could be trusted to remain loyal if Singapore were ejected from the Malaysian federation.[58]

Lim Kim San, the minister of defence between 1967 and 1969, recalled two incidents that illuminated Singaporean leaders' concerns about their Malay soldiers in the mid-1960s. The first took place during the 1964 racial riots when a British officer charged into a Malay crowd without noticing that his Malay soldiers had refused to follow him. The second, and more serious incident, occurred in 1965 when a senior Malay military officer refused to take an order from Dr. Goh, since he, like many of his compatriots, believed that Singapore would soon return to the federation and that orders would continue to flow from Kuala Lumpur.[59]

The behavior of Malaysian leaders and parties exacerbated fears that the Singaporean Malay population might become a Trojan horse during a Malaysian invasion. Singapore's leaders knew that Malaysian leaders were concerned that they had "let down" the Malay community in Singapore by allowing them to be ruled by a Chinese-dominated government.[60] The ruling UMNO party, and other Malay and Muslim organizations in Malaysia, proclaimed themselves guardians of Singapore's Malay minority on numerous occasions after the separation.[61] On several occasions, Malay newspapers hinted that Malays were being "victimized" in Singapore. In response, the Singaporean Special Branch focused most of its efforts on supervising what Bogaars called "Malay

---

Mohamed, who in 1965 was a platoon commander in 2SIR, estimates that 80 percent of the soldiers in his regiment were Malays.

57. Singapore, *Legislative Assembly Debates* 25, no. 17 (March 14, 1967), col. 1201.

58. Interview with George E. Bogaars, pp. 300–302.

59. Interview with Lim Kim San.

60. Interview with George E. Bogaars, p. 320.

61. Tim Huxley, "Singapore and Malaysia: A Precarious Balance?" *Pacific Review* 4, no. 3 (1991): 207.

extreme politics" in Singapore, rather than on the alleged internal Communist threat.[62]

The gravest fear of Singapore's leaders was that if Malaysian forces invaded Singapore, a Malay-dominated Singaporean military would surrender without a fight.[63] Dr. Goh recalled, "Early on, we thought that if we had many Malays in the army, then what would happen in case of war with Malaysia?"[64] He revealed that Singapore's leaders even planned to give Malay soldiers the choice of opting out in the event war broke out, though these plans were never put to paper.[65] At any rate, the scheme was clearly impractical and bordered on suicidal. Allowing 50–80 percent of the military to choose not to participate in the event of a foreign invasion would have amounted to surrender.

This was Singapore's security predicament between 1965 and 1975. On the one hand, the official ideology dictated that Malay youth, like Chinese, Indian, and Eurasian youth, should be conscripted, integrated, and promoted within the SAF on an equal basis. On the other hand, security concerns suggested that the military needed to exclude Malay youth from service, bring in Chinese, and find ways to clear its ranks of the high number of Malays. The dictates of multiracialism were at odds with the security concerns of Singaporean leaders.

PUSHING MALAY SERVICEMEN OUT

The task of building a new multiracial military in 1965 thus appeared daunting, since Singaporean Malay soldiers and NCOs swelled its ranks.[66] Increasingly concerned about the loyalty of Malay soldiers, Singaporean leaders sought at first to "racially balance" the military by recruiting more Chinese, Indian, and Eurasian soldiers and officers.[67] But local recruitment officers on aggressive campaigns encountered many more Malay than non-Malay volunteers. Frequently the officers had to

62. Interview with George E. Bogaars, pp. 320, 322.
63. Interview with Lt. Gen. Winston Choo.
64. Interview with Dr. Goh Keng Swee.
65. Interview with Dr. Goh Keng Swee.
66. Singapore, *Legislative Assembly Debates* 24, no. 10 (December 23, 1965), col. 346.
67. Interview with Dr. Hussin Mutalib, Department of Political Science, National University of Singapore, Center for International Affairs, Harvard University, May 21, 1992. The concept of racially balancing the military was used by Dr. Goh. See Singapore, *Parliamentary Debates Singapore* (February 23, 1977), cols. 398–399.

choose "less eager Chinese volunteers over more eager Malay volunteers."[68]

In January 1966, some Malay youths suspected that they were being singled out for dismissal when the recruitment officer decided to send them home although they had already signed official recruitment papers. A riot almost broke out. This incident illustrated how sensitive Malays were to the issue of military recruitment. For many Malays, the military was an important means of employment and the only channel for social mobility. Aware of this, Dr. Goh was determined to minimize racial conflicts concerning the government's recruitment policy, and so, after this near riot, he asked H. R. Hochstadt to take over the position of director of manpower from Colonel Law, whom he held accountable for the incident. Since Hochstadt was a Eurasian and a civilian, Dr. Goh believed that his appointment would best serve the highly delicate and sensitive goal of racially balancing the new military.[69]

One of Hochstadt's principal tasks was to recruit non-Malay candidates for officer courses. His problem was that Chinese were reluctant to commit themselves to lifelong careers as professional officers. To partially offset the shortage of Chinese candidates, Hochstadt resorted to recruiting officer cadets from among the small Singaporean Indian and Eurasian communities. The commanders of the new military included Ceylon merchants and Catholic citizens of Portuguese and Spanish descent. Though they constituted barely 2 percent of the population, Eurasians commanded roughly 10 percent of all ranks of major and above in the new SAF. Indians, who constituted only 8 percent of the population, commanded about 25 percent of the senior officer positions.[70] Moreover, of the first two chiefs of staff, one was Eurasian (Brigadier Campbell), the other Indian (Kirpa Ram Vij).

Among the rank and file, the task of diluting the Malay-dominated military was even more difficult. The recruitment drive between 1965 and 1967 did not change the racially skewed composition of the SAF, as only several hundred new soldiers joined the military. Singaporean politicians had two fears: that the presence of Malay soldiers in sensitive units and military posts would breach security, and that a concentration of Malay soldiers in one or a few military professions would severely

68. Interview with H. R. Hochstadt.
69. Interview with H. R. Hochstadt.
70. Interview with Kirpa Ram Vij.

damage the military's fighting capability in the event of war. The politicians were concerned that if all military drivers were Malays, during a Malaysian invasion they could virtually cripple the military's mobility.

Racially segregating the military was not a viable solution for two reasons. First, racial segregation was the antithesis of the official multiracial ideology. Had Singapore's leaders attempted such a segregation, it would have been noted immediately, and severely damaged their credibility both at home and abroad. Moreover, Singaporean citizens loathed the despicable colonial technique of racially segregating security forces, as exemplified by the British policy of segregating the Singaporean Voluntary Corps (the native Singaporean military unit) before World War II.[71] Second and more important, Malay soldiers and NCOs made up the majority of the army's rank and file and were also the most experienced servicemen. Orders to transfer all Malay soldiers into new segregated units ran the risk of embittering these soldiers, who might then lose their motivation to fight. If Malay units decided not to fight a Malaysian invasion, the SAF could lose more than 50 percent of its fighting force and—what was more serious—might have to leave the fighting to the mostly inexperienced and poorly trained non-Malay units.

Segregated Malay units also could become a serious source of trouble, agitation, and possibly even a coup d'état. If the latter were to happen, Lee had no other military units strong enough to contain the well-trained, highly armed, and experienced Malay battalions. In addition, the danger of a coup d'état palled in comparison with what Lee would face if the Malaysian military ever invaded his island nation. In such an event, collaboration between Singaporean Malay units and a Malaysian invading force could eradicate Lee's vulnerable regime even more quickly than happened in the Iraqi conquest of Kuwait in 1990. The solution to the Malay dilemma, therefore, had to be politically more subtle and militarily more effective to soothe the Singapore leaders' security anxieties and insure the new military's fighting capability.

The leaders decided to spread Malay soldiers thin in the new military, and installed racial damage-control mechanisms. First, they limited the range of Malay military vocations to the infantry, thereby restricting ultrasensitive positions (intelligence or planning of operations) in which even a single breach of security could result in disaster. Next, they ordered the commanders of the new military to "racially balance" the rank

71. Interview with Dr. Goh Keng Swee.

and file of the existing infantry battalions. Each infantry unit (battalion, company, and platoon) was to have a similar ratio of Malays and non-Malays. Moreover, within each unit, commanders were instructed to spread Malays and non-Malays evenly across the entire spectrum of infantry professions (e.g., drivers, mechanics, and riflemen). Such racial balancing was the key to insuring that units would fight even after "racial attrition" in a war with Malaysia.[72]

Naturally, no written documents or public orders instructed officers along the chain of command on such sensitive racial matters. Through oral instructions, battalion commanders learned what the expected "racial keys" were, and then allocated Malay and non-Malay soldiers to the various units, orally informing their subordinate officers in turn how to balance their units and subunits. Senior commanders visited units and closely supervised their makeup.[73]

The SAF installed additional racial "damage control" mechanisms to minimize the potential for Trojan horses in a Malaysian invasion. It no longer sent either veteran or new Malay soldiers to officer courses. Instead, many non-Malay civilians were transferred from their civil posts to the SAF and commissioned as officers. Thus, Malay NCOs, who constituted the majority of infantry NCOs, were further "sandwiched" between a racially balanced rank and file and new non-Malay officers.[74] In addition, the military sent a significant number of the new Malay soldiers to the logistics corps, where there was minimal danger of security breaches.[75]

All of these race-balancing efforts depended ultimately on the willingness of more Chinese to volunteer for military service. As mentioned above, the problem was that Singapore's Chinese population, like other Chinese minority groups across Southeast Asia, disdained military service, preferring to pursue careers in trade and commerce.[76] By 1967, Singaporean leaders were becoming increasingly alarmed by this disinclination

72. Interview with H. R. Hochstadt.
73. Interview with H. R. Hochstadt.
74. Interview with Samuel.
75. Interview with Philip Yeo, former permanent secretary of defence, Economic Development Board Office, Raffles City Tower, Singapore, July 9, 1992; interview with Dr. Hussin Mutalib.
76. Lee Kuan Yew, "A Speech Made at the Sree Narayana Mission in Sembawang," September 12, 1965 (University of Singapore, Singapore, 1976, photocopy); "Speech to Senior Civil Servants at the Victoria Theater," September 30, 1965 (University of Singapore, Singapore, 1976, photocopy).

to volunteer for the military. One PAP Parliament member bitterly responded to the traditional Chinese epigram, "Good iron is never used for making nails, and good men are never made into soldiers": "If good men are not turned into soldiers, then it follows that the nation will have to depend on good-for-nothing people for its defence."[77]

Most disturbing, the SAF suffered from an acute shortage of Chinese cadets in its first two officer courses (January 1966 and June 1966). As usual, too many officer cadets in these courses were members of Singapore's small minority groups, the Indians and Eurasians.[78] At the beginning of 1967, since it appeared that the voluntary military service system had failed to achieve its goal of attracting enough Chinese soldiers and officers, Lee announced his intention to institute conscription. He rejected military recommendations to build a professional military gradually during the next three years: "I will not be able to carry on politically for three years without an army."[79] The first National Service Bill (March 14, 1967) was designed to provide Singapore with a credible defense shield and compel more Chinese participation in the military.

To tackle opposition, especially among the Chinese, an unprecedented public relations campaign followed the enactment of conscription. The Singapore Chamber of Commerce, dominated by Chinese businessmen, assembled 120 to 150 merchants every Sunday morning to spend a day with the new conscripts in the camps of 1SIR and 2SIR. Similar visitation programs for Community Center Committees [CCCs], management committees, community centers, and principals of secondary schools followed. Within three months, two thousand visitors, mainly prominent Chinese merchants, community politicians, and educators, had completed a "tour of duty" to gain firsthand knowledge of what the military was doing with its new conscripts. In addition, cabinet ministers, members of Parliament, and senior civil servants volunteered to serve in the new military. Even the scholarly Dr. Goh began showing up to official functions wearing the uniform of a colonel in the Artillery.[80]

77. Singapore, *Legislative Assembly Debates* 25, no. 16 (March 13, 1967), col. 1169.

78. Military Heritage Department, Singapore Armed Forces Archive, "Significant Events of National Service," 1992; interview with Kirpa Ram Vij.

79. Interview with Tan Tek Kim, former chief of general staff, SAF, Mandarin Hotel, Singapore, June 25, 1993. Israeli advisors (referred to as "the Mexicans" back then) were brought in to assist with the training of the army and the establishment of SAFTI. See *Far Eastern Economic Review* 241 (August 19, 1967): 277.

80. Interview with Samuel; Yeo, "Buildup of Singapore Armed Forces," p. 37.

In 1967, events on the Malay Peninsula forced Singapore's leaders to redesign their ethnic military manpower policy. After a Chinese street demonstration in June, full-scale racial riots erupted in the Chinese-dominated district of Penang due to the December decision of the Malaysian government to devaluate the old Straits dollar. The behavior of Malaysian military and police units during these riots alarmed Lee. Given orders to shoot troublemakers on the spot, Malaysian security forces killed at least twenty-seven people—all of them Chinese. The ratio of Malaysian Chinese citizens was very high among the wounded, detained, arrested, and banished victims of the riots. Southeast Asian newspapers reported on "the shattered edifice of racial togetherness" in Malaysia.[81] Political analysts predicted that the December riots were just the beginning of a much larger racial explosion in Malaysia. It seemed that Singaporeans were living next door to a ticking racial time bomb.[82]

In May 1969, this time bomb exploded when the country's Malay majority and Chinese minority battled each other throughout the Malay Peninsula. This time the riots had a direct and immediate effect on Singapore, as Malaysian Chinese who escaped from Johore to Singapore spread horror stories about the behavior of the Malay-dominated security forces. Determined to avoid a "Bangladesh predicament," the Singaporean government closed the causeway and swiftly deployed multiracial military units to guard the property and lives of Singaporean Malay citizens from the rage of Chinese street gangs.[83] This damage-control strategy appeared to have succeeded, since only a handful of minor local incidents were reported. One Parliament member summarized the performance of the military: "The Malay soldiers reacted against the Malays, and the Chinese against the Chinese, who were causing trouble."[84]

Yet while they praised the performance of their multiracial security forces in public, Singaporean leaders' actions after the riots revealed their

---

81. *Far Eastern Economic Review* 233 (June 15, 1967); 258 (December 9, 1967): 425–427; 259 (December 14, 1967): 507–509.

82. *Far Eastern Economic Review* 224 (April 13, 1967): 90.

83. Interview with Prof. Lau Teik Soon; interview with Encik Othman Bin Wok, pp. 40–41.

84. Interview with Encik Othman Bin Wok, p. 42. One academic researcher accepted Wok's argument that this riot-control exercise was successful; interview with Ernest C. T. Chew, dean of the social sciences, National University of Singapore, June 30, 1992.

real, entirely different conclusion. The 1967 and 1969 riots served as a powerful reminder to these leaders that even an efficient intelligence organization, such as the Malaysian Special Branch, could not defuse the "communal danger." Although their own intelligence organization had developed great expertise in penetrating the ranks of established underground organizations in Singapore, such as the Communist Party, it was mostly helpless against racial riots, which could be instigated by any individual.[85]

Singapore's leaders therefore decided to tighten security measures within the military even further. After 1969, the conscription of Malay youth virtually stopped, and senior defense officials were instructed to carefully screen out Malays from enlistment lists.[86] When informally discussing the issue of Malay conscription among themselves, senior politicians used the analogy of a dam and holes. The dam was the general guideline, to halt the recruitment of Malay youth. As any builder of a good dam knows, however, the water pressure should be occasionally eased by opening small holes at the bottom. Thus, recruitment officers were told to allow a small trickle of Malay youth into the military whenever frustration in the Malay community reached a dangerous level. Informal instructions to "open" or "close" holes in the racial-recruitment dam were passed down the chain of command, beginning with the senior echelons of the Ministry of Defence.

Since the system was not computerized, local recruitment officers sent hand-written lists of new draftees to their supervisors. Senior officers then perused these lists as the last step in a tedious and prolonged inspection process. Meanwhile, recruitment officers were still facing a shortage of Chinese draftees as a result of the generous education and employment deferrals granted before 1970. To fill their quotas, they were occasionally tempted to enlist Malay youth, and it was the role of senior defense officials to curb such temptations. Nonetheless, in 1970, Bogaars, the permanent secretary of defence, failed to examine the hand-written lists submitted for his inspection, despite direct orders from Lee. Bogaars' seniority and Lee's own high regard for him were of

85. Interview with Lim Kim San.
86. Stanley S. Bedlington, "Ethnicity and the Armed Forces in Singapore," in Ellinwood and Enloe, *Ethnicity and the Military in Asia*, p. 136. Several dozen young Malays who had a good command of the English language were conscripted after 1969, but they were just about the only Malays called to perform their military duty.

no avail, as he was permanently removed from his position in the Defence Ministry for "losing control" over this sensitive issue.[87]

A new lingo developed among officials and officers to describe the mistakes—and fate—of those who failed to comply with the informal racial manpower policy. The term "setback" was used to describe the lot of an official or officer who on a few occasions did not abide by the informal policy. Those who "suffered from a setback" were reprimanded but usually allowed to continue in their current jobs. The term "loss of control" was used to describe the behavior, and usually the end of the career, of those who on too many occasions did not execute the policy: officials and officers who suffered from a "loss of control" quickly found themselves out of a job. Bogaars, for example, suffered from a "loss of control," and therefore was removed from his prestigious position.

Additional security measures within the SAF complemented the policy of halting Malay conscription. The few Malay youth who were recruited served as firemen and policemen and, after the mid-1970s, were posted in Civil Defence units.[88] New incentives were offered to encourage Malay soldiers and policemen to retire. At the end of the 1960s, for example, the government created a new civilian guard organization, named CISCO, that provided financial institutions with sentinels, mostly veteran Malay soldiers and policemen.[89] Additional Malay field commanders were transferred to administrative positions.[90] Prestigious new military vocations, courses, and high-tech corps were sealed off to Malay soldiers.[91] After 1975, Mandarin Chinese replaced English as the language of senior commanders in the military, and officers who were candidates for promotion to the rank of captain and above had to pass an oral Mandarin exam. This policy gave a clear advantage to Chinese officers in military promotion.[92]

87. Interview with Lim Kim San; interview with Col. (Ret.) Aeria.

88. Interview with Zainul Abidin Rasheed, chief executive officer, Yaysan Mendaki, Mendaki Building, July 14, 1992.

89. Interview with Dr. Hussin Mutalib.

90. Ismail Kassim, *Problems of Elite Cohesion: A Perspective from a Minority Community* (Singapore: Singapore University Press, 1974), p. 58.

91. Malays staffed certain intelligence vocations because the military needed their language skills. The commando, air force, and officer courses, however, were "closed shops" for Malay youth. Interview with Lim Kim San.

92. Samuel, the former head of the National Education Department in the Ministry of Defence, stated that Mandarin replaced English because the efforts to teach English in the military were unsuccessful, and the military suffered from a chronic shortage of English

By the end of the 1960s, the ethnic composition of the SAF was very different from that in 1965. Chinese soldiers now almost exclusively manned new units. The Third Infantry Brigade, which was launched shortly after the 1969 riots, comprised two new Chinese-dominated National Service regiments (3SIR and 4SIR). The importance of this brigade—the first full-time, non-Malay unit—for Singapore's leaders became evident when Lim Kim San, the minister of defence, in a most unusual move, asked Kirpa Ram Vij to give up his position temporarily as the director of general staff (the most senior staff position of the SAF at the time) and take personal charge of constructing the new brigade's buildup. Vij completed this task in nine months and, after attending a short staff course, returned to his newly named post of chief of staff.[93]

Fears of renewed racial riots on the island were also quite intense during the mid-1970s.[94] In light of such fears, Singaporean leaders were determined to continue exempting Malay youth from military service, even though the SAF faced an acute manpower shortage. Instead of recruiting Malays, the Ministry of Defence outsourced close to 70 percent of the military's logistics positions to civilians, and used women to replace Chinese conscripts in noncombatant roles. Philip Yeo, the head of the Logistics Department of the Ministry of Defence, who personally launched many of these manpower innovations and later became the permanent secretary of defence, said that "eligible Chinese males went to Winston [the chief of staff]," referring to the unwritten policy of allocating all medically fit Chinese draftees to combatant positions.[95]

REPLACING PROFESSIONAL OFFICERS WITH CIVIL SERVANTS

If South African officers succeeded in promoting racial integration within the military despite the dictates of apartheid, why were Singaporean officers unable to promote the status of their Malay soldiers un-

---

teachers. In contrast, he argued, after 1975 the SAF had a large pool of potential Mandarin teachers. Interview with Samuel.

93. Interview with Kirpa Ram Vij.

94. Rajaratnam, "Non-Communist Subversion in Singapore," p. 119.

95. In this comment, Yeo referred to Lt. Gen. Choo, the chief of staff of the SAF after 1974, and the latter's ultimate responsibility to build credible and efficient fighting units; interview with Philip Yeo.

der conditions of multiracialism? The answer is that after 1965 Singapore had no class of professionally autonomous military officers equivalent to that of South Africa. To secure enough officers for the new military in Singapore, politicians transferred many civil servants to military posts. Thus, when Singapore's leaders decided to systematically control, check, and finally halt the recruitment of Malay youth, they faced no opposition from within the armed forces. In stark contrast to the situation in South Africa, the senior ranks of the Singaporean military were staffed with obedient civilians accustomed to executing the orders of their political masters in the most efficient manner, without questioning the wisdom of these policies.

During the 1966 military manpower exchange with Malaysia, Singapore returned about seven hundred Malaysian personnel, including many NCOs who might have served as new SAF officers. The Malaysians allowed a much smaller number of Singaporean servicemen to return home, and only three of these were experienced Chinese officers whom politicians were willing to trust with the mission of building the new military.[96] To complicate matters even further, experienced Singaporean officers who were serving with 1SIR and 2SIR were reassigned to staff positions in the new Ministry of Defence. Thus, in 1965, the SAF had very few professional senior officers to command, staff, and operate the military.[97]

The SAF's Operation Boxer I (early 1966) and Operation Boxer II (June 1966) recruited 1,120 new rank-and-file soldiers.[98] Such quick solutions, however, were unavailable at the senior-officer level. The SAF built a new officer school, but its first 117 home-trained junior Singaporean officers graduated only in July 1967, and therefore could not immediately resolve the problem of securing sufficient qualified and experienced mid- and senior-level officers for the ranks of captain and above.[99]

To resolve this dilemma, Dr. Goh selected a few civil servants whom he personally trusted, appointed them to senior positions in the new military, and selected several dozen additional officers from lists of qual-

96. These three officers were Jimmy Yap, Edward Young, and Winston Choo; interview with Kwa Chong Guan, director, National Museum, MINDEF, Singapore, July 1, 1992.
97. Maj. Singh Gill, "History of the Singapore Infantry Regiment," *Pointer Supplement Edition* (September 1990): 57.
98. Interview with Kwa Chong Guan.
99. Gill, "History of the Singapore Infantry Regiment," pp. 57–59.

ified civil servants that his aides prepared for him.[100] Dr. Goh admitted that when the Singaporean military was born in 1965, he considered the regular officers "inexperienced and intellectually weak," and therefore preferred to bring in his own men in spite of their minimal military experience.[101]

Nearly every officer appointed to a senior position had little or no pre-1965 military experience. Tan Tek Kim was serving as the senior assistant to the police commissioner in 1965, when he was temporarily transferred to the military to become its first director of general staff. In 1968, he returned to the police, and later became its commissioner. Likewise, Kirpa Ram Vij, who became the second director of general staff in June 1968, was a part-time junior officer in the Singaporean Volunteer Corps (SVC) who was commissioned during the Federation years after completing a six-week officer course conducted mostly on weekends. Observers jokingly nicknamed officers who graduated from this course "six-week wonders"—the wonder being that one could become an officer in that time.[102] And James Aeria, the first commander of the Singaporean navy, was a member of the Naval Volunteer Corps during the Federation years.

Other senior defense officials did not have even this limited paramilitary exposure. The first director of manpower was Hochstadt, who worked as a civil servant under Dr. Goh in the Ministry of Finance and was asked to follow his boss to the new Defence Ministry. Samuel, the head of the SAF's National Education Department, was a teacher transferred to the military. Philip Yeo, who graduated from engineering school in May 1970, was first posted in the System Analysis Branch of the Ministry of Defence and then promoted after a few years to command the entire logistics apparatus of the new military.

Transferred civil servants, even those in senior military positions, hesitated for long periods before formally joining the permanent force of the military. Aeria assumed command of the navy in 1965, yet waited until 1969 to officially join the permanent force. Colonel Armugam, who served in 1966 as the head of manpower proceedings and classification of personnel and built the Central Manpower Base, became a full member of the SAF only after 1966, when the military acknowledged his ten

---

100. Interview with George E. Bogaars, p. 320.
101. Interview with Dr. Goh Keng Swee.
102. Interview with Kwa Chong Guan.

years of experience as a teacher. Naturally, under such conditions, officer ranks reflected neither military experience nor seniority. Vij, for example, was promoted from captain to lieutenant colonel in order to build SAFTI (Singapore Armed Forces Training Institute). A year later, at the age of thirty-three, he was promoted to the rank of colonel and assumed command of the entire military. And Samuel the teacher was given the ceremonial rank of colonel in 1972.

Not surprisingly, the first civilian officers of the SAF were told that their task was to build a "civil service in uniform."[103] Military professionalism was to have no autonomous domain, as Lee sought to build a politically loyal military. A military coup d'état in Indonesia, and the deposing of Sukarno in May 1967, further strengthened Lee's conviction that an independent officer corps was dangerous to the state. Most important, Lee sought to create a new breed of senior officers who were certain to follow orders if racial riots broke out again. Bogaars, the permanent secretary of defence, described what kind of political officers Singaporean leaders sought after 1965: "I felt that what was becoming quite important in our kind of environment for the five years between '65 and '70 was the need to have officers with very strong political kinds of experience and knowledge and backgrounds to deal with the new types of security problems which were being created by larger issues, the fundamental issues that exist in plural societies. Things like the problems which relate to a small area of land with a high density of population, problems which result from the social reactions between members of communities who lived in a very small confined area, the continued problem of races, the major races, Malay and Chinese."[104] In short, in 1965 Singaporean leaders searched—and found—officers who were not too narrowly focused on professional military matters, and who shared a common mindset about race relations. Unquestionable loyalty, ideological affinity, and non-Malay racial background were the principal selection criteria for officers, not military experience or combat training.

Thus, as the government gradually increased efforts to control Malay soldiers within the new military, and halted Malay conscription after 1967, there were no professional officers who could have objected to this policy. Unlike the case of South Africa, civilians and officers could not have disagreed over the ethnic military manpower issues because, by

103. Interview with Kirpa Ram Vij.
104. Interview with George E. Bogaars, pp. 329–330.

1967, everyone was a civil servant in Singapore, including those in uniform. The power of Singaporean politicians vis-à-vis the military was absolute, and top civilian commanders were obsequious and unquestionably loyal.

"Divided We Stand": The Malay Leadership

The contradiction between the dictates of multiracialism and the government's blatantly exclusionary manpower policy against the Malay community resulted in feelings of bitterness, frustration, and, ultimately, social alienation among Malay youth. To many Malay citizens, the government of Singapore was a disguised "Chinese" government whose call for multiracialism was a mere cloak for its policy of favoritism toward the Chinese majority. Historical circumstances further fueled the hostility of Singaporean Malays toward their new government. Because of British "divide and rule" colonial practices, Malays were significantly less educated than the Chinese when Singapore was born. The adoption of the principle of meritocracy and the elimination of the Malaysian practice of granting Malays "special privileges," such as job quotas on the Malay Peninsula, left the Malay minority in Singapore far behind the well-to-do Chinese majority. For many young Singaporean citizens of Malay origin, the military provided the only channel of employment and social mobility. Moreover, the consequences of excluding Malays from military service spilled over to the civilian sector as Malay youth who did not serve in the military faced, in the short term, employers who refused to hire them and, in the long term, second-class citizenship.[105] Throughout the 1970s, this issue emerged as the focal point of contention between the government and the Malay community and was even discussed publicly during the 1972 and 1976 electoral campaigns.[106]

Bedlington reported that many Singaporean Malays were either "dis-

---

105. In 1970, the government passed the National Servicemen (Employment) Bill, which forced employers in certain sectors to employ only discharged national servicemen. The law also compelled employers to get special permission if they wished to recruit an employee who had not served in the military. Moreover, in order to gain such permission, the employer had to demonstrate that there were no veterans who qualified for the job opening. This law curtailed even further the already limited job market for Malay youth. See Singapore, *Legislative Assembly Debates* 30, no. 3 (June 26, 1970), col. 88.

106. Interview with Dr. Goh Keng Swee; Kassim, *Problems of Elite Cohesion*, pp. 121–122.

satisfied or downright alienated from the political system" as a result of the government's policy: "The government's actions have made many young Malays suspect—rightly so—that they are not trusted as responsible citizens by the very government to whom and by whom they are constantly exhorted to be loyal; as a consequence, many Malays told me, they are beginning to ask themselves whether, in fact, it is worthwhile extending any loyalty at all."[107] The alienation and frustration of young Malays who were excluded from military service raise another interesting enigma: Why were Malay leaders so unsuccessful in challenging the government's exclusionary policy toward Malay soldiers and Malay youth who wished to serve in the military? What accounts for the failure of Malay leaders to change the government's policy on this important matter? Why did not Malay leaders negotiate for their youth the kind of military arrangements that South African Indian and colored leaders achieved for theirs?

The solution to this puzzle lies in the historical weakness—and internal division—of the Malay leadership in Singapore.[108] Accusations that Singaporean Malay leaders were co-opted into the government and had betrayed the trust of their community were voiced even before Lee declared independence in August 1965. For example, when UMNO, the leading Malaysian Malay party, lost the 1964 Singapore elections to PAP Malay candidates, it condemned the latter as "traitors to the Malays in Singapore."[109]

Indeed, after 1965, many Singaporean Malay citizens continued to believe that Singapore's independence would not last for long and that eventually Lee would be forced back into the Malaysian federation.[110] Alarmed by such political sentiments, Lee carefully selected and promoted Malays who had worked with the PAP before 1963 to serve in parliamentary, governmental, and civil service posts. Thus, ideological affinity with the PAP, rather than grassroots support, characterized Singaporean Malay leaders throughout the 1970s.[111] Feelings of alienation intensified among Malay citizens as they were forced to resettle in high-rise buildings and the government eliminated their "special priv-

---

107. Stanley S. Bedlington, "The Singapore Malay Community: The Politics of State Integration," Ph.D. dissertation, Cornell University, 1974, pp. 244, 248.

108. Kassim, *Problems of Elite Cohesion*, pp. 41–42, 44–45.

109. Interview with Encik Othman Bin Wok, p. 30.

110. Interview with Encik Othman Bin Wok, pp. 31–32.

111. Kassim, *Problems of Elite Cohesion*, pp. 107–108.

ileges." The Malay PAP leaders who supported these policies grew further apart from the Malay community they supposedly represented.[112]

Accountable to the PAP leaders rather than to their constituents, Malay leaders were thus in no position to aid Malay youth when the government halted their recruitment after the 1969 racial riots. They voiced only a few weak, unofficial complaints against the new policy. On one occasion, Malay PAP leaders sent a letter asking for the recruitment of one hundred random Malay youth but received no answer.[113] Malay PAP leaders had only one success in their weak attempts to reverse the informal ban on Malay recruitment: they convinced the Ministry of Defence to provide Malay youth with official discharge cards.[114] But when young Malays finally received their formal military service deferral documents in the early 1970s, civilian employers still refused to hire them because they feared that their new Malay employees would be called to serve at a moment's notice.[115]

In public statements, Malay leaders unconditionally committed themselves to the official ideology of meritocracy above all, which many among their Malay constituents considered a disguise for state-sanctioned discrimination. Malay PAP leaders publicly defended even the most fatuous official explanations of why Malay youth were being exempted from military service. For example, they sanctioned the arguments of the government that Malay youth lacked education and did not command the English language (the same was true for the majority of Chinese Hokkien youth who were drafted), and that Malay males needed to spend more time at home with their families.[116] Sometimes Malay PAP leaders contributed their own inane explanations for the Malay exemptions. They argued, for instance, that the government did not have enough facilities to train Malay soldiers (it certainly had enough facilities to train everyone besides the Malays).[117] Later on, Malay PAP leaders shifted from excuses to outright lies by telling their constituents that a new racial balance in the military had finally been

112. Interview with Encik Othman Bin Wok, pp. 35–36.

113. Kassim, *Problems of Elite Cohesion*, pp. 59–62; interview with Dr. Hussin Mutalib.

114. Interview with Zainul Abidin Rasheed.

115. Interview with Abu Bakar Maidin, president, Muslim Missionary Society Singapore (JAMIYAH), Islamic Center Jamiyah, Singapore, July 15, 1992.

116. Kassim, *Problems of Elite Cohesion*, pp. 60, 110–111.

117. Interview with Encik Othman Bin Wok, p. 22.

established and that Malay youth were now again being inducted (they were not).[118]

It would be unfair, however, to place too much blame on the shoulders of Malay PAP leaders. During the 1970s, Lee held them under a tight grip. For him, few issues, if any, were as sensitive as that of military discrimination against Malay citizens. This was the Achilles heel of his campaign to convince Malaysia that Singaporean Malays supported his government and received fair treatment from it. Information on the recruitment of Malay youth and their fate within the new military was therefore scant, and discussion of the issue was restricted to university campuses and occasional question-and-answer periods during electoral events in 1972 and 1976. Proposals to discuss the issue in public were instantly rejected.[119]

Despite these obstacles, it seems that Malay PAP leaders could have done more to alleviate the Malay recruitment problem during the 1970s. The total and unconditional submission of Malay PAP leaders was matched only by the indifference and passivity of other Malay organizations, which did not even place the issue on their agendas. The principal opposition party, the Barisan Sosialis, which had more Malay supporters and officers than the PAP, did not even mention the issue in its official antigovernment publications. Other Malay organizations, such as the PKM, were completely silent on the matter. Two scholars who conducted research in Singapore during the early 1970s on the local Malay community argued that Malay organizations even back then could have built a united front to place the issue on the national agenda.[120]

By the second half of the 1970s, Malay exasperation with military recruitment and discrimination policies reached an all-time high. Even without official data, Malay parents knew that their children alone were not called upon to serve. Malay officers and NCOs who had been transferred from field command positions to the logistics corps were also frustrated. Nearly every officer knew that military units had informal quotas on Malays.[121] The Malay PAP leaders, who failed even to place this problem on the national agenda, were portrayed by their constitu-

118. Interview with Encik Othman Bin Wok, pp. 44–45.
119. Interview with Zainul Abidin Rasheed.
120. Kassim, *Problems of Elite Cohesion*, pp. 59–60; Bedlington, "Singapore Malay," pp. 245–246.
121. Interview with Kirpa Ram Vij; interview with Philip Yeo; interview with Dr. Hussin Mutalib.

ents as unresponsive and incompetent.[122] The time was ripe for a change of guard within the ranks of Singapore's Malay leadership.

In 1982, Mendaki, representing the second generation of Malay leadership, was founded as a Malay self-help organization with a mandate from the government to improve the poor educational standards and the dismal economic status of the Singaporean Malay community. Though the leaders of Mendaki had to pay their political dues to the PAP, they were younger, bolder, and, most important, more politically sophisticated then the older Malay PAP leadership. In the early 1980s, for instance, these young Malays convinced the government that the military, by enlisting Malay youth, could assist in the war on drugs, which plagued the Malay community.[123] Indeed, during the 1987 debate on Malays in the SAF, several of the older Malay PAP leaders admitted in Parliament that the young generation of Malay MPs was already succeeding where they had failed, by placing the issue of Malay military discrimination on the national agenda.[124]

Toward the end of the 1980s, a third generation of Malay leaders pushed the new assertiveness one step further. This new breed was composed of independent white-collar professionals (university professors, lawyers, doctors, and businessmen) rather than professional politicians. Using strong language, they condemned the previous two generations of Malay leaders: "The practice of co-opting Malay grassroots leaders into the PAP . . . not only constricts the leadership pool in the community but such leaders are, by and large, no longer accepted to lead Malay/Muslim organizations."[125] This new generation argued that total submission to every whim of the PAP leaders had resulted in "the gradual loss of effectiveness of Malay and Muslim organizations." They also argued that there was a growing sense of "leaderlessness" among Singaporean Malays.[126] More assertive, aggressive, and independent than their predecessors, these young professionals were successful in negotiating with the government and promoting the interests of the Malay community.

122. Kassim, *Problems of Elite Cohesion*, p. 81.

123. Interview with Abu Bakar Maidin; interview with Dr. Hussin Mutalib.

124. Singapore, *Parliamentary Debates Singapore* 49, no. 4 (March 17, 1987), cols. 366–367, 372.

125. "Forging a Vision—Malays/Muslims in 21st Century Singapore: Prospects, Challenges and Directions," conference paper, National Convention of Singapore Malay/Muslim Professionals, Singapore, October 1990, pp. 21, 58–59.

126. "Forging a Vision," pp. 21, 58–59.

The new leadership condemned the old practice of "shutting out many Malay youth from National Service as part of an official security policy." The ultimate result of this policy of "institutional discrimination," they argued, was the "alienation of Malay-Muslim society."[127] The arguments used by these leaders and their supporters were modern and sophisticated. One non-Malay Singaporean opposition member reminded the government that distrusting Muslim Malay citizens because of their Muslim religion was hypocritical, as Muslims were fighting and killing each other in the Iran–Iraq war.[128] But the most interesting charge of the new Malay leadership concerned the long-term effects of a scarce pool of Malay veterans on the development of a genuine Singaporean Malay leadership: "The larger impact of this [the exemption of Malay youth from military service] was to contribute to a brain-drain on the Malay/ Muslim elite, and eventually a narrowing of the pool of able people to lead the community."[129] By 1990, therefore, independent professional Malay leaders recognized that an additional price was being paid long-term for past submission to the government's ethnically discriminatory manpower policy: the loss of a generation of Malay veterans.

THE SOCIAL COST OF MILITARY EXCLUSION

The Trojan horse dilemma haunted the minds of Singaporean politicians until very recently. As late as 1987, Brig. Gen. Lee Hsien Loong, a prominent leader and Lee Kuan Yew's son, addressed the issue of Muslim soldiers' loyalty in the event of a war with Malaysia. The first to speak on this subject in Parliament since the state's establishment, Lee Hsien Loong said, "If there is a conflict, we don't want to put any of our soldiers in a difficult position where his emotions for the nation may be in conflict with his emotions for his religion. . . . We don't want to put anybody in that position where he feels he is not fighting a just cause, and perhaps worse, maybe his side is not the right side."[130] Indeed,

127. "Forging a Vision," pp. 21, 52.
128. Chiam See Tong, in Singapore, *Parliamentary Debates Singapore* 49, no. 4 (March 17, 1987), col. 381.
129. "Forging a Vision," pp. 21, 52.
130. See *Straits Times*, February 23, 1987; Singapore, *Parliamentary Debates Singapore* 49, no. 4 (March 17, 1987), col. 375. This unusually frank statement from such a prominent leader was extensively quoted in Singapore's newspapers, and launched a heated debate

throughout its early history, the government adopted strong measures to ensure that Malay youth would never have to make a choice between their "emotions for the nation" and their "emotions for the religion." Malay servicemen were pushed out of the military, and young Malays found that the military doors, once their prime avenue for social mobility and a promising career, were firmly closed. Years of exclusion resulted in social bitterness, frustration, and a major collision between the state and its principal ethnic minority group.

In contrast to the South African Defence Forces, the SAF did not have a group of autonomous professional officers. In Singapore, the senior officers were civilians transferred to the SAF and the Ministry of Defence from other ministries. The goal of Singaporean leaders was to build a "civil service in uniform" that would be loyal, obedient, and, most important, sensitive to the ethnic concerns of these leaders. Thus, when the politicians decided to rid the military's ranks of Malays after the 1969 riots, there were no professional senior officers present to defend the interests of their Malay soldiers in the name of combat readiness.

Consistent with their policy on staffing the senior SAF posts, Singaporean leaders took strong measures to ensure that the leadership supposedly representing the interests of the Malay community was obedient to the state and supportive of the government's policies. The co-opted, divided, and weak Malay leaders chose not to resist the government's exclusionary ethnic military manpower policy and in many cases even supported this policy publicly. Kassim, who studied the divisions among Singaporean Malay groups and leaders during the 1970s, concluded that the amorphous ethnic leadership structure of the Malay community there made it easier for the government to manipulate the community and employ co-opting techniques.[131]

After 1977, as the Malaysian invasion threat was diminishing and as the Singaporean military was becoming stronger and more professional, Lee Kuan Yew's fears of Malay Trojan horses within the military subsided. Singapore then adopted a policy of phased integration towards its Malay citizens, and between 1977 and 1985, the proportion of Malays in the SAF doubled. After 1985, all eligible Malays were reportedly being

---

in the country and with its Muslim neighbors (Malaysia and Indonesia) about the historical discrimination against Malays in Singapore's Armed Forces. See *Straits Times*, March 18, 1987; April 4, 1987; April 9, 1987.

131. Kassim, *Problems of Elite Cohesion*, pp. 6–7.

called up for national service. More Malays were posted during the 1980s in sensitive positions, including the Commando Battalion. Most important, more Malays began graduating from the officers' academy. The number of these officers remained low, as only 6 of 174 officers who graduated in March 1987 were Muslims. But the overall trend was progressive: Malays were finally being taken into the SAF and given a chance to succeed within its ranks.[132] Malay recruitment remained a forbidden issue for public discussion, but in 1987 B. G. Lee broke this taboo with a public comment on Malay dual loyalty. During the debate that followed his speech, Chiam See Tong, the lone opposition member in Singapore's Parliament, asked the government, "Is it really necessary to employ mercenaries [Gurkhas] in place of our citizens? Is that not a smack on the face of our citizens? . . . We trust all kinds of foreigners but we do not trust our own Malay citizens."[133]

These strong words gave voice to the frustrations of a lost generation of Malays who were denied the opportunity to serve in the military. Chiam See Tong's words also capture well the alienation, frustration, and feelings of betrayal that characterized the Malay community during the first decade of Singapore's history. Although it is too early to predict what will become of Malay servicemen in the SAF, two important lessons can already be gleaned. For the history of the Malays in the Singaporean military between 1965 and 1977 illustrates the harsh social consequences a country may face, first, if its leaders cannot overcome their Trojan horse fears and, second, if both military officers and ethnic leaders lack sufficient professional or political autonomy to challenge an important official exclusionary ethnic manpower policy.

132. Singapore, *Parliamentary Debates Singapore* 49, no. 4 (March 17, 1987), cols. 376–377; "This Is a Singapore Problem, We Will Solve It Ourselves," *Straits Times*, March 18, 1987; "Dr. Yeo: To Each Its Own Racial Solution," *Straits Times*, March 22, 1987; "Malays in the SAF: Singapore Will Be Closely Watched, Says Pelita," *Straits Times*, March 29, 1987.

133. See Singapore, *Parliamentary Debates Singapore* 49, no. 2 (March 13, 1987), col. 133; 49, no. 4 (March 17, 1987), col. 381. See also "Opposition MP Would Have SAF Policy on Malays Abandoned," *Straits Times*, March 18, 1987.

[4]

Israel: Between Inclusion and Exclusion

THE ZIONIST NATION-BUILDING IDEOLOGY

The Zionist ideology and movement emerged as products of the three great ideologies that conquered the human mind in the nineteenth century: liberalism, nationalism, and socialism. The liberal ideas of the Enlightenment emancipated Jews from their traditional segregated shtetls, shifted them from the periphery to the center of European society, and allowed them to penetrate and influence European culture to a greater degree than ever before. The rise of nationalism forced the newly emancipated Jews to come to terms with the dilemma of their ambiguous national identity in Europe, as illustrated by the Dreyfus affair and its effect on Herzl, the founding father of Zionism. Socialism defined the secular, humanistic, universalistic ideas that characterized the Zionist theory until very recently.[1]

David Ben-Gurion (1886–1973), Israel's first prime minister and minister of defence, converted Zionism from a nascent political doctrine and a voluntary movement into an official state ideology after 1948. As Avineri states, "To a very large extent, the State of Israel, with its achievements and failures, is a mirror as well as a monument to Ben-Gurion's own achievements and failures."[2] On numerous occasions, Ben-Gurion expressed his definite ideas about the nation-building essence of the Zi-

1. Shlomo Avineri, *The Making of Modern Zionism: The Intellectual Origins of the Jewish State* (New York: Basic Books, 1981), pp. 3–13. Avineri's work remains the best concise history of the Zionist ideology.
2. Avineri, *Making of Modern Zionism*, p. 199.

onist ideology and how to implement it in the Jewish state. He summarized what he thought Zionism meant in practice: "It [Zionism] means taking masses of uprooted, impoverished, sterile Jewish masses, living parasitically off the body of an alien economic body and dependent on others—and introducing them to productive and creative life, implanting them on the land [of Israel]."[3]

Thus, unlike Lee, who sought to integrate various cultures into a new composite Singaporean identity, Ben-Gurion promoted a Zionist ideology that was highly assimilative. While Lee sought to create the new Singaporean society as a mosaic of languages, cultures, and religions, Ben-Gurion was determined to obliterate traditional Jewish identities in the quest to build a new Israeli identity. The dozens of Jewish Diaspora identities would be rooted out through an intensive assimilation campaign directed at the massive influx of Jewish immigrants who arrived in Israel after 1948. Ben-Gurion insisted that there could be one—and only one—Israeli identity. Israeli citizens had to speak Hebrew, work the land, be disciplined, and be knowledgeable about Jewish history. Only such new Israeli citizens, Ben-Gurion argued, could "build one nation in language, consciousness, courage, and devotion to land and independence."[4] The essence of his national ideology was to cast the new Jewish immigrants in the mold of the heroic East European Jewish Zionist pioneers who came to Palestine around the turn of the century and built the first institutions of the future state.

Haunted by the lessons of the bloody War of Independence, Ben-Gurion asserted in 1949 that the task of building the new unified Jewish nation was extremely urgent, since the state had to defend itself against imminent Arab attacks: "We have no time to follow the natural historical process of becoming a nation."[5] In 1949, this task appeared daunting. Observing the massive influx of sorrowful Jewish refugees who had escaped burned-out Europe and persecution in Arab lands, Ben-Gurion commented, "The vast majority of our people, from a Jewish perspective, are nothing but human dust, with no language, no tradition, no roots, no linkage to normal state life, no habits of living in an independent society."[6] The new immigrants had little or no command of the modern

3. Avineri, *Making of Modern Zionism*, p. 200.
4. Israel, *Divrei Haknesset* 2 (August 15, 1949): 1567.
5. Israel, *Divrei Haknesset* 2 (August 15, 1949): 1567.
6. Israel, *Divrei Haknesset* 2 (August 15, 1949): 1337–1338.

Hebrew language, knew virtually nothing about Jewish history and the Zionist ideology and history, and were, for the most part, coming to Israel because other countries had refused to take them. Ben-Gurion prescribed the medicine for what he conceived to be the illness of the new state: "We must blend in a melting pot various diaspora immigrants and communities that differ from us, and create a new unified nation."[7]

Unfortunately, the new state was poor and lacked the financial and institutional resources to execute Ben-Gurion's melting-pot ideology. In 1949, the new Israel Defence Forces (IDF) appeared to be the only available nation-building tool, for several reasons. First, it was the only unified institution. The educational system was splintered along partisan lines, with key political groups maintaining their own elementary and high schools. The IDF appeared to be the one institution that could instill unified national values in all citizens while they were still young and malleable.[8] Second, the military was an efficient institution, compared with the other organs of state bureaucracy. Finally, and most important, in 1949 nothing seemed impossible for the triumphant army; this included the ability to accelerate the long historical processes that are usually required to create a nation out of immigrants.

THE ZIONIST IDEOLOGY AND THE MILITARY MELTING POT

Presenting Israel's first conscription bill to the Knesset (Parliament) on August 15, 1949, Ben-Gurion vowed to turn the new IDF into a national melting pot in which Jewish immigrant and native youth, blended together, would abandon ancient Diaspora identities and adopt a new Israeli character. The army alone, he argued, could be "the workshop of the new nation," and "an integrating institution to create the new character of the nation." In the military, Ben-Gurion promised, "the sons and daughters of the elite" would be equal to immigrant children who grew up under conditions of "ignorance, dirtiness, and valuelessness."[9]

Ben-Gurion also pledged to the Knesset that the IDF would teach its draftees to be true pioneers: to settle the land, work the fields, conquer nature, and love hard work. New immigrant soldiers would learn the He-

---

7. Israel, *Divrei Haknesset* 2 (August 15, 1949): 1337–1338.
8. Israel, *Divrei Haknesset* 2 (August 15, 1949): 1338.
9. Israel, *Divrei Haknesset* 2 (August 15, 1949): 1338.

brew language, Jewish history, Israeli geography, Jewish friendship, valor, mutual responsibility, habits of culture, and even hygiene.[10] In addition, Ben-Gurion promised that conscripts would shed the traditional "fault of Jewish individualism" and instead adopt a healthy disciplined character.[11] To achieve this goal, all draftees would serve their first year in the army in an agricultural settlement, thereby "blending the warrior with the settler."[12] In performing all of these functions, the new IDF would be the production line for a self-confident, heroic, and inspired "pioneering nation" endowed with a "combatant and creative" spirit.[13]

Naturally, Ben-Gurion argued, such a military melting pot had no place for segregated units. Members of the Mapam Party, the leading left-wing opposition party, attempted to defend their kibbutz-affiliated elite units, the Palmach. They argued that Ben-Gurion's new "barracks army" would inculcate idleness and careerism. They also denigrated the Military Jurisdiction Law, asserting that Ben-Gurion was enforcing a "Prussian mentality" and "dog's discipline" on the new draftees, and that the new military would therefore be "foreign" to "our own Jewish history."[14] In contrast, they highlighted the potential of the Palmach brigades, an exemplary Jewish force based on highly devoted volunteers, to serve as a model for the rest of the nation.[15]

Ben-Gurion was determined, however, to eliminate all partisan units, even those, such as the Palmach, that had demonstrated great valor during the War of Independence. He also asserted that, since the recently ended war had exhausted the country and people were yearning to return to normal life, it would be impossible to secure enough volunteers to fill the ranks of the new army.[16]

Only a handful of Knesset members dared criticize the idea of using the military as a melting pot. For example, Yosef Sapir, a member of the centrist General Zionist Party, argued that Israel needed to build the best

10. Israel, *Divrei Haknesset* 2 (September 5, 1949): 1567, 1571–1572.

11. Israel, *Divrei Haknesset* 2 (September 5, 1949): 1340.

12. Israel, *Divrei Haknesset* 2 (August 29, 1949): 1442. For similar statements, see Israel, *Divrei Haknesset* 2 (August 29, 1949): 1443; (August 30, 1949): 1448; (September 1, 1949): 1520–1521, 1527; (September 5, 1949): 1557, 1562; 3 (January 16, 1950): 533.

13. Israel, *Divrei Haknesset* 2 (September 5, 1949): 1572.

14. Israel, *Divrei Haknesset* 2 (August 10, 1949): 1313, 1316, 1318–1319; (August 15, 1949): 1347, 1349–50.

15. See, for example, Israel Galili, "People's Army," address to a town meeting in Tel Aviv, 1948, pp. 8–9.

16. Israel, *Divrei Haknesset* 3 (January 16, 1950): 536.

army possible in a short time and that training for the so-called educational agriculture would waste precious military training time.[17] But Sapir stood almost alone.[18] Ben-Gurion's supporters used metaphors from ancient and modern Jewish history to generate excitement and political consensus for his nation-building vision of the new military.[19] Members of the Knesset enthusiastically received Ben-Gurion's bill as "the most daring law ever brought to the Knesset," and as "a new social experiment that has no historical precedent."[20] This "unprecedented historical experiment" was designed, of course, to blend together more than fifty-five different Jewish immigrant groups into one Jewish nation, not to include the Arab citizens of the new Jewish state, who would remain outside the boundaries of this military melting pot.

ISRAELI ARABS: THE MILITARY MELTING POT AND ETHNIC IDENTITY

Ben-Gurion's vision of the new nation-building military did not encompass Israeli Arabs, but focused exclusively on instilling Jewish values in Jewish draftees. Nonetheless, the universal-conscription bill, which included even women, had no special clauses exempting Israeli Arabs from compulsory military service.[21] In 1949, therefore, only a few months after the conclusion of the bloody 1948 war, Arab Knesset members sought to ensure that the state would not compel their young Arab constituents to serve against their brethren across the border in enemy countries.

Like the Singaporean Malays, Israeli Arabs have constituted about 15 percent of their country's population since 1948. And like Singaporean leaders, Israeli politicians were convinced they could not trust their Arab citizens with arms. In 1949, Itzhak Ben-Zvi, Israel's second president,

17. Israel, *Divrei Haknesset* 2 (August 29, 1949): 1441.

18. Several young religious Zionist soldiers developed a comprehensive program for a Jewish army whose sources lay in the Bible, not socialism. This vision never reached the Knesset's debates. See Rabbi Amital, "To the Path of the Religious Soldier during the Independence War," *Moreshet: The Journal of Battalion 79's Synagogue*, 1949; reprinted in Yehuda Amital, *Hamalot M'maamakim* (Jerusalem: Society of Yeshivat Har Etzion, 1986), pp. 96–107.

19. See, for example, Israel, *Divrei Haknesset* 2 (September 5, 1949): 1519, 1552.

20. Israel, *Divrei Haknesset* 2 (August 29, 1949): 1442; (September 1, 1949): 1526; (September 5, 1949): 1551, 1563; (September 8, 1949): 1619.

21. Israel was the first—and is, so far, the only—country in modern history to conscript women during peacetime.

argued that Arab citizens were a fifth column within the state's ranks: "The real intention of the Arab countries is fairly obvious: they want to introduce a Trojan horse into the enemy's camp. . . . When the Arab governments will find the right time to attack Israel, they will have an immediate and readily available fifth column, playing the same role as the Sudets did in Czechoslovakia, aiding the Nazis."[22] Accordingly, after the 1948 war, the government placed all the Arab villages in its territory under military rule. Arabs were given the vote, and a few Arabs have even served in the Knesset and as deputy ministers in the government, but since 1948 Arabs have been second-class citizens. To this day, Arab citizens continue to point out the tension between the collective Jewish nature of the state and the promise of the Israeli Declaration of Independence to treat all citizens equally, regardless of racial, gender, and religious differences. To complicate things even further, Arab countries and Arab organizations have claimed guardianship of Israel's Arab community.

In 1949, therefore, Arab Knesset members faced a difficult dilemma. On the one hand, they wished to present themselves to the larger Israeli public as loyal citizens in order to be treated as equals by the state. After all, several Arab leaders argued, surely the military could not continue to rule Arab villages if Arab youth joined its ranks. On the other hand, the Arabs did not wish to serve in a military whose declared enemies were their kin across the border.

Israeli Arab leaders therefore were forced to walk a thin line. They applauded the new conscription bill, but requested "temporary exemptions" from military service for Arab citizens until the problem of Arab refugees was settled. One Arab Knesset member requested that the government defer call-up notices for Arab youth by five years. This period, he explained, would serve as a "transition period," during which stability and calm would be restored among Israeli Arabs and their feelings of alienation and discrimination, together with problems of Arab unemployment, would be eliminated.[23] Only the Communist Knesset members demanded the conscription of both Arab men and women alongside their Jewish peers.[24] The government heeded the plea of the non-

22. Quoted in Uzi Benziman and Atallah Mansour, *Subtenants: Israeli Arabs, Their Status, and the Policy toward Them* (in Hebrew) (Jerusalem: Keter Publishing House, 1991): 19.

23. Israel, *Divrei Haknesset* 2 (September 1, 1949): 1525, 1529.

24. Israel, *Divrei Haknesset* 2 (September 1, 1949): 1531; 3 (January 16, 1950): 525, 534.

Communist Arab members: annual deferments have been granted to Muslim and Christian Arab citizens since 1949.

Not all Israeli Arab leaders, however, wished their groups to be exempted from military service. Their community has been traditionally divided among five subethnic groups: Muslims, Christians, Bedouins, Druze, and Circassians. Druze, Bedouin, and Circassian citizens had already served in the IDF during the 1948 war. Leaders of these three Arab groups supported initiatives to recruit their youth, but were concerned about the effects of this military melting pot on them. Druze leaders, in particular, felt trapped. The desire to be part of the new nation and its military clashed with their fears that such cooperation would ultimately result in the complete assimilation of young Druze and the loss of their group's collective identity.

Similarly, Jewish religious Knesset members feared that their youth would abandon their religious lifestyle under the pressure of such a melting pot. Zerach Warhaftig, a representative of the Religious Front Party, warned the Knesset against Ben-Gurion's attempts to cast off Jewish history and create a new pioneering spirit in the army. Pioneerism, he argued, should not imply the destruction of the Jewish tradition; the ancient ought not be sacrificed for the sake of the modern. He rejected the vision of the new military as a national school, and pleaded with Ben-Gurion to entrust the issues of education and national values to the hands of professional educators and teachers.[25] And M. Onna, another religious Knesset member, warned that Israel should not repeat the mistakes of the "American melting pot": ancient identities ought not be destroyed in order to build a new and questionable identity that people might resent.[26] Since Ben-Gurion's political power in 1949 was overwhelming, some religious Knesset members decided to appeal to him by using his language rather than their own. Rabbi Kalman Khana tried in vain to exploit Ben-Gurion's own allegorical language. "Pioneerism" in

25. Israel, *Divrei Haknesset* 2 (September 5, 1949): 1558–1559. Unlike Warhaftig, other religious Knesset members joined the initial euphoria surrounding the nation-building conscription bill, but they were quickly disillusioned. See the supportive speeches of religious Knesset members in the first debate (1949): Israel, *Divrei Haknesset* 2 (September 1, 1949): 1522 (Onna); 2 (September 5, 1949): 1561 (Pinkas); 2 (September 1, 1949): 1523–1524 (Shag). In comparison, see the disillusioned speeches of religious Knesset members during the debate over the law's first amendment in 1950: Israel, *Divrei Haknesset* 3 (January 16, 1950): 525–526 (Khana); 3 (January 16, 1950): 428 (Norok).

26. Israel, *Divrei Haknesset* 2 (September 1, 1949): 1523.

the new military, he argued, should refer not only to its designated agriculture meaning but also to the "spiritual life" of the Jewish soldier.[27]

The unusual coalition between Jewish religious and Arab Knesset members against Ben-Gurion's demand to conscript women between 1949 and 1955 provides an additional example of the dilemma ethnic leaders face when asked to support a nation-building military. Jewish religious members were concerned that the modesty of Jewish women, particularly religious Jewish women, would be violated in the new secular military. Arab Knesset members were equally worried that the military would shake the very foundations of the traditional Arab village by conscripting Arab women who were—and still remain—restricted to their customary roles in the house. Thus, in a most unusual temporary coalition, Arab Knesset members joined forces with Jewish religious members to protest against Ben-Gurion's efforts to conscript women. Ben-Gurion agreed to let Arab women off the hook, but he was adamant in his decision to conscript Jewish women.

In pursuit of his conscription plans, Ben-Gurion cleverly placed religious Jewish Knesset members on the horns of the following dilemma. On the one hand, religious Knesset members resisted his idea of conscripting women. On the other hand, many among the religious leaders expressed support for some educational features of Ben-Gurion's vision of the new military, especially Hebrew instruction for new conscripts. Thus, when the religious Knesset members raised a demand that women receive exemptions from compulsory military service, Ben-Gurion asked them why they were willing to allow men to learn Hebrew in the military but sought to deprive women of the same experience.[28] His question remained unanswered, but it serves as a powerful illustration of the predicament ethnic leaders may face when required to support the military recruitment of their youth: reconciling the traditions of their groups with the military melting pot. Put differently, how can ethnic leaders secure the continuity of their groups if their youth are to be "melted" with other youth in the military and inspired to adopt a new, secular, and modern identity?

Occasionally, this dilemma becomes even more painful when ethnic leaders simultaneously negotiate other issues with the government, in

27. Israel, *Divrei Haknesset* 2 (August 29, 1949): 1445.
28. Israel, *Divrei Haknesset* 2 (September 5, 1949): 1569–71.

addition to that of military service.[29] For example, in 1949 the fragmented and weak Israeli Arab community had to negotiate with the Jewish state a host of important issues, such as the status of their religious courts, and the return of Arabs who fled the state during the 1948 war and wished to return to their families. A decision to resist cooperation with the state concerning military service nowadays amounts to a declaration of war on the state, and thus precludes progress on other issues. (Ben-Gurion often emphasized that the military service obligation should precede all discussions of political rights and social benefits.)[30] Thus, some form of negotiation and compromise appears necessary.

Only a few Israeli Arab groups—Druze, Bedouins, and Circassians—have found the golden mean between resistance and submission, between ethnic identity and the military's melting pot. These groups chiefly owe their success to a phased-integration policy allowing for their gradual recruitment and increased integration into a military organization primarily staffed by servicemen from the dominant Jewish ethnic group. Most of this chapter is devoted to the fascinating history of phased Druze integration into the IDF. But before we turn to this history, I will discuss briefly three other policy choices: immediate egalitarianism, collective exemption, and a separate ethnic civil service. As the following section shows, Israel has tried these policies at various times since 1948. In all cases, these attempts have failed.

Immediate Egalitarianism, Ethnic Civil Service and Exemption

In countries where the Trojan horse dilemma endures for many years, statesmen suspect the loyalty of ethnic youth, and ethnic leaders suspect the intentions of statesmen toward their youth. Thus, the idea of a color-blind recruitment policy is unlikely ever to materialize. Demands for the conscription of all Israeli Arabs were heard after the 1948 war, but Arab citizens and all Israeli governments nonetheless resigned themselves to the fact that an immediate, full, and egalitarian draft call for the state's

29. In 1949 and 1950, the Religious Front Party negotiated with Ben-Gurion a law guaranteeing the Orthodox rabbis in Israel absolute monopoly over personal-status matters. A strong objection to Ben-Gurion's conscription bill, therefore, might have cost the Religious Front Party Ben-Gurion's support on an equally vital issue. Interview with Dr. Zerah Warhaftig, former minister of religious affairs, Bar-Ilan University, Israel, December 19, 1991.

30. See, for example, Israel, *Divrei Haknesset* 3 (January 16, 1950): 537.

largest ethnic group was not a viable option. The grim fates of several plans to conscript Israeli Arabs can shed light on why naive recruitment attempts must fail in a maze of mutual hostility, suspicion, and distrust.

During the 1948 war, an Israeli official had already proposed an unrealistic plan to recruit all Israeli Arabs immediately. This anonymous official from the Ministry of Minority Affairs suggested that young Israeli Arabs be recruited into the army in order to strengthen their commitment to the new state and improve their image among the Jewish majority. His proposal offered potential Arab conscripts the option of serving far from the front. The official went to great pains to remind his readers that Arab volunteers currently were serving in the Israeli Defence Forces and fighting on the Jewish side in the war. But the Ministry of Minority Affairs was an unusually progressive institution in a country born in a long and bloody war with its Arab neighbors. When, therefore, the ministry was closed down nine months after its creation, and its responsibilities were assigned to other ministries, this proposal was buried in the state's archives.[31]

During the 1949–1950 parliamentary debate over the first draft bill, members of the Communist Party called again for the immediate and equal recruitment of Israeli Arabs. One member even proposed that conscripting Arab men and women would fight enslavement and tradition within the Israeli Arab community.[32] But this idea was unpopular, even among the Communist Party's Arab voters, and the Communists in the Knesset later reversed their demand, from total conscription to full exemption for Israeli Arabs. During the 1949–1950 parliamentary debates over conscription, Arab Knesset members from more mainstream parties asked for a temporary exemption for their constituents until the problem of Arab refugees was resolved.[33] Ever since those exemptions were granted in 1950, the idea of immediate and egalitarian conscription for Israeli Arabs has not received serious attention or debate in the Israeli Parliament.[34]

The third plan to conscript all Israeli Arabs is the most interesting in the state's history. This long-forgotten episode exemplifies the problems

31. Elie Rekhess, "Initial Israeli Policy Guidelines towards the Arab Minority, 1948–1949," in *New Perspectives on Israeli History: The Early Years of the State*, ed. Laurence J. Silberstein (New York: New York University Press, 1991), pp. 112–119.

32. Israel, *Divrei Haknesset* 2 (September 1, 1949): 1531; 3 (January 16, 1950): 525, 534.

33. Israel, *Divrei Haknesset* 2 (September 1, 1949): 1525, 1529.

34. Benziman and Mansour, *Subtenants*, p. 117.

inherent in an immediate and equal draft call for members of distrusted ethnic groups. In July 1954, the Israeli Ministry of Defence decided to test for the first—and last—time the idea of calling Arab youth to the flag. Young Arab citizens, like their Jewish counterparts, received notices to register for the draft. In addition, Israeli diplomats were instructed to give equal treatment to expatriate Jewish and Arab citizens in matters concerning the fulfillment of their draft duty.[35]

At first, excitement on all sides was evident. The Hebrew newspapers reminded their readers that the Arab youth required to register had been only eleven to fourteen years of age during the 1948 war. Newspaper stories highlighted Arab volunteers who had served in the Israeli army since 1949.[36] Pinchas Lavon, the defence minister, declared that this registration was being done "in accordance with the decision to equalize the rights and duties of members of all groups in the state."[37] Left-wing Israeli newspapers reminded the government that if Arab citizens were to serve in the army, it was only fair to abolish the military government imposed on Arab villages after 1948. Young Israeli Arabs showed some initial excitement.[38]

Yet this goodwill on all sides did not last long, and was replaced by overwhelming suspicion and distrust of the state's real intentions. Though the potential new recruits appeared fairly enthusiastic about the prospect of joining the army, their parents distrusted the state's intentions. More mundane economic reasons also contributed to opposition to the draft. As conscripts, young Israeli Arabs would not have been able to provide subsistence to their families. Some analysts believed that the state was just "testing the loyalty of its Arab citizens"; others even argued that the registration campaign was nothing but a crude plan to intimidate Israeli Arabs and push them to leave the state in fear of conscription.[39] In addition, foreign Arab newspapers argued that Israel was planning to recruit Arabs and send them into "slave-labor segregated units only."[40] Whether these accusations were true or not, the whole

---

35. P. Leshem, "The Law of Defence Service, 1949 (Conscription: Drafting Minorities Holding Israeli Citizenship)," Foreign Ministry, Tel Aviv, December 12, 1954; R. Palphul, "Conscription of Israeli Minority Citizens Abroad," Foreign Ministry, Tel Aviv, January 2, 1955.

36. "Registration of Minorities to the IDF Begins," *Hador*, July 1954.

37. Benziman and Mansour, *Subtenants*, p. 117.

38. Benziman and Mansour, *Subtenants*, p. 117.

39. Benziman and Mansour, *Subtenants*, pp. 117–118.

40. Benziman and Mansour, *Subtenants*, p. 119.

event came to naught. There also were rumors that in 1955 Israel approached Archbishop Hakim in Beirut, requesting his support for the conscription of young Christian Arabs, and that Archbishop Hakim consulted the pope and declined the offer. The wall of distrust and mutual suspicion was too high for a direct approach. With few exceptions, Israeli Muslim and Christian citizens did not serve in the military until recently.

Israeli governments have resorted to two lines of argument to justify the historical exemption of most Arab citizens from military service. First, they argued that Israeli Arabs were "just waiting for another round" of warfare between Israel and its Arab neighbors and that the recruitment of Arabs thus would breach security. Second, they argued that it would be cruel, even inhuman, to force Israeli Arabs to fight their fellow Arabs on the other side of the border.

These two principal lines of argument—the danger and cruelty in forcing Israeli Arabs to serve in the military—were used by officials throughout the history of the state even when evidence suggested that neither was holding water. For example, the Sofer report of March 1987 reminded the government that Arabs were fighting other Arabs throughout the Middle East. Thus, the report argued, Israeli Arabs were perfectly capable of fighting other Arabs in the service of the state.[41] But such arguments had little effect on distrustful statesmen. Most statesmen have refused to adopt immediate and equal conscription for all in states experiencing the Trojan horse dilemma.

After the failure of the 1954 initiative, Israeli Muslim and Christian citizens were never again called to perform their military duty as prescribed by the law. Ben-Gurion decided to exempt collectively Muslim and Christian citizens from military service, and every minister of defence religiously adhered to this policy until 1989. Hayyim Israeli, who has served as a personal assistant to every Israeli minister of defence since 1949, argued that Israel's top defense officials shared a consensus that its Muslim citizens were simply too unreliable to be enlisted.[42] Several IDF officers who served in key manpower positions during the 1950s recalled that the General Staff debated the issue of Muslim and Christian enlistment on a few occasions. According to these officers, however, most of the IDF's senior officers questioned the loyalty of Muslim and Chris-

41. Benziman and Mansour, *Subtenants*, p. 121

42. Interview with Hayyim Israeli, assistant to the minister of defence, Tel Aviv, August 6, 1992.

tian citizens and argued that allowing them in the military would amount to assisting a fifth column to penetrate its ranks.[43]

Formally, Muslim and Christian Arab citizens had the option of volunteering for military service. But the conditions for the acceptance of such volunteers were difficult to satisfy. To gain approval, Arab volunteers had to command the Hebrew language, complete at least ten years of schooling, have paternal approval, and be twenty-two years of age or less. They were also required to serve in field units because the IDF had enough conscripts and regulars staffing its headquarters.[44] Arab volunteers had to serve under conditions similar to those of their Jewish counterparts, including very meager pay; but this hit poor Arab families harder than the better-off Jewish families. Finally, Arab volunteers needed strong Jewish recommendations to support their applications.[45] Needless to say, none of the these requirements was ever applied to Jewish conscripts. On the contrary, Jewish citizens were drafted even when they were above twenty-two years of age, with minimal or sometimes no educational background, and, during the state's first decade, with minimal or no command of the Hebrew language. Jewish youth also did not need recommendations and were not required to make advance commitments to serve in frontal units.

Throughout its history, the IDF remained loyal to Ben-Gurion's vision of serving as a melting pot for Jews only. Arabs who wished to become more involved in Jewish society through service in the army were rejected. Colonel Moshe Ya'ari, a former overseer of the draft in the IDF Manpower Division, reversed Ben-Gurion's demand that the army serve as a melting pot for new draftees. Explaining the criteria for the recruitment of Arab volunteers into the IDF, Ya'ari said, "We won't take someone who wants or needs a new identity in order to serve in the army."[46]

---

43. Interview with Col. Yehuda Nitzan (Ret.), former head, Personnel Department, IDF, Tel Aviv, August 14, 1992; interview with Lt. Gen. Zvi Zur, former chief of staff, IDF, Tel Aviv, August 6, 1992; interview with Lt. Col. (Ret.) Shevach Lerner, former head, Manpower Division, IDF, Afeka, August 16, 1992; interview with Dr. Nathanael Lorch, historian, Jerusalem, August 20, 1992.

44. Jack Katzenell, "Minorities in the IDF," *IDF Journal* 4, no. 3 (Fall 1987): 45; Huggi, "Arab Soldiers in the IDF," *Ba'mahane*, October 21, 1987, p. 17.

45. The second Arab Christian officer in the IDF, for instance, came from a family with close friendship ties to Ezer Weizman, a former air force commander and defence minister; Arye Kyzel, "The Recruitment Officer Asked Where I Wish to Serve. I Said: Only in Golani," *Yediot Aharonot*, October 6, 1991.

46. Katzenell, "Minorities in the IDF," p. 17.

In light of such conditions, the number of Muslim or Christian volunteers during the first four decades of the state was close to nil. A former senior officer in the IDF Manpower Division asserted that the IDF approved around thirty Muslim and Christian volunteers for enlistment annually throughout the 1950s.[47] But the actual number of enlisted Muslim and Christian volunteers was probably even smaller.[48] For all practical purposes, Muslim and Christian youth remained virtually excluded from IDF service until 1989.

As with the Singaporean Malays, closing the Israeli armed forces to Muslim and Christian youngsters resulted in deep alienation between the state and its principal ethnic minority group. Since 1954, the division between the Jewish citizens who have served in the military and Arab citizens who have not has grown in importance. On the one hand, members of the Jewish majority increasingly identified good citizenship with military service, and therefore became increasingly hostile toward ethnic groups that did not serve in the military. On the other hand, the Arab minority developed comprehensive ideological systems to justify their exemptions, such as the demand that Israel establish full peace with its Arab neighbors before young Israeli Arabs were called to the flag. A vicious ideological cycle evolved. As more emphasis was put on military service as a precondition for full citizenship, the anti-state ideologies of groups that did not serve became more comprehensive and nonnegotiable. Proposals to Israeli Muslim citizens such as, "Do not serve, and accept residency status rather than citizenship," are examples of this vicious ideological cycle, not sincere solutions for its resolution.[49] Instead of serving as the nation builder, military service turned into the great nation divider between citizen-soldiers and citizen-civilians.

A handful of Israeli politicians raised the idea of allowing Israeli Arab citizens to serve the state in nonmilitary functions. If members of a distrusted ethnic group cannot be fully trusted with arms and if total exemption is socially undesirable, they argued, why not open a special channel, such as a civil national service, through which ethnic citizens could contribute to society and demonstrate their loyalty to the state? A

---

47. Interview with Col. Yehuda Nitzan (Ret.).

48. Lt. Gen. Refael Eitan (Raful), the chief of staff of the IDF between 1978 and 1983, claimed that he personally approved only four to five Arab recruits annually, on the basis of recommendations evaluating the volunteer, his family, and their ties to the state; Huggi, "Arab Soldiers in the IDF," p. 16.

49. Ariel Sharon, a former minister of defence, proposed this idea on October 22, 1992.

system allowing Israeli Arabs to perform their duty of national service in the police, fire brigade, and civil-defense units or in hospitals and schools, these politicians maintained, could satisfy the security concerns of the political leadership while promoting the image of Israeli Arabs, and later facilitating their the integration into the state.

Plans for separate civil national service for Israeli Arabs never materialized, however. Too many politicians used this idea to threaten Arab citizens rather than as a genuine mechanism for integration. Unscrupulous Israeli politicians have proposed Arab civil national-service programs in the aftermath of conflicts between Israeli Arabs and the state—for example, after Land Day (1976), when Israeli Arabs engaged the authorities in a bloody struggle over land expropriation in the Galilee, and, under the right-wing Likud government, after the Intifada broke out in December 1987. The timing of these proposals and the political stands of their authors naturally have led Israeli Arab leaders to distrust the very idea of nonmilitary national service for their youth. Politicians proposing such plans frequently have ignored the demands of Israeli Arab leaders to participate in the decision-making process. Even today, Israeli Arabs regard the idea of civil national service as nothing but a trick to test their loyalty or, even worse, to enslave them without the provision of equal status and rights.[50]

Every other plan for nonmilitary national service for Israeli Arabs also has failed, for other reasons. The proposal for a separate ethnic national service for Arabs citizens contradicted the legal principle of equality pledged in the Israeli Declaration of Independence. Moreover, even if this legal barrier had been overcome, Israeli leaders feared that instituting an Arab civil service would raise Israeli Arabs' level of expectations for state benefits and equal rights, ultimately resulting in increased social tensions. One Druze leader maintained that, for precisely such reasons, Ben-Gurion deferred judgment for a long time before accepting the Druze leaders' 1955 request to conscript their youth. Ben-Gurion was worried that media reports of Druze conscripts defending their country would contrast starkly with their slim prospects of gaining employment in the Jewish sector after discharge.[51]

Like Ben-Gurion, Moshe Arens, Israel's minister of defence (1988–

---

50. *Ha'aretz*, December 12, 1990.

51. Interview with Kammal Manssur, special advisor to the Israeli president on minority affairs, Osfya, December 18, 1991.

1992), was very concerned that large military intakes of Arab youth would lead to growing frustrations among the ranks of discharged and unemployed Arab soldiers. He therefore shrewdly chose to speak of "duties first, then rights" when addressing Jewish audiences, and of "rights first, then duties" when discussing the prospects for enlisting more Arab youth.[52] Similarly, in South Africa, Botha in 1982 argued that whites could not expect coloreds to do military service as long as coloreds did not have a say in the government.[53]

All plans to establish a separate Arab civil service however, have failed mainly because of the fear that it would develop a life of its own and eventually turn against the state. Proposals for an Arab "self-help" organization (in which Arab national servicemen would work in Arab villages, hospitals, and schools) were interpreted as signs that the state had failed or, worse, did not wish to serve the needs of its minority population.[54] Thus, Israeli politicians feared that the existence of such an organization sponsored by the state would intensify calls for social autonomy among Israel Arabs and contribute to political irredentism. In Israel, as in all other ethnically divided states, politicians refused to help their minority groups attain self-sufficiency.

It is important to note that even if such a self-help organization existed, it was not likely to change the general social climate regarding the Arab minority in Israel. Since the Israeli public refused to accept the idea that civil national service was a "fair substitute" for military service, it rebuffed ideas of Arab national service time and again as an insufficient contribution to society or an unreliable test of loyalty.[55] The conscription of limited numbers of Malay national servicemen into the fire brigade or civil defense in the mid-1970s likewise did little to alleviate the frustration of the Malay community, for the public in Singapore, as in Israel,

52. Katzenell, "Minorities in the IDF," p. 45.

53. *Cape Times*, March 26, 1982.

54. Binyamin Gur-Arye, a former advisor on minority affairs to the Israeli prime minister, argued that the formation of state-sponsored Arab ethnic service would amount to supporting the demand for Israeli Arabs' autonomy. See Benziman and Mansour, *Subtenants*, p. 120.

55. Recent plans for an Arab civil national service suggest that in the long run such a program will become part of a larger scheme in which Jews and Arabs are given an equal choice to serve in either the military or the civilian plan. See Shlomo Ginosar, "The Katz Plan," *Davar*, February 9, 1989. Alternatively, one scholar suggested integrating a plan for an Arab civil national service into a scheme of gradual recruitment to the IDF. See Yoav Gelber, "Palestinians Deluxe," *Ha'aretz*, September 14, 1990. This idea is close in spirit to my argument for phased recruitment.

held that civil national service was too lenient a way to serve the state, compared with the willingness to sacrifice one's life required by military service.

In societies where members of the majority serve in the military and some members of the ethnic minority serve in hospitals and schools, the social divisions are redrawn among those who fully serve their country

in the military, those who "half-heartedly" serve their country as civil servicemen, and those who do not serve at all. The society then is redivided into first-, second-, and third-class citizens, rather than first- and second-class citizens. There are no good alternatives to military service in countries that have conscript citizens and expect them to sacrifice their lives in defense of the state.

PHASED INTEGRATION: DRUZE SOLDIERS IN THE IDF

Phased integration is a military manpower policy that delineates special conditions under which ethnic soldiers will be recruited, trained and deployed. This policy can include introductory measures, such as voluntary service within a conscript-based military, segregated units, and limited promotional avenues. Phased integration serves as a measure to build confidence between the state and an ethnic group, and should gradually lead to greater inclusion of ethnic soldiers within the armed forces. This policy should be abandoned eventually (usually after one generation, or twenty years) in favor of equal treatment of ethnic soldiers. Israel successfully applied phased integration to Druze citizens in the IDF.

The vast majority of the 91,700 Israeli Druze citizens reside in the Galilee district (the northern part of the state).[56] The Druze population is rural, secular, poor, underdeveloped, and undereducated compared to the Jewish majority. The Druze speak Arabic among themselves, though today many are bilingual, speaking both Hebrew and Arabic.[57] Dispersed throughout the Middle East, the Druze are loyal to the different states

56. Israel, Central Bureau of Statistics, *Statistical Abstract of Israel, 1995* (Jerusalem: Central Bureau of Statistics, 1995), p. 43.

57. See Gabriel Ben-Dor, *The Druze in Israel: A Political Study* (Jerusalem: Magnes Press, 1979), p. 9.

where they reside. Thus, for example, Druze officers serve in high-ranking positions in the Syrian armed forces.[58]

Although historians concur that Jews and Druze had been natural allies since Israel was founded, absorbing Israeli Druze youth into the IDF was not a guaranteed success.[59] Newly released documents suggest that conflict dominated the relationship between the state and its Druze community in the first few years. One enemy Druze battalion from Syria and Lebanon fought with the army of Fawzi Kaukji against Israel, although it retreated soon after its failure in the battles of Ramat Yohanan (April 12–17, 1948). In the worst incident between Druze and Jews during the 1948 war, the people of Jat and Yanuh, two Druze villages occupied by Kaukji's army, betrayed their oral promise to cooperate with the Jews, and slaughtered a mixed Druze-Jewish IDF unit that was approaching their villages (October 28, 1948).[60] After the war, Israel imposed military rule over its Arab and Druze villages. Like other Arab villagers, Druze needed special permits to travel within Israel. Thus, the conditions for developing a full-fledged Trojan horse syndrome involving the Jewish state and its Druze minority were present from the outset. But the Druze differed from other Israeli Arab communities in one crucial aspect: some Druze soldiers had served in the IDF during and after the War of Independence.

Between April and June of 1948, the IDF, desperate for manpower, began recruiting minority volunteers. As the war in the northern part of Israel raged on, influential Druze sheikhs either cooperated with Kaukji's army or remained neutral. In July 1948, Yigal Yadin, IDF chief of staff, assigned Tuvia Lishanski to command the first Minority Unit. This company, originally composed of three distinct ethnic platoons (Druze, Circassian, and Bedouin), swore allegiance to the IDF on October 10, 1948. The unit participated in Operation Hiram (October 29–31, 1948), in which the IDF liberated Galilee from Kaukji's army. To avoid ethnic strife during this operation, the IDF deployed Druze soldiers in Druze villages

58. Donald Horowitz, *Ethnic Groups in Conflict* (Berkeley: University of California Press, 1985).

59. See, for example, David Coren, *Steadfast Alliance: The Druse Community in Palestine and the "Hagana"* (Tel Aviv: Ministry of Defence, 1991). Unsubstantiated descriptions—such as "Traditionally the persecuted victims of Moslem Arabs, the Druze accepted their new Israeli rulers with gratitude and assurances of ironclad loyalty"—can be found in many history textbooks on the early days of the Jewish state. See Howard Sachar, *A History of Israel: From the Rise of Zionism to Our Time* (New York: Alfred A. Knopf, 1979), p. 532.

60. Coren, *Steadfast Alliance*, pp. 51–59, 70–74.

and Circassian soldiers in Circassian villages. On December 6, 1948, a second batch of Druze volunteers swore allegiance to the army.[61]

With attitudes similar to those of South African officials towards the first nonwhite soldiers (1963–1972), Israeli politicians and high-ranking IDF commanders questioned the allegiance of these newly recruited Arab soldiers. But in stark contrast to the high professional standards that characterized the South African military in 1963, the IDF was far from being a professional military institution at its inception. Indeed, between 1948 and 1954, it was much closer to being an underground guerrilla organization than a professional military institution. Ben-Gurion's dream of establishing an "army of farmers" was embedded in Israel's first Defence Service Act (1949), which required that, after some preliminary military training, each soldier devote his or her first twelve months to agricultural training. The NAHAL, a military unit, was established as the successor of the Palmach, the underground organization that played a heroic role during the struggle for independence. The NAHAL quickly adopted the principal virtues and vices of its predecessor. Charged with high morale, motivation, and strong ideology, NAHAL soldiers were short on discipline. Every NAHAL private, for example, had the right to oppose an officer and dispute his orders. On one occasion, soldiers in one of the NAHAL's settlements refused their commanders' orders to remove pictures of Stalin they had posted in the barracks, arguing that in a democratic army soldiers were entitled to "freedom of expression."[62]

The massive waves of Jewish refugees that doubled the young state's population in five years (between 1949 and 1953) exacerbated the problem of building a professional military. Since most of the military's instruction manuals and technical literature were in Hebrew, a language many of the new immigrants did not command, the best soldiers were sent to support, logistics, and headquarters units. The ranks of the fighting units were swamped with so-called leftovers—soldiers who barely spoke the state's language and who lacked motivation and fighting spirit. In addition, the eclectic arsenal of weapons the IDF acquired before and during the 1948 war was far from suitable to meet its future challenge: a second round of warfare with several Arab countries.[63]

61. Coren, *Steadfast Alliance*, p. 67.

62. Ze'ev Schiff, *A History of the Israeli Army, 1874 to the Present* (London: Sidgwick & Jackson, 1987), pp. 58–63.

63. The IDF had only sixteen tanks, and the Arabs forty-five, during the 1948 war. In contrast, by the mid-1950s, Israel and the Arabs owned and operated about a thousand

The problem of acquiring a cadre of young, talented, and motivated men and training them to become professional officers was the toughest dilemma the IDF faced after the 1948 war. The IDF lost the best of its officers during the war, and many of the remaining officers left the military immediately after to pursue less demanding careers. Foreign Jewish officers who had volunteered to aid the IDF in 1948 returned to their home countries. A survey conducted immediately after the war revealed that only a tiny percentage of the IDF officer corps (about four hundred officers) had some kind of professional military training, and an even smaller number of officers had completed an officer course in either the British army or the Haganah (the largest Jewish underground military organization before establishment of the state). To make matters even worse, during the war thousands of officers were commissioned with no professional training. The military, therefore, launched a massive campaign to upgrade the professional standards of its officers. In the early 1950s, it opened thirty military schools with the goal of training a cadre of twenty-seven thousand officers within eighteen months. But it could not alleviate some of the root problems in such a short period. For instance, because only a tiny group of officer cadets spoke English, the military could not use advanced foreign military textbooks in its training courses. This was a grave problem because Israel's War of Independence was fought according to World War I textbooks. Bloody infantry clashes and personal weapons characterized this first Israeli-Arab war, not the tank divisions, blitzkrieg warfare, and air combat that were hallmarks of World War II. Lacking the linguistic skills to read the textbooks summarizing the lessons of World War II, new officers continued to prepare for the last war rather than the next one.

Commanded by poorly trained officers, Israel's "army of farmers and new immigrants" suffered great losses and humiliating defeats on the battlefield in its first years. During the six years following the 1948 war, the IDF failed time and again in reprisal actions against Arab infiltrators. IDF units that were sent to strike infiltration bases behind enemy lines often failed even to locate or reach their targets, and soldiers aborted missions prematurely, occasionally abandoning valuable equipment in enemy territory. In one shocking incident in May 1951, a large force of IDF soldiers failed to repel a small Syrian force that dug itself into a hill

---

tanks and five hundred combat airplanes. See Israel Tal, *National Security: The Few against the Many* (Tel-Aviv: Dvir, 1996), pp. 125–126. See also Sachar, *History of Israel*, p. 479.

inside Israeli territory. The Syrians were finally pushed back, but twenty-one Israeli soldiers were killed. On January 28, 1953, twelve riflemen from the Jordanian National Guard held down an entire Israeli battalion from the elite Givati Infantry Brigade. The Israeli battalion finally aborted its mission and withdrew. By the end of 1953, the Israeli Defence Staff concluded that almost half of its reprisal activities (forty-one of eighty-five) were "unqualified failures," with six other missions considered "partially successful" and the rest of the combat missions "successful." Indeed, IDF performance on the battlefield during its first five years was so abysmal that commanders preferred to send out small units on reprisal actions, hoping that the failure of only a few men would cause less psychological damage among the ranks.[64]

During this crucial period of IDF battlefield failures due to poor professional standards, Druze and Circassian soldiers did not have the level of professional military support that the first colored soldiers received from senior SADF commanders, and no "professional military shield" guarded the first Arab soldiers from xenophobic politicians fearing Trojan horses within the IDF. But the poor status of the infantry Minority Unit differed only slightly from that of the other Jewish infantry units.[65] In each of a series of crises that characterized its first years, between 1948 and 1954, the Minority Unit, lacking a "professional shield," came close to being disbanded. The only defense for this unit and its right to exist came from an unexpected source: its junior Jewish commanders.

This small group of officers took upon themselves the important role of ensuring that their minority soldiers remained in the IDF despite external political pressure to expel them. These officers also zealously protected the interests of their minority soldiers against greedy state institutions interested in confiscating the assets of their communities.[66] Among other things, the officers succeeded in securing food supplies, weapons licenses, and travel passes for their soldiers' villages. More important, the officers battled state bureaucrats to insure that their soldiers' lands would not be confiscated. On one occasion, a Jewish officer from

---

64. Schiff, *History of the Israeli Army*, pp. 54–55, 72–73.

65. Mordechai Makleff, the chief of staff of the IDF in the early 1950s, was frequently approached by Israeli officers who complained about the abysmal education, training, and motivation of their soldiers. Makleff used to answer that the average enemy Arab soldier was likely to be even more backward than the average Israeli soldier. See Schiff, *History of the Israeli Army*, p. 53.

66. Coren, *Steadfast Alliance*, p. 67.

the Minority Unit organized resistance in Kfar Kama, a Circassian village, against the State Guardian for Absentee Property, which intended
to survey property left behind by villagers who fled or were expelled
from the country during the war.[67] On another, military authorities decided to close down the Minority Unit after a serious incident of inter-
ethnic violence between Druze and Bedouin soldiers. Once again, the
Jewish officers of the unit saved the day and revived the unit.[68]

In April 1950, a new crisis evolved. Ben-Gurion ordered the reduction
of the IDF budget by one-third. Laskov, the new chief of staff, reorganized the army and ordered the dismantling of several units, including
the Minority Unit. Once again, present and former Jewish officers of the
Minority Unit convinced Ben-Gurion that the unit served an important
social goal that transcended its military utility. The unit was therefore
not abolished, even though IDF correspondence from the period clearly
indicates that its military value had decreased to an insignificant level.[69]
But its junior Jewish commanders, who succeeded in saving the unit,
lacked the power, authority, and influence to change its status.

In 1953, the Minority Unit faced yet another crisis, this time instigated
by the Druze community. At that time, the Minority Unit had four reserve companies: three Druze and one Circassian/Bedouin. It drew its
manpower from among soldiers discharged from a fifth full-time Druze
company in the Minority Unit. But since the meager pay kept all but a
handful of Druze soldiers from volunteering to serve in the IDF after the
1948 war, the unit continued to lose soldiers (because of age or medical
reasons), with no new reservists available to replace them. The remaining
Druze reservists in the unit believed that the burden of service was unfair. After all, they had served during the war, and, in "compensation,"
were called upon annually to perform their reserve duty, while other
Druze never served in the military. In addition, Amnon Yanai, the Jewish
commander of the Minority Unit, described another deterrent to attracting new reservists—the discrimination against his soldiers: "The soldiers
are permanently employed in the Negev [Israel's southern desert]. They
view this mission, and justly so, as discrimination in comparison to Jew-

67. "Circassian Absentee Property in Kfar Kama," March 30, 1949; "Confiscation of Absentee Property in Kfar Kama, Kinneret District," March 4, 1949; March 16, 1949; in Israeli
State Archives: Ministry of Minority Affairs, 302/91.

68. Interview with Kammal Manssur.

69. "A Proposal to Economize and Change the Standards of the Minority Battalion Headquarters," December 24, 1952, IDF Archives, 79/54/71.

ish units that serve only for short periods in the Negev and on a rotation basis. . . . The soldiers are bitter because they have to stand in line with other minorities to receive transport licenses."[70]

Yanai suggested several ways to alleviate his soldiers' frustrations.[71] To replenish his unit's ranks, he proposed that older Druze who had not served during the 1948 war be recruited for a short period of basic training and then join the reserves.[72] In June 1953, the IDF gave Yanai permission to proceed with his plan. Yanai's recruitment efforts faced immediate opposition from the Druze traditional leadership. Several of the prominent Druze sheikhs banned their clansmen from joining the military. Sheikh Salaman Tariff admitted, "Volunteering to serve in the IDF is a delicate political matter with great effect abroad. Thus, it requires careful calculation before accepting it."[73] Yanai concluded that Druze leaders were afraid they would appear to neighboring Arab countries as too enthusiastically allied with Israel. Only two hundred Druze volunteered to serve in mid-1953. They were mostly followers of Sheikh Salah Hanfies, a longtime ally of the Jews in Palestine.[74] This incident illustrates the limits of officer activism in the face of resistance from traditional community leadership.

In late 1953, after a series of humiliating battlefield failures, the IDF finally began an intensive campaign to upgrade its professional standards. In November 1953, Ben-Gurion appointed the young and energetic Moshe Dayan to command the military, and Dayan immediately began revamping the IDF. New weapon systems and training methods were introduced, and Unit 101 (predecessor of the Israeli paratroops corps) set new standards of performance on the battlefield. Dayan also ordered the assignment of the best recruits to fighting units instead of

70. "Report on the Condition of the Unit," January 9, 1953, IDF Archives, 79/54/71.

71. Yanai proposed equalizing the pay of Jewish and Druze soldiers, allowing Druze soldiers to use their military reserve cards as licenses for travel outside their villages, and discharging the Circassian/Bedouin reserve company because of the advanced age of its members and the tensions between the company's ethnic elements. The Circassian/Bedouin reserve company was dismissed in December 1953. See "The Reserve of the Minority Battalion: The Circassian and Haib Company," December 7, 1953, IDF Archives, 63/55/74.

72. "Report on the Condition of the Unit," January 9, 1953, IDF Archives, 79/54/71.

73. Amnon Yanai, "The Recruitment of Druze to the IDF," October 15, 1953, Israeli State Archives, file 130, 2402/28.

74. Yanai, "Recruitment of Druze to the IDF."

headquarters and logistics units. Most important, he decided to rejuvenate the military by compelling officers to retire at the age of forty. He then conditioned all promotions in rank on leadership on the battlefield, and restructured the IDF officer career path to compel officers to attend tough military training courses and to command field units. Dayan emphasized that the IDF needed constant movement up the chain of command to make way for a younger, bolder, and more innovative generation of officers, which in turn would introduce fresh ideas and elevate the combat performance of the military. By then, Ben-Gurion, who was still the most powerful politician in Israel despite his eighteen-month retreat from politics to the Negev Desert, had completely abandoned his original vision of an "army of farmers." He now enthusiastically supported Dayan's efforts to revamp the IDF and to turn it into a first-class fighting machine. The impact of this new professionalism on the Minority Unit was almost immediate.

Dayan and his reinvigorated General Staff scrutinized the professional standards of every IDF unit, including the Minority Unit. Zvi Zur, the head of the IDF Manpower Division in the mid-1950s and later the chief of staff, recalled several senior staff meetings convened to discuss the absorption of Druze soldiers.[75] The principal decision from these meetings was to bring the Minority Unit one step closer to equal status with similar Jewish units. The military established new schedules for military training, operational deployment, maneuvers, and vacation time in accordance with its decision to promote the unit's professional standards. The IDF obliged the unit to undergo periodic examinations of military preparedness, like Jewish units. In addition, it subjected the new minority battalion to the regional military command under which it operated, taking away from the Operations Department of the IDF its traditional direct command over the unit.

It is important to remember that, while the junior Jewish officers of the Minority Unit succeeded in ensuring its survival from 1948 to 1953, they did not have the power to convince the higher echelons of the military to upgrade its status. Only after the IDF was infused with a younger and more innovative generation of commanders did things begin to change for the unit. Dayan's efforts, beginning at the end of 1953, to upgrade the professional standards of the IDF encompassed all units,

75. Interview with Lt. Gen. Zvi Zur.

including the Minority Unit. Dayan himself embodied the power of a professional military mind over ethnic emotions. The young chief of staff lost his only brother, Zohar "Zorik" Dayan, during the IDF's bloody Ramat Yohanan battles against an enemy Druze unit in April 1948. Despite his personal loss, he chose not to discriminate against the Minority Unit, even though it consisted mostly of Druze men, some of whom had fought against the IDF in the Ramat Yohanan battles.[76] Still, even after the Minority Unit was promoted to a regular military unit in 1954, the distrust gap remained, exemplified by the IDF's decisions to maintain Jewish command of the unit, to allow Druze volunteers to serve only in this one unit, and to assign the unit border-guard duties along Israel's southern border, far away from its home villages in northern Israel.[77]

DRUZE CONSCRIPTION

In 1955, the groundwork was laid for the next step in closing the distrust gap: conscription. By then, the traditional Druze leadership had become convinced that the Jewish state was there to stay. One prominent leader explained their historic decision to become the first Israeli Arab ethnic group to accept conscription: "We joined the IDF because the IDF was the nation. The nation was the state, and we wanted to be part of the state."[78] For their part, senior IDF officers described the decision to conscript Druze youth as the culmination of a growing mutual trust between the military and the Druze community. One officer said, "We knew that they [Druze] were loyal, but there was a siege atmosphere in the state and we needed time to allay our fears."[79] Another officer noted that the voluntary recruitment of Druze youth from 1949 to 1955 had been crucial in combating and overcoming "inertia and psychological

76. Coren, *Steadfast Alliance*, p. 56.

77. "The Headquarters of the Minority Battalion," January 25, 1954; "An Exhibition of Company 300," January 27, 1954, IDF Archives, 63/55/74. See also "A Proposition for the Structure and Standards of a Minority Battalion," April 15, 1954; "An Invitation to the Exhibition of the Minority Unit," May 2, 1954; "A Proposal for Discussion Concerning the Subjection of the Minority Battalion and Company 300," July 19, 1954; "Subjection of Battalion 300," August 22, 1954; September 3, 1954; "An Examination of the Preparedness of Company 300," October 17, 1954, in IDF Archives, 8/56/79.

78. Interview with Amal Nassar A-Din, former Knesset member, Dalyat El-Kermel, December 18, 1991.

79. Interview with Lt. Gen. Zvi Zur.

5. IDF Circassian soldiers darken their face for night maneuvers, 1958. From the first, the IDF provided standard infantry equipment to members of the Minority Unit. Photo by *Ba'mahane*, the IDF journal, courtesy of the IDF Archives, Tel Aviv

barriers."[80] A third officer described the decision to conscript Druze as a "process that grew naturally."[81]

In the ongoing negotiations between politicians, officers, and ethnic leaders, the advent of conscription is the time for ethnic leaders to negotiate exemptions. For example, ethnic leaders often demand exemptions from military service for their women and religious youth before they grant their support for conscription. A failure to settle the issue of group exemptions in advance will result in bitter struggles between the state and the community over individual exemptions. This point is demonstrated by comparing Israeli Druze leaders' failure to secure such exemptions in advance with the Jewish Orthodox leaders' success in obtaining extensive military exemptions for members of their group dur-

80. Interview with Gen. (Res.) Refael Vardi, former head, Manpower Division, Tzahala, August 13, 1992.

81. Interview with Col. Yehuda Nitzan (Ret.).

6. Soldier from the Minority Unit with "infiltrators," February 1958. In its first decade the unit was stationed in the southern Negev desert, where grazing is rare. Photo by *Ba'mahane*, the IDF journal, courtesy of the IDF Archives, Tel Aviv

ing negotiations with Ben-Gurion over the first conscription bill and its immediate amendments (1949–1954).

For decades the Druze community suffered the consequences of its leaders' failure to secure such exemptions in advance. Ben-Gurion first presented his initiative to conscript Druze youth in informal discussions with Jaber Ma'adi and Saleh Hanfies, two Druze Knesset members in his Mapai Party. Ma'adi and Hanfies then communicated the idea to other Druze leaders. In 1955, a group of sixteen sheikhs publicly endorsed the new plan without attaching any conditions. They did not even negotiate with the state on whether, and how, to exempt religious Druze students from military service. The first Druze conscripts were inducted in 1956.[82]

A year after the first induction, young Druze men demonstrated in

82. Interview with Amal Nassar A-Din; interview with Kammal Manssur.

7. Desert navigation, February 1958. After 1954 the IDF intensified its efforts to upgrade the Minority Unit. Navigation became one of the most important skills that soldiers had to master. Photo by *Ba'mahane*, the IDF journal, courtesy of the IDF Archives, Tel Aviv

Haifa, demanding that the state exempt religious Druze from military service. In response, the government established a Druze committee to determine which religious Druze were eligible for exemption. In 1958, every Druze village established a committee to recommend which draft-eligible Druze should be exempted.[83] Sheikh Amin Tariff had the final word on all men recommended for exemption by the committees. Since then, the issue of military exemption on religious grounds has turned into the great battle zone between Druze political leaders who support conscription and Druze religious leaders who oppose it. Druze youth who resist the draft now can easily obtain an exemption from military service on religious grounds. Two years before their call-up day, they begin their studies in the *hilwaa* (the Druze place of prayer). When they reach eighteen years of age, the imam (religious leader) recommends to the spiritual leaders of the Druze community that these students be exempted from military service so they may continue their religious studies. The spiritual leaders usually provide the young men with an approval letter, and the IDF exempts them from military service. During the next five years, the religious students are required to submit letters to the IDF confirming that they are indeed pursuing religious studies;

83. Interview with Amal Nassar A-Din.

8. Druze soldiers of Minority Unit deployed in the southern Negev, far from their villages in the north, February 1958. Their mission was to patrol the desert and to stop infiltrators from crossing the Egypt-Israel border. Photo by *Ba'mahane*, the IDF journal, courtesy of the IDF Archives, Tel Aviv

the process is similar to that for Jewish yeshiva students.[84] Despite this seemingly rigorous procedure, few of these religious exemptees actually participate in religious studies after their exemption. Although Druze religious leaders are well aware of why many Druze males discover their religious roots two years before their call-up dates, the leaders support these young men because they themselves object to the draft.[85]

There are no agreed-upon figures for how many Druze have chosen to evade the draft on religious grounds since the IDF began conscripting Druze youth in 1956. The IDF has a stake in maintaining that the numbers are marginal and insignificant, while Druze leaders opposed to the draft insist that the numbers are much higher. Recently, the IDF claimed that only 3 percent of eighteen-year-old Druze men evade the draft, similar to the percentage of draft-eligible Jewish men. In contrast, a Druze journalist who studied Druze draft evasion estimated that 18–20 percent

84. Gabi Zohar, "One Sided Alliance," *Ha'aretz*, October 21, 1991.
85. Interview with Mohammed Naffa, Knesset member, Jerusalem, January 1, 1992.

resist the draft, and that in 1988 a record high 42 percent evaded their call-ups.[86] The issue of draft evasion on religious grounds has marred the relationship between the IDF and the Druze community. Young Druze leaders who took over leadership positions within their community during the 1970s condemned the 1955 failure of Druze sheikhs to resolve the issue of religious exemption at a time when Ben-Gurion genuinely sought their support for conscripting their youth.[87]

There may be several explanations for why the Druze leaders did not settle the issue of draft exemptions before accepting Ben-Gurion's initiative. Some argue that in 1955 the Druze leaders were not yet accustomed to the political-bargaining rules of the new democratic regime. Others argue that the Druze Knesset members feared losing their next election, and hoped to win back the confidence of party bosses through unconditional submission to the state's conscription demands.[88] Finally, a few Druze leaders opposed to conscription argue that the sixteen sheikhs sought to enhance their own prestige and status at the expense of their community.[89]

It is interesting that the few Druze leaders who have been opposed to conscription since 1955 have received almost no exposure in Israel for their views. They have enjoyed many opportunities to discuss their agenda with foreign correspondents, but such foreign news stories rarely reach Druze youth.[90] Ethnic leaders opposed to conscription have preferred to use the legal means of religious exemption to ensure that those who choose not to serve do not have to. Ironically, the IDF also is quite content with this solution. It has no use for poorly motivated soldiers, and since Druze religious exemptions do not attract media coverage, this arrangement satisfies everyone.

But not all choose the path of least resistance. Every year since 1954, a few dozen Druze have chosen to turn their refusal of service into a public campaign and to serve as an example for others, who will then follow in their footsteps. Such cases continue to pose a dilemma for the IDF. On the one hand, the military does not wish to punish Druze draft resisters too harshly because it would risk turning them into martyrs. On the other hand, light punishment could tempt other Druze to resist

86. Zohar, "One Sided Alliance."
87. Interview with Amal Nassar A-Din; interview with Kammal Manssur.
88. Interview with Kammal Manssur.
89. Interview with Mohammed Naffa.
90. Interview with Mohammed Naffa.

service. The IDF therefore continues to pursue a pragmatic policy in all such cases. Druze draft resisters usually serve several terms of up to a year in military jails before they are granted an exemption from military service.

The most effective strategy for ethnic leaders who choose resistance is the establishment of public institutions to support draft evasion. During the 1970s, for example, young Druze established the Druze Action Committee. This organization argued that Israeli Druze citizens were Arabs, and thus ought to receive exemptions like those enjoyed by other Israeli Arab communities (Muslims, Christians, and Bedouins). Located in Yarka, a Druze village in Galilee, the committee maintained close ties with the Israeli Communist Party, and focused most of its efforts on providing assistance to Druze draft resistors. It also attempted to convince the Israeli Druze community that their traditional leaders were wrong to support conscription in the mid-1950s, and that the community ought to decide the question of military service through a referendum.[91]

DRUZE SOLDIERS: FROM GUARDS TO FIRST-LINE COMBAT

After the idea of conscription was accepted with relatively little debate over exemptions or organized resistance, the only question remaining was whether to allocate Druze draftees to Jewish units or, alternatively, to continue channeling them into the Minority Unit. Both the Druze leaders and the IDF feared the social consequences of mixing the undereducated Druze draftees with Jewish soldiers. One Druze leader said, "We did not want our soldiers to become the servants of Jewish officers."[92] The Jewish commander of the Minority Unit explained his support for the segregated unit: "This human material [Druze soldiers] suffers from an inferiority complex and suspicion, and they would not be able to overcome these problems serving in one unit with Jewish soldiers. On the contrary, the Druze soldier will find and point out events in the unit's life as directed against him and as discrimination against him. This will result in social bitterness and decline of morale."

The concluding lines of this officer's letter confirmed that the distrust gap was still far from being closed: "It seems to me that for security

91. Interview with Mohammed Naffa.
92. Interview with Kammal Manssur.

reasons it is desirable to have separate units to improve their control."[93] The military continued to send Druze draftees to the Minority Unit between 1956 and 1972, but the existence of this unit, and its allegedly inferior service conditions, served as a rallying point for Druze leaders opposed to conscription. These leaders claimed, for instance, that between 1956 and 1968 the IDF assigned Druze draftees to do its "dirty work," with guard duty along Israel's southern desert border.[94] At the same time, however, the Minority Unit was also a highly visible symbol of the alliance between the Druze and the state. During the 1950s, Israeli politicians identified that unit with the Druze community. On one occasion, when Ben-Gurion sent an official apology to the Druze community, he addressed his letter to the Druze unit.[95]

Between 1956 and 1972, Druze sheikhs exercised strong influence over the segregated Druze unit. They wasted much energy and political capital lobbying IDF officers to promote one Druze officer at the expense of another, instead of pursuing more important military-integration issues. Clan and family membership was a consideration, though not the most important, when the IDF discussed military promotions. IDF officers sensitive to the political struggles among various Druze clans, for example, presented Druze leaders with lists of eligible candidates before making historic decisions about promoting the first Druze officers to the ranks of captain, major, and so on. On one occasion, the Druze sheikhs long debated over which Druze major should become the first IDF Druze lieutenant colonel. The problem was that the most prominent Druze officer was Saed Abdul Haq, who came from a small, humble Lebanese family. The traditional sheikhs preferred a choice from a more prominent family. Finally, one leader stated that they should give their blessing to promoting any Druze officer, because that would ensure that "the community as a whole is taking a step forward."[96] Saed Abdul Haq ultimately became the first IDF Druze lieutenant colonel, but the incident illustrates what ethnic leaders should avoid in negotiations with the military.

The contrast between the Druze sheikhs and South African colored leaders is illuminating. While the veteran colored leaders ceaselessly

---

93. "Druze in Mixed Units," February 22, 1955, IDF Archives, 8/56/79.
94. Interview with Mohammed Naffa.
95. Interview with Kammal Manssur.
96. Interview with Kammal Manssur.

worked to remove bottlenecks blocking the promotion of colored servicemen in the SADF, Druze sheikhs chose to bicker over which young
Druze was "noble enough" to become the first major or lieutenant colonel. The IDF and Israeli officials therefore could easily manipulate divisions among Druze leaders throughout the 1950s, letting Druze leaders
argue over lists of names instead of discussing principles and policies of
integration. From the military's viewpoint, there was always a sheikh,
or even several sheikhs, willing to sanction cooperation with the military.
The military thus was able to obtain just enough Druze servicemen without considering how their treatment would impact the willingness of
younger Druze to serve in the future.[97]

In 1960, Ben-Gurion formally reviewed the Druze Minority Unit and
recorded in his personal diary the unit's problems and his impressions.
The segregated battalion at that time included three hundred and twenty
soldiers (80 percent Druze, the rest Circassian and Christian), and had
five Druze officers (a captain and four first-lieutenants). Some old frustrations surfaced. Druze soldiers detested their guard duty in the south
and demanded operational duties like those of other IDF infantry battalions. Ben-Gurion also noted in his diary tensions between the very
young Jewish officers of the unit and their Druze soldiers, and that the
level of Hebrew fluency among Druze soldiers was poor. He ordered
the army to address the complaints of Druze soldiers, writing in the
diary, "We must firmly uproot all discrimination. We must allow every
Druze to progress like the Jew. Every Druze officer must serve in the
paratroops [the elite unit of the IDF at the time]."[98]

Despite Ben-Gurion's awareness of discrimination in the operational
duties of the unit, the Minority Unit was denied participation in the
battles of the 1956 and 1967 wars. During this period, the Druze became
increasingly vocal in their insistence on contributing to Israel's war efforts. In 1967, Druze leaders encouraged the disabled and exempted
members of their community to demonstrate in front of the Israeli Defence Ministry in order to convince the IDF to recruit them so they could
help in the war.[99] Neither the military nor the Druze leaders seriously
believed that several dozen Druze would make a difference in a war that

97. Interview with Kammal Manssur.
98. David Ben-Gurion, personal diary, August 25, 1960, and October 10, 1960; quoted in
*Studies in the Establishment of Israel: A Collection of Problems in Zionism, the Yishuv, and the
State of Israel* (in Hebrew) (Sede Boker: Ben-Gurion Center, 1992), pp. 452–454.
99. Interview with Kammal Manssur.

turned out to last only six days. Nonetheless, the Israeli press covered this demonstration, and thereby conveyed a simple and clear message of Druze loyalty to the state.

Although never publicly admitted by any Israeli official, one reason for keeping Druze soldiers off battlefronts was that the Druze community was vulnerable to suffering disaster in battle, since most of its sons were restricted to one unit. One Druze leader, Mohammed Naffa, has charged that such fears ultimately led the IDF to exempt the Minority Unit from fighting in the 1956 and 1967 wars: the loss of several dozen Druze soldiers in battle would fracture the delicate and special relationship between the Druze community and the state.[100]

Despite such fears, the moment of truth for the unit came between 1968 and 1970, when the IDF was combating the Palestine Liberation Organization's fierce infiltration attempts in the Jordan valley. The military called in the Minority Unit, and when Druze soldiers suffered many casualties,[101] the media and the larger Israeli public rediscovered and enthusiastically embraced the Israeli Druze community. The death of a Druze Knesset member's son in battle was turned into a national event.[102] Ben-Gurion's words in 1956 were quoted time and again: "The pact between the Druze people and the Jewish people is not written on a scrap of paper. It is sanctified by the blood of Druze fighters."[103] Druze leaders were quick to adopt this philosophy, and they turned the central Druze military cemetery in the village of Osfya into the focal point of the relationship between the Druze community and the state.[104]

The increasing Druze participation in combat duty brought new dilemmas for the Druze leaders. The fear that ethnic soldiers would be manipulated to serve a bad cause ran high, especially during wartime. During the Lebanon War, Israeli Druze citizens were dismayed to discover that the IDF took the side of Lebanese Christian villages against

100. Interview with Mohammed Naffa.

101. By March 1971, ninety-five Druze were killed in battle (sixty-four soldiers and thirty-one border police servicemen). See Ben-Dor, *Druze in Israel*, p. 132.

102. Major Sergeant Lutfi Naser A-Din, son of Amal Nassar A-Din, died on May 7, 1969, only a few hours before his discharge from the army, in pursuit of a terrorist squad in the Jordan Valley.

103. Katzenell, "Minorities in the IDF," p. 41.

104. Because the Druze believe in reincarnation, they do not bother to mark the burial grounds of their dead, so there are no signs indicating who is buried and where. The military cemetery in Osfya is immaculately kept, however, and granite headstones mark the graves of fallen Druze soldiers.

their neighboring Druze villages. Israeli Druze leaders feared that the IDF would make Druze soldiers launch a war against their kin in Lebanon. Druze established a small organization called the Druze Oversight Committee to supervise the IDF's activities in Lebanese Druze villages. Senior Druze leaders were likewise alarmed during the early stages of the Intifada (1987–1988), when the Israeli press published stories about Druze soldiers repressing Palestinian riots. One leader even accused the Israeli government of deliberately employing divide-and-rule tactics to separate the Druze and Palestinian people, and set one against the other.[105] The great Druze religious leader, Sheikh Amin Tariff, even called upon Druze soldiers to "fulfill your duty but to be human and not do anything that contradicts our tradition," after an official Palestinian complaint about the behavior of Druze soldiers in Palestinian villages.

Druze concerns also increased when Israel formally annexed the Golan Heights in 1981. Many among the local Druze community refused to serve in the IDF because their leaders feared that the Syrians would return one day to rule the Golan Heights and punish them. Israeli Muslim leaders have also noted on several occasions how Arab officials on the other side of the border closely monitor their statements about Druze youth serving in the IDF.[106]

DRUZE OFFICERS: BREAKING THE GLASS CEILING

Although they proved their loyalty on the battlefield in the face of these difficulties, the promised opportunities for Druze soldiers did not materialize quickly. During 1971 and 1972, their tensions and frustrations grew. The Minority Unit by then had grown into a reserve-based infantry brigade, but many Druze officers and soldiers began to opt out. Believing they had proven themselves beyond any doubt, they demanded full integration into all of the IDF corps and branches. Facing this pressure, the IDF began opening the doors step by step. In 1972, the pioneers who broke the old pattern of sending all Druze to the minority brigade belonged to the first class of Druze academics, who demanded and, after

105. Interview with Mohammed Naffa.
106. *Jerusalem Post*, January 11, 1992.

a struggle obtained, positions in the IDF in accordance with their skills and backgrounds.[107]

Young Druze officers then, in a two-step process, followed the example set by Druze academics. First, during the early 1970s, Druze officers took over senior command positions within the Minority Unit, a promotional process that accelerated during and immediately after the 1973 Yom Kippur War as the IDF tripled in size. The Minority Unit expanded significantly, and additional command positions became available for new Druze officers, including a lieutenant colonel who built the first regular Druze battalion during the 1973 war. Second, during the late 1970s, more Druze officers enrolled in advanced military courses. The military's School for Staff and Command admitted its first Druze officer in 1978, and Druze officers began to receive command positions over Jewish units after completing these courses. Today the highest-ranking Druze in the IDF is a brigadier general, and Druze regularly command Jewish brigades, divisions, and elite units.

During the 1970s, many of these young officers began to challenge the traditional authority of the sheikhs. One scholar who interviewed the first discharged Druze officers during the early 1970s commented, "The political potential of a generation of discharged officers of that stature is enormous."[108] These words were written when the highest-ranking Druze officer was a major and Druze officers were still confined to serve exclusively in the Minority Unit. Since the late 1970s, the group of discharged Druze officers has included several colonels who have commanded elite and regular Jewish units. Many have returned to their villages and assumed local political positions. These leaders were not willing to play by the rules of the old bargaining game. In 1978, Kamal Manssur noted that "the era of monologue with a small Druze group that had modest demands was over."[109]

During the 1980s, criticism of the traditional Druze leadership and its bargaining methods became even more explicit. One young Druze leader

---

107. The IDF recruits academics (students of law, engineering, medicine, and any other academic program useful to the military) through a special program called the Academic Reserve Force (Atuda Akademit). This program allows high school graduates to continue their studies in one of the state's universities, while their fellow classmates are drafted. After graduating from university, the participants in this program are conscripted into the IDF and serve an additional two years, usually as officers. In 1972 the IDF conscripted the first class of university graduate Druze soldiers.

108. Ben-Dor, *Druze in Israel*, p. 147.

109. *Ma'ariv*, August 18, 1978.

[161]

wrote, "The [traditional] Druze leaders who established the relationship with the Jewish people before the birth of the state and after did not have a sufficient understanding of a democratic regime like ours. Under such a regime, it is not enough to be a loyal citizen in order to get one's rights. One should fight and struggle, using every available democratic means to ensure that demands for such rights will be fulfilled. Objectively speaking, it is impossible to blame them [the sheikhs] because their requests and demands were small and symbolic."[110]

The new Druze leaders (academics, mayors of Druze villages, and veteran senior officers), highlighting the fact that their people were the only Israeli Arab citizens to be conscripted, early on demanded preferential treatment. "Why do we not have the courage to fully admit that the Druze who are brothers-in-arms with the Jews deserve special privileges, without being ashamed of such an admission?" Manssur asked in 1972.[111] This new veteran leadership, together with the threat of growing resistance to conscription among young Druze, finally forced the state to move away from symbolic gestures and adopt concrete actions to improve Druze villages.

During the 1970s, as the ranks of Druze officers burgeoned, long-held suspicions and old barriers began crumbling for rank-and-file Druze as well. In February 1972, the army decided to allow a limited number of Druze soldiers into all of its corps except the air force and intelligence. In 1974, Colonel Binyamin Ben-Eliezer, the new commander of the Minority Unit, abolished the Druze leaders' external influence over his unit. Promotions now were determined solely on the basis of merit, and Druze servicemen quickly learned that promotions no longer depended on closed-door negotiations between the IDF and the sheikhs. When he was asked if young Druze soldiers would be admitted to the highly prestigious Israeli air force and intelligence corps, the first Israeli Druze general responded, "The young Druze have to realize that our future progress depends on our performance. We must not fail. If we fail, doors will be closed. If we succeed more doors will be opened."[112] In March 1978, the Minority Unit, for the first time in its history, gained an independent role during the Litani Operation in Lebanon. After the operation ended, the military opened new vocations and corps for Druze soldiers

110. *Ma'ariv*, September 29, 1986.
111. *Ma'ariv*, June 5, 1972.
112. Katzenell, "Minorities in the IDF," *IDF Journal* 4, no. 3 (fall 1987): 42.

outside the Minority Unit.[113] The Minority Unit itself went on to fight in the Lebanon war.

In 1982 the IDF began posting many more Druze conscripts among different Jewish units. This was not an overnight process. Brig. Gen. Hail Salah, the first Israeli Druze general, noted, "We must not forget that Israel is still a young country, and if we Druze look around the world at other peoples in our situation we can see that they did not reach every position of authority overnight. It took time."[114] To support this gradual manpower innovation, the IDF created a staff department for minority soldiers, headed by a Druze officer. Its goal was "to aid young Druze to integrate into the IDF with greater ease," since such "integration . . . will eventually result in better absorption of Druze veterans in the civil market."[115]

Finally, in April 1991, Moshe Arens, the defence minister, declared all IDF units open to the Druze. When attacked by opponents who considered his decision to open the ultrasensitive air force to Druze reckless, Arens responded, "Vanunu [the Jewish man who tried to sell Israel's nuclear secrets] was not a Druze."[116] As more Druze soldiers joined Jewish units, the Minority Unit began suffering from an acute shortage of manpower. To replenish its ranks, the IDF assigned Jewish draftees to serve in this unit. New Druze draftees are now given a choice: to serve either with their fellow Jewish conscripts or in a special Druze battalion. As most choose to serve in mixed units, the last Druze battalion will probably be abolished.[117]

The legal, political, and social status of the Druze community improved along with the advance of Druze soldiers within the IDF. Between 1957 and 1964, the government granted the request of traditional Druze leaders and promoted the Druze community to the status of an independent religious community.[118] In the mid-1970s, as Druze servicemen were making headway within the IDF, the government decided that Druze citizens would receive services directly from government ministries rather than from the Arab departments of these ministries. A new

---

113. Interview with Gen. (Res.) Refael Vardi.

114. Katzenell, "Minorities in the IDF," p. 42.

115. Lt. Col. Laviv, head of the department, quoted in Huggi, "Arab Soldiers in the IDF," p. 17.

116. Mordechai Vanunu, a former Jewish employee of the Israeli nuclear plant in Dimona, attempted to sell information concerning Israel's nuclear capacity to a British newspaper. He later was arrested by Mossad agents and sentenced to jail.

117. "The Druze in the IDF: Equal Rights," *Ba'Mahane*, November 27, 1991, pp. 52–59.

118. Jacob Landau, *The Arabs in Israel: A Political Study* (London: Oxford University Press, 1969), pp. 13–14.

committee under the general director of the prime minister's office was established to implement this decision. Among other actions, the committee decided to employ Druze veterans in the military and aircraft industries, and the military store chain, and it also established a special fund to make loans to Druze veterans. To promote further the status of the Druze community, Asad Asad, a Druze who previously served as a senior commander in the IDF, was appointed special advisor to the prime minister for Druze affairs.[119] Druze villages still remain underdeveloped compared to similar Jewish communities. Nonetheless, the Druze political leaders interviewed for this book were united firmly in their belief that military service did much to promote the interests and status of the Druze community in Israel.

EXPANDING THE DRUZE EXPERIMENT TO OTHER ARAB COMMUNITIES

By the late 1980s, the success of the phased integration of Druze soldiers led to expansion of the experiment. In 1989, Moshe Arens, the defence minister, who was educated in America and had served as Israel's ambassador to the United States, launched a personal campaign to extend the policy of phased integration to other Israeli Arab groups. Influenced by the American experience, Arens declared on one occasion, "Very few states have no minorities. We are compelled to live with minorities and we will be better off viewing it as a challenge rather than as a necessity."[120]

Arens strongly believed that Arab citizens had to serve in the IDF in order to improve their status in Israeli society, but he understood very well the deeply rooted historical opposition to an immediate draft call for all Israeli Arab citizens. Israeli Arab leaders, for example, have often expressed fears that, if drafted, their youth would be compelled to serve as no-cost menial laborers. One bluntly stated that Arab youth do not wish to serve Jewish soldiers in military kitchens.[121] Even Arab leaders who supported some form of Arab recruitment conditioned their consent on the IDF's not turning Arab recruits into "slaves" of the Jewish mili-

119. Interview with Gad Hitman, assistant to the advisor on minority affairs, Ramat-Gan, December 27, 1991.

120. Moshe Arens, "Education for Living Together in the Israeli Reality," *Skira Hodshit*, January 1992, p. 8. (*Skira Hodshit* is the IDF monthly officer journal.)

121. *Ha'aretz*, July 25, 1991.

tary. Yitzhak Rabin (chief of staff 1964–1968, minister of defence 1984–1986, prime minister 1974–1977, 1992–1994) admitted that on several occasions he rejected plans for Arab conscription because he feared that Arab draftees would ultimately become the IDF's "hewers of wood and drawers of water."[122]

Arens also faced the legacy of decades of nonservice: the chasm between those who serve and those who do not, and the well-developed ideological justifications of those who do not serve. As time passed, the national division between the dominant ethnic group serving in the military and ethnic groups not serving grew in importance; the question of military service divided the nation between members of dominant and subjected ethnic groups. As we have seen, Ben-Gurion continued to preach his military melting-pot vision throughout the 1950s and 1960s, and politicians, army commanders, and scholars, embracing his normative ideas uncritically, turned them into an axiom of Israeli life.[123] In response, leaders of the Muslim and Christian Arab minority communities again raised their arguments that peace must prevail throughout the Middle East before Israeli Arab citizens could fulfill their military obligations. They also maintained that the military's efforts to recruit Druze and Bedouin Arabs while exempting other Arabs was part of an insidious government policy of "divide and rule."

Faced with this ideological impasse, Arens advocated a policy of phased integration, successfully exploiting the experience with Druze servicemen to open the gates of the IDF to other ethnic groups. He began with a gradual and small-scale program that did not require the approval of the government and could be initiated under the sole authority of the defence minister:[124] He increased the rate of Bedouin volunteers into the IDF by recruiting older Bedouins for short-term conscription followed by reserve service.[125]

---

122. Benziman and Mansour, *Subtenants*, p. 119.

123. For an example of this uncritical acceptance of Ben-Gurion's ideas, see Tom Bowden, *Army in the Service of the State* (Tel Aviv: University Publishing Projects, 1976). See also Maurice M. Roumani, *From Immigrant to Citizen: The Contribution of the Army to National Integration in Israel—the Case of Oriental Jews* (The Hague: Foundation for the Study of Plural Societies, 1979).

124. Benziman and Mansour, *Subtenants*, p. 121.

125. This program ("Giyus Shlav B' ") usually applies to older Jewish immigrants, twenty-eight years of age and above. See "The Adults Want to Serve in the Military," *Kol Hatzafon*, Acre, November 29, 1991; "Forty Years Old to Basic Training," *Yediot Aharonot*, August 9, 1991; Ori Binder, "Dozens of Bedouins Volunteered to Serve on the Reserve,"

Arens then launched the second step of his phased-integration program: state officials traveled to Arab villages, explaining the new initiative and encouraging young Arab Christians to volunteer. In 1992, the IDF recruited 1,589 Arab citizens, compared with 730 in 1991.[126] Israeli newspapers highlighted the dramatic increase in Arab Christian volunteers.[127] The Christian volunteer program also contained a political element. Many of the Israeli Christian youth who volunteered to serve in the IDF between 1991 and 1993 came from villages with mixed Muslim and Christian populations. These volunteers claimed that the rise of a militant Islamist movement in their villages had spoiled the traditional live-and-let-live relationship between Muslim and Christian residents. Some Christian residents believed that the presence of armed and uniformed Christian youth in the villages might help restore relaxed relations.[128] Israeli politicians, who likewise feared the rise of the Islamist movement, no doubt were content to see more Christians joining the IDF. In addition, many young Christian citizens admitted that they finally had decided to enlist in order to improve their economic lot.[129]

THE SUCCESS OF PHASED INTEGRATION

Not a single Israeli politician was willing to place the goal of social integration of Israeli Arabs above the need to make secure the ranks of

---

Ma'ariv, August 9, 1991; Avi Beniaho, "35 Bedouins Volunteered to Reserve Duty and Were Recruited for Basic Training Level B," *Al Hamishmar*, July 29, 1991.

126. Advisor to the Prime Minister on Arab Affairs, *Israeli Arabs* (Jerusalem: Government Printing Office, 1992), p. 44.

127. See, for example, Zohir Andraus, "In the Name of the Flag and the Holy Spirit," *Natania*, July 12, 1991; Mazal Mualem, "Christians Wish to Join the IDF," *Ma'ariv*, July 31, 1991; Muhammad Halilia, "More Than 200 Arab Christians Asked to Serve in the IDF," *Davar*, July 26, 1991; "200 Christian Youngsters Join the IDF," *Kol Haemek ve'Hagalil*, July 26, 1991.

128. Interview with Gad Hitman. Hate and mistrust among members of different ethnic groups may be present even when they serve together in the same military unit. A foreign correspondent who visited a southern military post in 1949, manned by soldiers from Israel's Minority Unit, described the relationship between the Druze and Circassian elements of the unit in the following unusual way: "They [Druze and Circassian soldiers] have no use for each other. The Circassians wouldn't even discuss their Druze NCOs, and a Druze sergeant qualified his Circassian men for me as 'dirty savages' "; Hal Lehrman, "The Arabs of Israel: Pages from a Correspondent's Notebook," *Commentary* 8 (December 1949): 528.

129. *Ma'ariv*, August 30, 1991; *Kol Ha'zaphon*, October 10, 1991.

the IDF. Thus, all plans for immediate egalitarianism and equal conscription of Jews and Arabs were classified as naive, utopian, or dangerous. A few of these egalitarian recruitment schemes generated some short-term excitement and goodwill, which eventually were replaced by deep suspicion, distrust, and hostility. Israeli politicians then resorted to the argument that it would be both cruel and unsafe to recruit Arab citizens to fight their kin across the border. Plans for immediate egalitarianism among Jews and Arabs in the IDF were not able to penetrate the high walls of mutual distrust between Israel and its Arab minority groups.

A few Israeli politicians sought to offer Israeli Arabs the option of serving in a separate ethnic civil national service, such as special labor brigades to assist hospitals and schools, or even in police, fire brigades, or civil defense units. This idea, however, quickly turned into a political minefield. Some Israeli politicians proposed such a national service for Israeli Arabs as a means of punishing young Arab citizens. Israeli Arab leaders were left out of discussions concerning plans to impose national service on their youth. In addition, Israel's legal code was at odds with the creation of an ethnically segregated national service. Israeli politicians also feared that this scheme would raise expectations among Israeli Arabs to a level that could not be fulfilled. Most important, the politicians were very concerned about the creation of segregated Arab labor brigades because such units might fuel calls for political irredentism among Israeli Arabs. For their part, the Israeli public never considered a civil national service for Arab youth a sufficient test of loyalty because it felt that only military service entailed the implicit obligation to sacrifice one's life for the state. For all its appeal, therefore, the idea did not alleviate the tensions between the state and its Arab minority groups. Occasionally, discussions of such plans in the media even further soured the relationship between the state and its non-Jewish communities.

Phased integration of Arab youth into the IDF was the only policy that bridged this distrust gap. It sought to absorb gradually members of the Druze and Circassian communities (and, later on, Bedouin and Christian Arab youth) into the military in order to build mutual trust among Israeli politicians, IDF officers, and the Druze community. The success of this policy toward the Israeli Druze community depended on senior IDF commanders's constant readiness to change their management of Druze soldiers as they gained more confidence in them. This point is illustrated by the IDF's gradually increasing willingness to allow Druze soldiers in battle after 1968, to let them serve outside their segregated unit after

1972, and to promote Druze officers to the ranks of senior commanders after 1975.

The phased integration policy was subject to many crises of distrust, as exemplified in the history of the IDF's Minority Unit throughout the 1950s. To overcome these crises, strong politicians such as Ben-Gurion (and Arens at the end of the 1980s) had to intervene personally to promote the status of non-Jewish soldiers. A group of Jewish IDF officers who were committed to their Druze soldiers also fought to alleviate many of the tensions characterizing the initial stages of the phased integration of Druze into the IDF during the early 1950s. Phased integration succeeded eventually, as Druze officers and soldiers found more and more doors open to them. Indeed, the ultimate measure of success for a policy of phased integration occurs when journalists, academics, ethnic soldiers, military officers, and even politicians begin to question why such a policy was needed in the first place.

[5]

Moving Toward Ethnic Integration

On April 6, 1994, a plane carrying President Habyarimana of Rwanda and President Ntaryamira of Burundi was shot down as it attempted to land at the Kigali airport in Rwanda. The plane crashed into the garden of President Habyarimana's residence, killing all passengers on board. Less than an hour after the assassination, all hell broke loose in Rwanda. Hutu civilian militias known as the Interahamwe ("those who stand together") set roadblocks, and the murder of Rwanda's Tutsi minority began.[1]

The first attacks on Tutsis that night appeared not to be different from previous rounds of Hutu massacres of Tutsis. The Belgian colonial regime (1918–1962) considered the Tutsi minority of Rwanda a "superior race," and therefore elevated Tutsi chieftains to rule the country. In 1959, however, the death of Mwaami Rudahigwa, the childless Tutsi king, prompted the Hutus to rise against the Tutsis and massacre thousands. Many Tutsis escaped the country to neighboring Uganda and became refugees for life. This massive 1959 exodus marked the beginning of vicious, violent cycles that continued to force rulers-turned-victims to flee their killers en masse into neighboring countries. Between 1959 and 1994, sporadic massacres of Tutsis erupted, frequently triggered by the Hutu majority's fears that the mythical "Tutsi nobility" would return to reenslave them.

But the new round of violence that began on the night President Ha-

---

1. Gérard Prunier, *The Rwanda Crisis: History of a Genocide* (New York: Columbia University Press, 1995), pp. 254–255.

byarimana was assassinated quickly evolved into something that even ethnically torn Rwanda had not experienced before: genocide. This time, the Tutsi minority had no place to hide. The "bush cleaning" (the Hutu euphemism for genocide) of the Tutsis took place in the countryside and in the city, in shops, at roadblocks, and inside churches, schools, and private homes. Unlike previous massacres, this ethnic cleansing campaign was to be the "final solution" for the Tutsi minority. No Tutsi was to be spared, and the killers proceeded from house to house, frequently returning to dig under piles of dead Tutsis in order to kill the wounded buried beneath. Schoolteachers of Hutu origin lined up their Tutsi pupils and shot them to death, and Hutu citizens cut down their Tutsi neighbors with machetes. Even mixed-race couples were not spared: Hutu husbands were forced to observe the killing of their Tutsi wives, and Tutsi wives of Hutu men were compelled to throw their mixed-race babies into rivers before being killed themselves. Within days, Lake Victoria was seriously polluted with forty thousand Tutsi bodies, and garbage trucks brought some sixty thousand Tutsi bodies to unidentified and unmarked collective burial grounds. All in all, between April and June 1994, five hundred thousand to eight hundred thousand Rwandan citizens, mostly of Tutsi origin, were brutally murdered by their Hutu neighbors.[2]

The military, the Forces Armées Rwandaises (FAR), was the only state institution that had the power to stop the rapidly escalating genocide. Indeed, at first, the FAR was reluctant to join the killers. On the night of April 7, sporadic fights broke out between FAR units and the presidential guard (GP) units, which were at the forefront of the genocide. The new commander-in-chief of the military, Colonel Marcel Gatsinzi (the former commander, Colonel Deogratias Nsabimana, was killed with President Habyarimana) attempted to keep the army out of the genocide. Many of his subordinates, however, had already begun joining the killers, acting against the orders of their officers. Finally, on April 8, Colonel Gatsinzi stopped the fighting between the military and the Interahamwe and the GP units. During the next two months, FAR units and soldiers joined the collective slaughter. For instance, when desperate Tutsi victims crowded a church and repelled the attacks of the Interahamwe militia, FAR units were brought in. The soldiers fired mortar shells through

2. Fergal Keane, *Season of Blood: A Rwandan Journey* (London: Viking Press, 1995), pp. 90–91.

the roof and threw hand grenades through the windows, forcing the helpless Tutsi citizens to leave the church and rush out into the machetes of the Interahamwe militia. In another incident, FAR soldiers entered a hospital in pursuit of wounded Tutsis. One employee of the Medecins sans Frontières organization described the behavior of the soldiers: "Any wounded person (assumed to be Tutsi, since he had been wounded) was killed. Right in front of our eyes, the army men would come inside the hospital, take the wounded, line them up and machine-gun them down."[3]

While these atrocities were taking place, the Rwandese Patriotic Front (RPF), the leading Tutsi-dominated guerrilla organization, launched a powerful assault on Rwanda from neighboring Burundi. The FAR, which by then was nothing more than a host of armed gangs of murderers, thieves, rapists, and thugs, collapsed. In July 1994, the RPF conquered Kigali, the capital, and set up an interim government. Fearing reprisals, Hutu officials and military officers escaped the country by hiding among the 2.5 million Hutu refugees who fled the RPF into neighboring Zaire. Inside the Hutu refugee camps in Zaire, the killing of Tutsis continued unabated. A cholera epidemic then swept the camps, killing thousands more Tutsis and Hutus.

The grueling tragedy of Rwanda's Tutsi minority, and the aftermath of this genocide, serve as a powerful reminder of the fate that may befall multiethnic states that fail to resolve the Trojan horse dilemma. In Rwanda, this dilemma had been the toughest problem Hutu and Tutsi politicians needed to resolve during their peace talks in Arusha, Tanzania, in August 1993. The final Arusha agreements contained detailed articles concerning the integration of Tutsi-dominated RPF guerrilla fighters into the Hutu-dominated FAR.[4] These articles called for the creation of a new military composed of 60 percent FAR forces and 40 percent RPF forces, commanded by an officer corps equally divided between Tutsi RPF officers and Hutu FAR commanders. The agreements even specified that no two hierarchically consecutive positions (for example, commander and second-in-command) in a given unit would be held by members of one group. Nonetheless, President Habyarimana could not

---

3. Prunier, *Rwanda Crisis*, p. 254.

4. Before the August 1993 Arusha agreements, Habyarimana entertained very strong fears about Tutsi Trojan horse soldiers. There was only one Tutsi officer in the whole FAR, and Hutu members of the armed forces were prohibited by regulations from marrying Tutsi women. Prunier, *Rwanda Crisis*, p. 75.

overcome his fears of Tutsi Trojan horses in the FAR.[5] He therefore continuously delayed implementing of the Arusha agreements during the next seven months. While he was stalling, extremist Tutsis and Hutus armed themselves and prepared for the next round of ethnic cleansing. Neither group could have anticipated how gruesome this round would be for all sides. For his failure to implement the agreements, Habyarimana paid with his life. Even more important, by refusing to resolve the Trojan horse dilemma along the lines of the agreements, President Habyarimana condemned his country and its citizens to long years of ethnic genocide, civil war, and the squalor of refugee camps.

The consequences of this failure to implement the Arusha agreements also serve as a powerful reminder that the Trojan horse dilemma is a double-edged sword lying against the neck of the state. On the one hand, the military, as the sole state institution with a monopoly on the legitimate use of collective violence, cannot afford Trojan horses and internal ethnic strife. On the other hand, the long-term exclusion of certain racial groups from the military can result in the slow degradation of the military from a supraethnic guardian of the state into a xenophobic and bloodthirsty ethnic militia. Politicians in multiethnic societies frequently tend to "secure the military's loyalty" by excluding allegedly disloyal ethnic groups from the armed forces. But the history of Rwanda clearly demonstrates that such an approach can be disastrous for both the political leadership and the state. In multiethnic countries where the military has become an ethnic militia, politicians have gained no security. Quite to the contrary, they have often been toppled in coup d'états led by ethnically xenophobic generals or, worse, have plunged their states into prolonged and horrific civil wars.

Yet even politicians and military commanders who wish to resolve the Trojan horse dilemma in an innovative way may find themselves paralyzed when faced with the following daunting questions: If allowed into the military, will young ethnic soldiers become Trojan horses, or will they serve loyally? Can young men with such strong blood, linguistic, religious, and cultural ties to the potential enemy be fully trusted with arms in the service of the state? If the state excludes them from the military, how can ethnic youth with kin across the border in an enemy country be integrated into the society if they have not fulfilled their military obligation, which is deemed by most citizens a precondition for

---

5. Prunier, *Rwanda Crisis*, p. 193.

citizenship? On the other hand, if the state allows them into the military, how can it supervise ethnic servicemen without turning them into distrusted second-class soldiers?

It is important to note that, given a chance to serve their countries, ethnic soldiers are almost always loyal soldiers. There have been but few and negligible incidents in which South African black soldiers, Singaporean Malay servicemen, and Israeli Arab troops actually conspired with external forces against the state. Indeed, whenever and wherever they were given a chance, ethnic soldiers have served their countries loyally, including on the battlefield. Nonetheless, the Trojan horse dilemma is a real one because it occupies the minds of senior politicians and military officers and shapes their decisions on military manpower policy.

These leaders will not overcome their fears overnight. No "magic" or immediate solutions will remove their concerns about ethnic Trojan horses in the military, as we can see in the failure of the Arusha agreements in Rwanda. The best approach seems to be a phased-integration strategy to absorb ethnic soldiers gradually into the military, and gradually promote them to first-class servicemen and officers. As this study has shown, such a strategy is more likely to work in professional military organizations where senior commanders are motivated not by political motives but by a desire to elevate the combat performance of the troops. Lessons gleaned from the historical experiences of South Africa, Singapore, and Israel on the hard and treacherous road to ethnic integration within the military can be divided among four target groups: officers, politicians, ethnic leaders, and ethnic servicemen.

GUIDELINES FOR OFFICERS

Above all else, professional officers who seek to integrate their troops ethnically must speak in terms of increasing combat readiness when they ask politicians to support their ethnic manpower experiments. They should refrain from arguing for integration on the basis of social justice and, instead, focus their conversations with politicians on the combat performance rewards the military would gain if allowed to integrate its ranks. Among other actions, professional officers should launch and evaluate comparative studies of segregated and nonsegregated units' performance, and present their findings to the politicians. In South Africa, for example, Fraser, Malan, and other senior officers provided Botha with documentation on this issue, and won his support for their efforts to return nonwhites to the SADF and, later on, to promote them. In Israel, Ben-Gurion copied into his personal diary data from military reports concerning the service records of Druze soldiers. After examining the data, he instructed the military to elevate the Minority Unit to a regular combat unit. Professional officers do not operate in a political vacuum and will not be able to carry out ethnic integration within the military against the wishes of their political masters. By educating the politicians on this issue, however, the military can acquire the political support needed to execute manpower innovations.

Senior commanders would also do well to prepare carefully and systematically for the inclusion and integration of new ethnic groups. They should also know that, far from being a cheap solution for acquiring additional manpower, ethnic integration is an expensive endeavor. Senior officers will need to devote time, effort, and funds to studying the unique problems of bringing in new groups. Among other steps, new general-staff departments exclusively devoted to the task of integrating ethnic soldiers must be established. The integration of Druze soldiers into the IDF, for example, accelerated after a special manpower department for Druze servicemen was established in the General Staff Headquarters. Moreover, high-quality, innovative, and open-minded officers should examine various alternatives for the integration of new ethnic soldiers. Officers should call upon experience gleaned from previous ethnic manpower experiments when new groups are brought into the military. During the mid-1970s, for example, when the SADF reopened its gates to black and Indian youth, South Africa successfully applied lessons learned from the integration of colored soldiers. The SADF also learned from its World War II experience, and assigned no less than sixteen seasoned officers and NCOs to supervise the training of the first ten black soldiers in 1973. In addition, if the military decides to establish segregated units to accommodate the first ethnic soldiers, it must also open its purse to ensure that these units are treated as equals in all matters concerning military facilities, training, and service conditions.

Military officers should also expect resistance from within the army to ethnic manpower innovations, and therefore should focus on sensitizing the younger generation of military officers to the need to change traditional military manpower policies. By its nature, the military is a conservative and tradition-bound institution. Change comes hard to militaries in the developing world, where most of the soldiers hail from rural communities, and where animosity toward potential Trojan horse ethnic groups runs high among the rank and file. Senior officers of such militaries should focus their efforts on the military school system, paying special attention to the selection of textbooks and to instruction and training methods. Most important, they should use military training schools as a forum for convincing young and malleable officers (at the ranks of captain and below) of the urgent need to change the ethnic composition of the military. These young officers are the backbone of the military, and they alone can impress upon the rank and file the idea that the military has to absorb new ethnic groups and treat them as equals. Since integration is likely to span more than one generation (twenty years), the careers of these young officers will become intertwined with the ongoing effort to integrate the military. Such officers first will serve as platoon and company commanders of segregated units, and eventually will move up the military chain of command to positions that enable them to abolish segregation within the military.

Senior officers also must understand the need to move slowly when a new ethnic group enters the military. For example, ethnic leaders are not likely to support the recruitment of their youth into a melting-pot military where soldiers from various groups are supposed to blend together and lose their distinct identities while acquiring a new supraethnic national identity. Above all else, ethnic leaders are concerned with the continuity of their group identity, and melting-pot militaries pose a grave danger to the source of this continuity—the younger generation. The segregation of ethnic youth in special units during their first years in the military is frequently acceptable both to senior officers who fear Trojan horses in the military and to ethnic leaders who fear that their youth in uniform will lose their ethnic identity. Such segregation may be a necessary first step in bringing a new group into the ranks.

Nonetheless, senior officers need to monitor personally and carefully the status of the ethnically segregated units they have created. In and of itself, segregation of ethnic soldiers is not necessary bad. Segregated units can be treated fairly, and gradually promoted in status, prestige, and assignments, as demonstrated by the history of colored, Indian, and black SADF units. On the other hand, segregated units can be brutalized and humiliated, as were the Shiite front-line units in Saddam Hussein's military during the Gulf War. Senior military commanders who wish to promote the ethnic integration of their troops must continuously ask themselves a series of tough questions: Why were the segregated units created in the first place? Are segregated units still serving the original purpose for which they were created? How do the morale, motivation, and performance of soldiers in ethnically segregated units compare with those of their nonsegregated counterparts? Segregation that lasts too long, with no clear purpose, becomes counterproductive. In Israel, for example, Druze officers and soldiers who excelled in the battle against terrorists in the Jordan Valley between 1968 and 1970 resented their confinement to one unit. Their morale and motivation quickly plummeted, and the IDF was then forced to terminate the traditional segregation of Druze soldiers and allow them into all corps, units, and schools.

War against a foreign power is usually an opportunity to accelerate the integration of ethnic soldiers. On the border or in enemy territory, ethnic segregation and discriminatory policies will not hold for long, as illustrated by the experience of nonwhite SADF units in South West Africa during the second half of the 1970s. Ethnic soldiers' loyal performance on the battlefield must be rewarded immediately with greater integration and promotions in rank and command. In addition, military officers should continue to monitor closely the missions assigned to ethnic soldiers. The IDF learned this lesson too late, and in 1983 had to withdraw its Druze soldiers hastily from their mission as guardians of the peace between feuding Druze and Christian villages in Lebanon. In Singapore, which, unlike South Africa and Israel, has not experienced a full-fledged war against an external enemy (since its 1965 independence), politicians had the luxury of disposing of their seasoned Malay Muslim soldiers. One can only wonder if the fate of Malay Muslim soldiers in the Singapore Armed Forces would have been different had Singapore clashed militarily with Malaysia after 1965. Officers who genuinely pursue integration during wartime will not be quick to dismiss war privileges granted to ethnic soldiers (such as access to new training facilities) because, in the minds of these officers, the soldiers have "earned these privileges on the battlefield." Even xenophobic politicians who oppose integrating new ethnic soldiers will have a difficult time opposing the concept of "rewards for heroes." With time, these rewards will be transferred to the next generation of recruits and become part of the new military standard of behavior toward ethnic servicemen.

Military commanders also must work hard to coordinate the pace of horizontal and vertical integration. One type of change will not benefit the military if not followed by the other. The mass recruitment of ethnic soldiers without their promotion to NCO and officer ranks will result in accusations that the military is merely recruiting cannon fodder. Similarly, the military will be blamed for tokenism if it chooses to promote a handful of ethnic officers without opening its gates to more members of their ethnic groups. Thus, a carefully plotted phased-integration strategy must combine horizontal and vertical promotions. In Israel and South Africa, recruiting Druze and nonwhite soldiers, respectively, eventually prompted the military to send many more ethnic soldiers to officer schools. In contrast, Singaporean leaders and their proxy civil servants in uniform first terminated the recruitment of new Malay soldiers in 1969 and then in 1974, with much less pressure from Malay rank and file, moved to restrict the entrance of Malay servicemen into officer courses.

Professional officers who seek to integrate the armed forces ethnically therefore will do well to heed to the following advice:

- Sensitize politicians to the military's need to integrate its ranks ethnically in order to improve combat readiness.
- Devote staff, funds, time, and effort to advance studies on how to bring in new ethnic groups. Properly executed, a phased-integration strategy will be costly.
- Expect resistance within the military to ethnic integration. Use the military school system to change ingrained attitudes on the issue. Focus on influencing the hearts and minds of young and junior officers.
- Move slowly at first. Segregation of the first ethnic soldiers may be a necessary step on the path toward future integration.
- Abolish ethnically segregated units as soon as they no longer serve the function for which they were originally created.
- Use the occasion of war to accelerate the process of ethnic integration.
- Do not rescind privileges granted to ethnic soldiers during wartime (such as access to military facilities that previously were off limits) after the fighting ends. Instead, engrave these privileges into the military's statute books and make them part of the new norms of behavior toward ethnic servicemen.
- Supervise and coordinate the pace of ethnic integration among both officers and the rank and file. Mix horizontal and vertical promotions of ethnic servicemen.
- Use the battle records of ethnic soldiers to convince politicians that the time is ripe to push the integration of the troops one step further.

[177]

One lesson that is hard to ignore is that politicians, everywhere and at all times, fear Trojan horse ethnic groups in the military. These fears cannot be eradicated overnight, just as the general public cannot immediately remove its general suspicion toward—and mistrust of—subordinated ethnic groups. The crux of the issue centers on three questions: Will politicians act on their Trojan horse fears? How dominant will these fears be in their decisions concerning the military? What will it take to soothe their fears? Politicians who prefer to leave ethnic groups outside the gates of the military must be made aware of the cost of this path. Excluding Malays from the Singaporean military (1965–1977), and Muslims from the Israeli armed forces (1948 to present), has exacerbated feelings of mistrust, alienation, and antagonism among the state, the general public, and the excluded ethnic communities. The role of the military in the April 1994 massacre of the Tutsi minority in Rwanda demonstrates what might be the ultimate cost of excluding permanently certain groups from the military: civil war, genocide, and national disintegration for members of all ethnic groups.

Since Trojan horse fears cannot be eradicated overnight, politicians would do well to abandon the nation-building-in-the-military rhetoric that characterizes their speeches. Rarely, if at all, does the military "build nations" in the developing world. More frequently, it "builds a nation" from some ethnic groups while leaving others outside its gates. Thus, rhetoric quickly clashes with the reality that some citizens serve in the military and some are excluded. In Singapore, for example, the Malay Muslim community reached its height of frustration and alienation from the state during the early 1970s because virtually every young Malay was being pushed away from the military precisely when all politicians appeared to be celebrating in public the new nation-building conscript military. Politicians must adopt humbler language, focusing on the need to accommodate all ethnic groups in the military and to proceed cautiously in all matters of military ethnic integration.

This study affirms that astute statesmen promote professional officers, not civil servants, to command positions in the military. Statesmen should also work to open the gates of foreign military academies to the officers of their armed forces. Such professionally trained officers will infuse the military with new ideas and doctrines learned in military colleges abroad. Professional officers also will place improved combat readiness of their troops above all other ends and, to achieve this, will eradicate traditional ethnic divisions in the military and replace them with modern functional divisions. Politicians may learn from these officers that the military will need to integrate its ranks faster than might be the pace of integration in the general society in order to combat a strong foe. The comparison between Singapore and South Africa illuminates this point. In Singapore, politicians installed obedient civil servants in the senior military posts, and these servants carried out unquestioningly their political masters' plan to exclude Malay servicemen from the military. As a result, the issue of Malay soldiers in the SAF became the focal point of antagonism between the Singapore Malay community and the state. In contrast, South African leaders were wise enough to promote a group of professional officers trained in Western military colleges, and then heed their advice about the need to recruit, promote, and deploy nonwhite soldiers. As a result, the SADF became the one and only state institution in which—even during the darkest years of apartheid—a young black, colored, or Indian man could advance his career. When the first-ever black government came to power in 1994, the armed forces were just about the only security institution in the state that did not need to be revamped or recreated from scratch (see more on this in the epilogue).

Politicians also can protect their professional officers from the media while the latter are experimenting with new ethnic manpower ideas. In South Africa, Botha, who was intimately familiar with—and supportive of—the bold ethnic experimentation of the SADF, took it upon himself to distract the media from what was happening to nonwhites in the military. His favorite trick was to announce "new" innovations to the media five years after the fact, when newer and much bolder innovations were already under way. Military officers who later become politicians are less skilled in keeping the media at bay however. Malan, who left his post as chief of the SADF in 1980 to became the minister of defence, infuriated black, colored, and Indian leaders during the 1980s with his hasty and careless statements that the time had come to conscript nonwhites into the SADF.

Political leaders also should avoid dragging the military into policing the very same ethnic enclaves from which ethnic soldiers are recruited. The temptation to assign ethnic troops to such internal tasks is great. After all, politicians may ask, who better to squelch ethnic riots than uniformed members of the communities in which the riots are taking place? But the military will quickly pay a dear price for getting its ethnic soldiers involved in such tasks. Its reputation as an ethnically neutral state institution will rapidly become tarnished. As a result, the number of ethnic volunteers for military service will drop, and ethnic units and servicemen will suffer the loss of motivation and morale. Eventually, fearing that ethnic soldiers will desert or refuse to obey commands, the military will be forced to withdraw ethnic units from policing duties in their own communities. Long-term losses, such as erosion of trust between the military and ethnic communities, will outweigh any short-lived gains, such as the suppression of a local riot.

Because of the enormous risk, politicians should avoid taking unilateral steps that have not first been negotiated with ethnic leaders—for instance, imposing conscription on ethnic youth. If ethnic leaders refuse to cooperate, politicians quickly will discover that they have no means at their disposal to enforce unilateral decisions. To execute its missions, the modern military requires willing and motivated soldiers, not legions of bitter and alienated conscripts. The seven-year-long failure of South African leaders to impose conscription on nonwhites against the wishes of ethnic community leaders (1977–1984), and the Singaporean politicians' success in convincing the leaders of the Chinese majority that military service was not a despicable profession (1967), illustrate this point. Politicians should therefore not attempt to short-circuit negotiations with ethnic leaders over the terms of military service for their youth.

Finally, politicians must continuously reinforce and support the military's ethnic manpower experiments, especially when the social climate in their countries becomes unstable. Specifically, during periods of ethnic riots and their aftermath, professional officers need plenty of political support in order to advance their ethnic manpower experiments. In South Africa, for example, when the military received such support after the Soweto riots, experimentation continued unabated and even intensified. In contrast, Singaporean leaders chose to close the military's doors to Malay youth after the 1969 racial riots in Malaysia, despite the impartial action of the multiracial SAF during these riots. Professional officers must endeavor to secure politicians' support in advance of such periods of upheaval. In South Africa, for example, senior SADF commanders labored hard to educate Botha and his ministers on the importance of letting nonwhites into the SADF. Their efforts paid off in 1976 during the Soweto riots, when the politicians supported the military's decision to keep blacks in the military. Racial and ethnic riots—within and outside the military—are a challenge to be confronted rather than a sign that ethnic manpower innovation within the military must end.

The list of advice for politicians who wish to support the integration of new ethnic groups into the military therefore includes the following:

- Acknowledge Trojan horse fears but be careful not to act on them.
- Abandon the nation-building-in-the-military rhetoric. Instead, adopt humbler expectations, focusing on the need to accommodate all ethnic groups in the military and to carefully experiment with increasing integration among various ethnic groups in uniform.
- Send officers to military academies abroad and, upon their return, support their efforts to infuse the military with new ideas and doctrines, including the need to revamp the military's ethnic manpower policy.
- Listen carefully to professional officers and understand that the military might have to integrate more rapidly than the society at large.
- Protect professional officers from the conservative media.
- Do not force the military to deploy ethnic units to police their own communities.
- Do not impose unilateral decisions, such as conscription, on ethnic communities. Consult and negotiate with ethnic leaders before taking such actions.
- Consistently support military ethnic experimentation, but make a particular effort to do so during periods of ethnic tension and unrest.

GUIDELINES FOR ETHNIC LEADERS

Leaders of subordinated communities whose members aspire to become first-class citizens would do better to negotiate the military service terms of their youth rather than resist cooperation on all military matters. The military's desire to recruit ethnic youth may not be a threat but, rather, an opportunity for leaders to improve the lot of their youth as well as the community's standing. If leaders pursue such an opportunity vigorously, it can evolve into an important engine of social mobility for ethnic youth, who, in the long term, will return to their villages and become the next generation of community leaders. Leaders must closely monitor the military's treatment of their youth in uniform however. If ethnic soldiers are maltreated or used as cannon fodder, community leaders should immediately withdraw their support for recruitment. All cooperation with the military concerning recruitment must be conditional on the military's fulfilling its part of the bargain (that is, fair treatment of ethnic soldiers). Leaders can use the military's ever-present fear of losing their cooperation as a powerful weapon to force it to open new gates for ethnic youth in uniform.

Ethnic leaders who choose to resist negotiation with the military over the terms of recruitment might also jeopardize their groups' long-term security.[6] Through service in the state's armed forces, ethnic groups acquire a pool of men experienced and trained in the use of arms. If civil order collapses, this pool will be the only effective communal defense line against other predatory ethnic groups. Moreover, in a society where every male is expected to serve in the military, ethnic groups are well aware of which groups do not serve, and such groups become easy prey. Politicians often play on racial fears to convince ethnic groups that their stake in the state's security should override all other considerations. For example, in 1974, Botha argued that the South African colored and Indian communities would be much safer under the white government than under a black regime. To bolster this argument, Botha highlighted the grim fate of Indian communities across the African continent under black governments.[7] Using this and similar examples, several scholars have maintained that politicians should be blamed for the bloody record of intergroup fighting because they set one group against the other. Yet even the most cunning politicians only manipulate intergroup rivalries that are already present. Bloody intergroup conflicts have existed since the dawn of history, irrespective of politicians. Thus, for members of a given ethnic group, military service in the state's armed forces may be an additional, and effective, way to deter other groups.

Ethnic leaders must attempt to be united and speak with one voice when negotiating with the military over service terms for their youth. This requirement is difficult to fulfill. Most subjugated ethnic groups are rural, their members lack education, and their leaders may be constantly feuding. Under such conditions, the military may not have to work hard to get a sufficient number of ethnic recruits: it can play one group of ethnic leaders against another to secure enough support from one faction

6. Simon Baynham, "Defense and Security Issues in a Transitional South Africa," *International Affairs Bulletin* 14, no. 3 (1990): 9.

7. South Africa, *Legislative Assembly Debates* 51 (September 9, 1974), col. 2491.

for its recruitment plans. The history of the divided and weak Druze leadership vis-à-vis the IDF is a case in point. Because of their internal divisions, the leaders of the Israeli Druze in 1956 missed a historic opportunity to negotiate their youth's service terms (including exemptions for military service on religious grounds) when the military began conscripting Druze for the first time. In contrast to the Druze community, the more united leadership of the colored community in South Africa was very successful in promoting the status of their youth after 1963.

The case of colored leaders and the SADF also illustrates another important lesson: ethnic leaders who are military veterans are more likely to know what to demand from the military and how to negotiate with generals. The progress of a given ethnic group in the military requires the constant removal of critical bottlenecks, such as those blocking the commissioning of the first ethnic officers or the promotion of the first ethnic unit to the status of a full-fledged combat unit. Ethnic leaders who have served in the military will quickly identify these bottlenecks and press top brass hard to remove them. In contrast, militarily inexperienced ethnic leaders will not know what to ask for in their negotiations. Between 1956 and 1972, Israeli Druze sheikhs with minimal or no military experience settled for selecting the next Druze officer promotion from a list of names presented to them by the IDF. And they failed to pressure the military into elevating the status of the Minority Unit, where all Druze conscripts served. In contrast, veteran colored leaders in South Africa pressured the SADF to obliterate discriminatory manpower policies, to equalize pay among white and nonwhite servicemen, to train and commission the first colored officers, and to upgrade the status of the colored unit from a service unit to a combat battalion. As a result, twenty years—or roughly one generation—after its establishment, the colored unit already was a seasoned combat brigade, with many colored officers and NCOs serving in it and other units across the military. In stark contrast to the negotiating success of these colored leaders, the Druze sheikhs still were browsing through lists of names to select the first Druze major twenty years after the Minority Unit was formed, and Druze servicemen still were confined to the Minority Unit and awaiting their first serious battle experience (which came in 1968).

Ethnic leaders also must keep a watchful eye on the kinds of military missions assigned to their youth in uniform. Colored leaders in South Africa became very bellicose after 1984 when the military attempted to deploy colored soldiers to pacify rebellious colored townships. Similarly,

[183]

a younger and much more assertive generation of Druze leaders—including veteran Druze officers—pressured the IDF in 1982 to remove Druze servicemen from policing duties in Druze villages in Lebanon. Most important, ethnic leaders must resist all premature plans calling for the conscription of their youth. Voluntary recruitment schemes serve as a better basis for negotiation from the perspective of ethnic leaders because the military is compelled to appeal for their support once or twice a year in order to ensure that a sufficient number of ethnic volunteers apply for military service. Ethnic leaders will have no problem justifying to the public why they support voluntary military recruitment but resist conscription. Since the state usually extends less than full and equal citizenship to members of subjugated ethnic communities, ethnic leaders also are entitled to extend less than full support for military ethnic recruitment plans.

Ethnic leaders who wish to support and monitor the integration of their youth into the military should consider the following:

- First, negotiate with the military the terms of ethnic recruitment. Resistance to negotiations may result in loss of a potentially important means of social mobilization for the ethnic group in the short term and, in the long term, deterioration of the group's status and power vis-à-vis other ethnic groups in the state.
- Take advantage of every chance to renegotiate with the military for improving the lot of ethnic youth in uniform. Do not miss historic opportunities, such as when the military seeks your support for an important change in the service terms of ethnic youth (for example, increasing the voluntary service period from one to two years).
- Once negotiations are successfully completed, encourage ethnic youth to volunteer for military service in order to improve their social mobility and ensure that the community acquires a pool of men with military training, in case a civil war erupts.
- Focus on improving service conditions and opening bottlenecks for integration rather than on promoting individuals.
- Let veteran ethnic officers negotiate service terms with the military if such veterans are available.
- Keep a watchful eye on the types of military missions assigned to ethnic youth. Resist cooperation with the military in all matters concerning the deployment of ethnic soldiers for policing duties in the community.
- Support voluntary recruitment and resist conscription of ethnic youth.

- Make it clear to military officials that support for ethnic recruitment is conditional on the fair treatment of such soldiers by the military. Immediately remove support for ethnic recruitment when the military does not keep up its end of the bargain.

GUIDELINES FOR ETHNIC SERVICEMEN

Ethnic servicemen do have a voice in matters concerning their treatment, promotion, status, and deployment in the military. But usually they must first establish their credentials on the battlefield. In both South Africa and Israel, the military accepted demands from ethnic servicemen to accelerate integration shortly before or after these servicemen were sent to battle. In Israel, the IDF agreed to open more doors to Druze soldiers soon after these soldiers completed an impressive tour of duty along the Jordan Valley, battling infiltrators. In South Africa, the SADF abolished the so-called no-salute clause just before the first colored officers were commissioned and after the first colored soldiers had already completed their tour of duty in South Africa.

Ethnic servicemen may not get a timely chance to establish their credentials on the battlefield, however. The first generation is usually assigned to segregated and service-oriented ethnic units. Twenty years may pass from the time the military commences the recruitment of allegedly Trojan horse ethnic soldiers to the moment it sends such soldiers to battle. Since military organizations are hierarchical, slow to change, and conservative by nature, it may take years to convince members of the armed forces to accept soldiers from subordinated ethnic groups as equals. In countries where the general public questions the very allegiance of these soldiers to the state, quick "no segregation" decrees such as the one Truman gave the American military in 1948 will not work. (We should keep in mind that it took the American military over one hundred and fifty years to desegregate black soldiers and elevate them to the status of first-class combat soldiers. Thus, even Truman's famous decree cannot be described as a "quick solution.") Frequently, the first generation of soldiers from mistrusted ethnic groups will have to sacrifice their own ambitions and career goals in order to buy the trust of the military and pave the way for the second generation to break away from segregated units and move up the chain of command.

Finally, ethnic servicemen must understand that the military can also change course in matters of ethnic integration. Under heavy political pressure, military commanders may be forced to move away from integration and toward exclusion, as shown by the history of Malay Muslim soldiers in the Singaporean military. Abundant signs for a reverse in policy will appear, including diminishing quotas for ethnic soldiers admitted for service; the removal of ethnic servicemen from sensitive missions, units, and schools; and the termination of promotion in rank for ethnic officers. With little or no voice, ethnic youth may wish to register their protest with their feet and leave the military. Militaries such as the one Saddam Hussein built for Iraq offer bleak prospects for ethnic soldiers.

Guidelines ethnic servicemen may wish to consider include the following:

- Pressure the military from within to include ethnic soldiers in combat missions. Remember that in a professional military the ultimate yardstick for promotion and status is performance on the battlefield.
- After battlefield performance, make demands to speed up integration; the military is likely to heed them.
- Be ready to vote with your feet if the military reverses its course of ethnic integration. Militaries that rely on volunteer ethnic recruits will quickly change course again if they discover that fewer ethnic youth are willing to serve.
- Have plenty of patience. It usually takes one generation before the first ethnic servicemen break out of the original segregated units and move up the chain of command.

A FINAL WORD

The history of the armed forces of every multiethnic state can be placed on a spectrum extending from integration to genocide. Though politicians are unlikely to consciously choose the so-called Rwanda model, many states end up with a politicized and xenophobic military because their leaders have not been able to marshal sufficient courage and determination to overcome their fears of ethnic Trojan horses in the military. In this book I have proposed one road for overcoming these fears: bring the youth of distrusted ethnic groups into the military through negotiation with community leaders over service terms and, under the close supervision and guidance of professional officers, gradually promote them in rank, status, and mission. Politicians and officers who are reluctant to adopt such a phased-integration strategy must reexamine their current ethnic military manpower policy carefully and consider its consequences for the military and society at large. The grim fate of Rwanda may await those who fail to do so.

Epilogue: The Political Motives of Ethnic Military Integration

Are soldiers with kin across the border marionettes that the state manipulates to divide and rule weak ethnic groups from within?

Several scholars answer this question with an unequivocal "yes." At least one drama unfolding as these lines are being written—that in South Africa—seems to suggest that they may be right. In April 1994, Nelson Mandela became that country's first black president, elected in the first ever elections in which all blacks were permitted to cast their votes. Torn between calls within his own party to bring the architects of apartheid to justice and his own pledge to achieve a historic reconciliation between whites and blacks, Mandela passed the National Unity and Reconciliation Act and established the Truth and Reconciliation Commission, popularly known as the Truth Committee. The committee offered former military, police, and civilian apartheid officials an opportunity to earn amnesty in return for revealing their human rights violations during the apartheid years. Three restrictions were placed on the work of the new committee: it could accept confessions from former apartheid officials only until December 15, 1996; it could not grant clemency for serious crimes, such as the murder of innocent civilians; and state prosecutors, who were barred from using the confessions as evidence in court, were permitted to collect other materials on their own to make indictments. As a result of these restrictions, the committee spent most of its time listening to and granting amnesties to low-ranking apartheid officials.

Then, at the beginning of December 1995, the attorney general for KwaZulu-Natal, Tim McNally, threw South Africa into spiraling political turmoil by submitting formal murder charges against the most senior and influential military architects of the apartheid regime. Notable among the accused was the former defence minister and chief of the SADF, Magnus Malan (this group of charged officials thus came to be known in South Africa as the Malan 20 group). But the Malan 20 group also included other highly influential former SADF commanders—General "Kat" Liebenberg, the former chief of the Defence Forces; General Tienie Groenewald, chief of military intelligence; General Jannie Geldenhuys, the retired chief of staff intelligence; and Vice Admiral Dries Putter—along with other former intelligence officers; military commanders; a former security police commander, Colonel Louis Botha; and four former KwaZulu policemen.[1]

Backed by an impressive collection of official documents from the state archives, McNally claimed that, in the mid-1980s, the members of the Malan 20 group initiated, supported, and sponsored an illegal military training camp not far from the Angolan border, on the banks of the Cuando River in the Caprivi Strip. Under the auspices of senior members of the Malan 20 group, the SADF trained two hundred black members of the Inkatha party whom Chief Buthelezi himself hand picked. Formally, the trainees and the new unit (known as the Caprivi 200) were to serve as personal guards for Chief Buthelezi. But McNally maintained that the archive documents clearly demonstrated that the Caprivi 200 unit was trained—with the complete blessing and support of the members of the Malan 20 group—to include an "offensive element." Among other things, members of the unit were trained to use AK-47s, RPG7 rocket launchers, G3 automatic rifles, Browning machine guns, and antipersonnel mines—clearly not the equipment and skills characteristic of bodyguard units.[2]

Upon completion of their training, members of the Caprivi 200 unit returned to KwaZulu and initiated a series of murderous attacks on leaders and supporters of the ANC, Chief Buthelezi's nemesis. The most heinous of these attacks took place in 1987, when the military gave the Caprivi 200 "offensive group" assault rifles and took it in a minibus to the home of Victor Ntuli, an activist of the United Democratic Front. Though Mr. Ntuli was not at home, the perpetrators carried out their plan and killed thirteen people, including women and five children under the age of ten. After the attack, the killers drove to the KwaZulu capital of Ulundi to attend a celebration organized by Chief Buthelezi's

---

1. *Mail & Guardian*, December 1, 1995.
2. *Mail & Guardian*, November 3, 1995.

personal assistant, Mr. Khumalo. A goat was slaughtered in honor of the attackers' "military achievement."[3]

Despite their knowledge of such atrocities, Mr. McNally charged in the indictment of the Malan 20 group, senior SADF and government officials—including Frederik de Klerk—continued to support the Caprivi 200 plan. The military dubbed support and training for the unit Operation Marion, deriving the name from "marionette," which, with its synonyms "dummy," "puppet," "mannequin," and "pawn," described how the State Security Council and SADF officers in 1985 viewed Buthelezi, a central component of their strategy to recruit surrogate black allies to act as a bulwark against the ANC. Minutes of meetings between senior politicians and SADF officers clearly demonstrated that although all the officials knew their actions were illegal, they deemed these activities vital to dividing and ruling the South African black community so that they could provide the international media with pictures of black-on-black violence, weaken the ANC, and prolong the life of the apartheid regime.[4]

On October 18, 1996, after a tense six-month trial, Judge Jan Hugo acquitted General Malan and the other fifteen defendants on all counts (in May, the judge had acquitted of all charges another four members of the Malan 20 group). In the acquittal proceedings, Judge Hugo argued that the prosecution case against the members of the Malan 20 group was sloppy and relied on questionable witnesses. Within hours after the conclusion of the trial, a bitter debate broke out. De Klerk and other members and supporters of the Afrikaner-based National Party celebrated the judge's decision, maintaining that Malan and other distinguished generals should not have been dragged to trial in the first place. But those who were convinced that Malan was guilty claimed that the justice system in South Africa still operated according to apartheid norms, and that politics, not the quest for justice, motivated Judge Hugo's decision. After President Mandela intervened to defend South Africa's justice system, both sides appeared to agree that the case against Malan was hastily composed and lacked sufficient evidence to charge the general on counts of murder.[5] The trial, however, only seemed to intensify, rather than resolve, a heated debate in South Africa about the role of the military in the formation and maintenance of apartheid pol-

3. *Mail & Guardian*, December 1, 1995.
4. *Mail & Guardian*, March 8, 1996; May 1, 1996.
5. *Mail & Guardian*, October 18, 1996.

icies during the 1970s and 1980s. From the perspective of this study, the Malan trial raises tough questions concerning the motives of politicians and officers who worked to bring new ethnic groups into the armed forces. These questions include the following:

- How could these professional military commanders—Malan, Geldenhuys, and Liebenberg—integrate nonwhite officers and soldiers into the SADF and at the same time launch murderous paramilitary units to spread black-on-black violence and terror?
- Did Malan and other SADF officers recruit and train blacks in the SADF in order to unleash them on the communities from which they hailed?
- Were conservative politicians such as Botha hoping to use the new nonwhite soldiers of the SADF as mercenaries to bring terror and violence to the black townships? Was this the real motive behind the support that Botha, and later de Klerk, gave the SADF during its campaign to integrate its ranks ethnically?
- Were the colored, black, and Indian leaders who negotiated with the government over the terms of recruitment and service of their ethnic youth mere government cronies whose job was to justify whatever the government and the SADF wished to do with ethnic servicemen?

To some scholars, the answers to these questions come quick and easy. They argue that during the last twenty years of the apartheid regime, and under the direct command of political figures such as Botha and de Klerk, senior SADF officers endeavored to divide and rule the black community, and to weaken and dissolve the antiapartheid movement from within. According to this line of argument, the recruitment and promotion of blacks in the SADF, and the establishment of the "third force" (as units such as the Caprivi 200 became known in South Africa), were merely tactical measures adopted and executed by SADF officers who single-mindedly pursued the goal of weakening and dividing the South African black community. The SADF, the police, and the third force thus would have been not professional institutions but state-sponsored paramilitary organizations whose goal was to play one black ethnic group against another to ensure the survival of one of the most racist regimes of the twentieth century.

Although these arguments merit serious discussion, they are historically inaccurate. The SADF was—and remains—an exemplary professional military organization. Throughout the apartheid years, it displayed all the hallmarks of military professionalism: a long-standing and distinguished tradition of warfare (including its participation in two world wars), a comprehensive system of military schools, a clear mission to defend the state against its external enemies (in the 1980s, close to fifty thousand Cuban soldiers and heavy equipment were deployed in Angola), established career paths for officers, elaborate training schedules for units, and a strong and proud esprit de corps. Indeed, in conversations held with senior SADF officers in 1993, one theme surfaced time and again: their contempt for organizations such as the South African police because of their brutal activities in the nonwhite townships.

Taking over from the police in 1974 the mission of defending the state's borders, the SADF spent the next thirteen years in war. To win this war, senior SADF officers did everything that could have been expected from a highly professional group of officers. They retrained their units to face both conventional and guerrilla warfare, purchased new weapon systems and trained with them, and analyzed their own failures to improve performance on the battlefield. One lesson they were quick to adopt was that the SADF needed to upgrade service-oriented nonwhite units to full-fledged combat units, and to integrate these units with white units. This lesson was not new; SADF officers had learned it abroad and in their own military schools beginning in the mid-1960s. Now the officers quickly implemented a lesson already known throughout the military. On the border, against a strong external foe, the professional needs of the SADF triumphed over the ideals of apartheid. The ethnic experimentation that characterized the SADF before 1973 became a campaign for an ethnically integrated military, (as described in chapter 2) because of military combat needs, not some cunning political plot.

In the mid-1980s, however, as the war in South West Africa was coming to an end, dramatic changes were taking place at home. The apartheid regime was on its last legs, and politicians who had turned this discriminatory ideology into a career were desperate. The external pressures on the military to save the failing regime intensified. Several senior SADF commanders yielded to these pressures when they launched Operation Marion. This should come as no surprise to students of civil-military relations: even the most professional military organization does not operate in a political vacuum. As illustrated by the fate of the military in Yugoslavia, no armed force is immune to political changes. There the professional legacy of the military ended when Communism collapsed,

[192]

and the state fell into a vicious civil war. In South Africa, a group of senior officers breached the legacy, standards, and ethics of military professionalism that had characterized the SADF since its foundation in 1910. Presiding over the trial of the Malan 20 group, Judge Hugo concurred with those who maintained that Operation Marion did not represent the true nature of the SADF, and violated its standards and ethics. It is clear that Operation Marion was a serious breach of the SADF's standards, but it was only that—a breach.

The Malan trial, and the debate over the political motives underlying ethnic integration in the military, should not divert attention from the important problem of bringing together different ethnic groups to serve as equals in the armed forces. On the verge of the twenty-first century, humanity once again faces the abyss of ethnocentrism, racial genocide, and ethnically driven atrocities. Countries that find a way for their ethnic groups to live with one another peacefully will prosper; states that fail to bring their various ethnic groups together will fall prey to racial hatred, ethnic disintegration from within, and civil war. Unfortunately, countries in the developing world often suffer from a scarcity of strong state institutions that can bridge the distrust gap between ethnic groups. Though the military is no panacea for healing internal ethnic hatred, it can contribute greatly to bringing together members of hostile ethnic groups for the common purpose of protecting the state against its external enemies. Turning the military into a supraethnic state institution, however, is likely to be a prolonged process, impeded by mutual suspicion between the state and those ethnic groups whose loyalty is questioned by the general public. Still, politicians, military commanders, and ethnic leaders have no alternative if they are concerned that the military might turn into a xenophobic ethnic militia. They must discuss, negotiate, and agree on ways to bring all ethnic youth into the military. They also must supervise closely the lot of these ethnic soldiers in the military, and constantly work toward opening more and more doors to them. As the fate of the military and the state in Yugoslavia and Rwanda demonstrate, a state may not survive the failure to integrate its ethnic groups into the military.

Interviews

South Africa

Belelie, Sgt. Maj. Liaison officer for instruction and basic training. Army Headquarters, Pretoria, South Africa, March 29, 1993.

Bernard, Col. W. Deputy director, Directorate Language Services. Defence Headquarters, Armscore, Pretoria, South Africa, March 25, 1993.

Bredenkamp, Lt. Col. J. D. Inquiry officer. SADF Archives, Pretoria, South Africa, March 24, 1993.

Claasen, Col. Head, Army Formal Training. Army Headquarters, Pretoria, South Africa, March 29, 1993.

Dlamini, 2d Lt. Nelson. Platoon leader, 21st Battalion. Lenz, South Africa, March 30, 1993.

Fieldhouse, Col. F. Director, Manpower Service Systems. Defence Headquarters, Pretoria, South Africa, March 27, 1993.

Fourie, Prof. Deon F. S. University of South Africa. Naval Officer Mess, Pretoria, South Africa, March 29, 1993.

Ganesan, S.Sgt. S. Naval Headquarters, Pretoria, South Africa, March 27, 1993.

Jacobs, Brig. Director, Army Personnel Maintenance. Army Headquarters, Pretoria, South Africa, April 2, 1993.

Jooste, Louise. Researcher. SADF Archives, Pretoria, South Africa, March 25, 1993.

Khoza, Maj. R. Public relations officer. Defence Headquarters, Pretoria, South Africa, March 25, 1993.

Le Crerar, Col. Commander, Group 18. Alexandra, South Africa, March 29, 1993.

Loedolff, Rear Adm. P. van Z. Deputy chief of staff personnel. Defence Headquarters, Pretoria, South Africa, March 25, 1993.

Mabuza, 1st Lt. Wayne. Company commander, 21st Battalion. Company barracks, Alexandra, Johannesburg, South Africa, March 30, 1993.

Maloba, Cpl. K. S. Rifleman, 21st Battalion. Lenz, South Africa, March 30, 1993.

Manning, Col. Former commander, SAS Jalsena. Naval Headquarters, Pretoria, South Africa, March 25, 1993.

Mapapa, S.Sgt. Z. 21st Battalion. Lenz, South Africa, March 30, 1993.

Moodley, Comdr. Yegan S. Former naval attaché. South Africa Embassy, Washington, D.C., U.S.A., June 12, 1992.

Nothling, Col. Head. SADF Military Archives, Pretoria, South Africa, March 24, 1993.

Pillay, Cmdr. Sagarem. Former deputy commander, SAS Jalsena. Naval Mess, Pretoria, South Africa, March 31, 1993.

Pretorius, Maj. Gen. Director of manpower provision. Defence Headquarters, Armscore, Pretoria, South Africa, March 27, 1993.

Rutsch, Col. M. Career Development of Personnel Division. Army Headquarters, Pretoria, South Africa, March 25, 1993.

Stoffberg, Col. D. P. Former director, Ethnology SA Army. Military Archives, Pretoria, South Africa, March 24, 1993.

Trainor, Rear Adm. Staff chief of naval support. Naval Headquarters, Pretoria, South Africa, March 25, 1993.

Van Der Vaag, Maj. I. Researcher. SADF Archives, Pretoria, South Africa, March 25, 1993.

Van Rooyan, Lt. Col. Deputy commander, 21st Battalion. Lenz, South Africa, March 30, 1993.

Singapore

Aeria, Col. James. Former commander, Singapore navy. Singapore's Technologies Building, Singapore, July 6, 1992.

Armugam, Col. Former SAF officer. Oral history interview, for the project "Political Development in Singapore 1965–1975."

Bogaars, George Edwin. Former permanent secretary, Ministry of Interior and Defence. CPF Building, Singapore, July 3, 1980. Oral history interview by Robert Chew, for the project "Political Development in Singapore 1965–1975," file B000032/030.

Chan Heng Chee, Prof. Director, Singapore International Foundation. PUB Building, Singapore, June 26, 1992.

Chew, Ernest C. T. Dean of the social sciences. National University of Singapore, June 30, 1992.

Choo, Lt. Gen. Winston. Chief of general staff, SAF. Harvard Business School, Cambridge, Mass., U.S.A., April 1, 1992.

Interviews

Goh Keng Swee. Former minister of defence. PSA Building, Singapore, July 3, 1992.

Hochstadt, H. R. Former director of manpower, MINDEF. PSA Building, Singapore, July 2, 1992.

Kwa, Chong Guan. Director, National Museum, MINDEF. Singapore, July 1, 1992.

Lau Teik Soon, Prof. Former head, Department of Political Science, and member of Parliament. National University of Singapore, Singapore, July 16, 1992.

Lim Kim Son. Former minister of defence. PSA Building, Singapore, July 9, 1992.

Maidin, Abu Bakar. President, Muslim Missionary Society Singapore (JAMI-YAH). Islamic Center Jamiyah, Singapore, July 15, 1992.

Menon, Col. Director of pubic relations, MINDEF. SAF Officer Club, Singapore, June 25, 1992.

Mohamed, Col. Syed Ibrahim bin Syed. Former SAF officer. Oral history interview, for the project "Political Development in Singapore 1965–1975."

Mahbubani, Kishore. Deputy permanent secretary, Ministry of Foreign Affairs. Center for International Affairs, Harvard University, Cambridge, Mass., U.S.A., February 5, 1992.

Mutalib, Hussin. Department of Political Science, National University of Singapore. Center for International Affairs, Harvard University, Cambridge, Mass., U.S.A., May 21, 1992.

Ong, Terrence. Directoriate for Legal Services. SAF Officer Club, Singapore, June 25, 1992.

Rasheed, Zainul Abidin. Chief executive officer, Yaysan Mendaki. Mendaki Building, Singapore, July 14, 1992.

Samuel. Former head, National Education Department. Central Manpower Base, Depot Road, Singapore, July 10, 1992.

Singh, Daljit. Editor, Institute for South East Asian Studies. Cricket Club, Singapore, June 29, 1992.

Singh, Maj. Kuldip. Head, Military Heritage Branch. SAF Officer Club, Singapore, June 25, 1992.

Tan, Teik Khim. Former chief of general staff, SAF. Manderin Hotel, Singapore, June 25, 1993.

Vij, Kirpa Ram. Former SAF chief of staff. NOL Building, Singapore, June 29, 1992.

Wok, Encik Othman Bin. Former minister of social affairs and ambassador to Indonesia. Singapore Tourist Promotion Board, Singapore, May 4, 1987. Oral history interview by Irene Lim, for the project "Political Development in Singapore 1965–1975."

Yee, Lai Meng. Deputy director, People's Association. People's Association Headquarters, Kallang Singapore, Singapore, June 25, 1992.

Yeo, Philip. Former permanent secretary of defence. Economic Development Board Office, Raffles City Tower, Singapore, July 9, 1992.

Israel

A-Din, Amal Nassar. Former Knesset member (Likud). Dalyat El-Karmel, Israel, December 18, 1991.

Amital, Rabbi Yehuda. Head, Yeshivat "Har Etzion." Jerusalem, Israel, December 19, 1991.

Hitman, Gad. Assistant to the advisor on minority affairs. Ramat-Gan, Israel, December 27, 1991.

Hovav, Meir. Editor. Jerusalem, Israel, December 30, 1991.

Israeli, Hayyim. Assistant to the minister of defence. Tel Aviv, Israel, August 6, 1992.

Lerner, Lt. Col. Shevach. Former head, Manpower Division, IDF. Afeka, Israel, August 16, 1992.

Lorch, Nathanael. Historian. Jerusalem, Israel, August 20, 1992.

Manssur, Kammal. Special advisor to the Israeli president on minority affairs. Osfya, Israel, December 18, 1991.

Naffa, Mohammed. Knesset member. Jerusalem, Israel, January 1, 1992.

Nitzan, Col. Yehuda. Former head, Personnel Department, IDF. Tel Aviv, Israel, August 14, 1992.

Vardi, Gen. Refael. Former head, Manpower Division. Tzahala, Israel, August 13, 1992.

Warhaftig, Zerach. Former minister of religious affairs. Bar-Ilan University, Israel, December 19, 1991.

Zur, Zvi. Former chief of staff, IDF. Tel Aviv, Israel, August 6, 1992.

Index

The Illogic of American Nuclear Strategy, by Robert Jervis

The Meaning of the Nuclear Revolution: Statecraft and the Prospect of Armageddon, by Robert Jervis

The Vulnerability of Empire, by Charles A. Kupchan

Anatomy of Mistrust: U.S.Soviet Relations during the Cold War, by Deborah Welch Larson

Nuclear Crisis Management: A Dangerous Illusion, by Richard Ned Lebow

Cooperation under Fire: Anglo-German Restraint during World War II, by Jeffrey W. Legro

The Search for Security in Space, edited by Kenneth N. Luongo and W. Thomas Wander

The Nuclear Future, by Michael Mandelbaum

Conventional Deterrence, by John J. Mearsheimer

Liddell Hart and the Weight of History, by John J. Mearsheimer

Reputation and International Politics, by Jonathan Mercer

The Sacred Cause: Civil-Military Conflict over Soviet National Security, 1917–1992, by Thomas M. Nichols

Liberal Peace, Liberal War: American Politics and International Security, by John M. Owen IV

Bombing to Win: Air Power and Coercion in War, by Robert A. Pape

A Question of Loyalty: Military Manpower in Multiethnic States, by Alon Peled

Inadvertent Escalation: Conventional War and Nuclear Risks, by Barry R. Posen

The Sources of Military Doctrine: France, Britain, and Germany between the World Wars, by Barry Posen

Dilemmas of Appeasement: British Deterrence and Defense, 1934–1937, by Gaines Post, Jr.

Crucible of Beliefs: Learning, Alliances, and World Wars, by Dan Reiter

Eisenhower and the Missile Gap, by Peter J. Roman

The Domestic Bases of Grand Strategy, edited by Richard Rosecrance and Arthur Stein

Societies and Military Power: India and Its Armies, by Stephen Peter Rosen

Winning the Next War: Innovation and the Modern Military, by Stephen Peter Rosen

Israel and Conventional Deterrence: Border Warfare from 1953 to 1970, by Jonathan Shimshoni

Fighting to a Finish: The Politics of War Termination in the United States and Japan, 1945, by Leon V. Sigal

Alliance Politics, by Glenn H. Snyder

The Ideology of the Offensive: Military Decision Making and the Disasters of 1914, by Jack Snyder